SQUARE METRE GARDENING

Mel Bartholomew

F

FRANCES LINCOLN LIMITED

PUBLISHERS

Frances Lincoln Ltd
www.franceslincoln.com

First Frances Lincoln edition 2013

A catalogue record for this book is available from
the British Library.

ISBN 978-0-7112-3452-9

UK consultant: Liz Dobbs
Design: Schermuly Design Co.
Proofreading and index: Marion and Michael Dent

Printed in China

SQUARE
METRE
GARDENING

Contents

Introduction

I know you will be successful with my Square Metre Gardening method, not only because I have spent over 30 years perfecting it but because of all the hundreds of people who have got in touch to let me know how much food they get from such a small space with such little effort. Here's a taste of how I figured it all out.

Lettuce is one of the easiest crops to grow and it comes in a variety of colours.

Introduction

Growing your own crops is a lot of work if you follow traditional methods. Luckily my observations and experiments on sowing and planting in garden situations show there is a better way.

Mel Bartholomew

It all started in 1975 after my retirement from my consulting engineering business, I decided to take up gardening as a hobby but I soon began to question the efficiency of all the conventional gardening practices we'd been taught. Why is fertiliser spread over the entire garden area, but the plants are only placed in long rows with wide paths on both sides? I wondered why you were supposed to cultivate all the soil in a garden even though plants in rows take up a fraction of the space. Then I pondered why you would walk all over the rest of the ground again, packing down all that newly cultivated soil? And, why, in this era of water conservation, is an entire plot sprinkled with water when the plants are only located in a 15-cm (6-inch) wide row in the centre of a 2-m (6-foot) wide strip?

As I analysed these traditional gardening methods, I realised there is only one outcome you can expect when you fertilise and water ground and paths with nothing planted in it – weeds!

PLANTING IN ROWS

Why plant an entire row of everything? Just because my kitchen garden is 10m (30ft) wide, for example, do I really want or need a whole 10m (30ft) row of cabbages? That would be at least thirty cabbages spaced 30cm (12in) apart. Why would I want thirty cabbages to be ready all at the same time? If everything is planted at one time, won't it also be ready to harvest all at once? It sounds like farming to me, but that's too much cabbage to enjoy at the same time for a homeowner. How many people go to the shops and buy thirty heads of cabbage once a year? Do you? So why grow it that way? There must be a better way to stagger the harvest, and the obvious solution is to stagger the time of planting whenever possible and to plant less.

I sought answers to all my gardening questions and, no matter where I travelled, I kept receiving the same answer, "Because that's the way we've always done it!" Right then and there I said, "I'm going to invent a better way to garden."

Part of the problem, I realised, was that single-row gardening was nothing but a hand-me-down technique from large-field arable

Planting in long rows is traditional but do you really want all those cabbages? My Square Metre Gardening method concentrates on growing family-sized portions in a smaller area so there is less wasted space and less work.

farming. Single rows make sense when you depend upon a tractor to plough up the soil but in a home garden, there is no longer a need for all that wasted space.

EXPERIMENTS WITH SPACING

Eager to test my reasoning, I planted two rows, 15cm (6in) apart, to see how well the plants would do. It worked! The plants grew just as well in two rows as they did in a single row, as long as each plant had 15cm (6in) all around. Next, I tried a triple row – three rows where I placed all the plants 15cm (6in) apart in all directions. Again, it worked! How wide could I make this, I asked? The answer is, as wide as you can reach in to maintain your garden; in other words, as long as your arms. But I still had a harvest too large to utilise.

So what was the obvious solution? Shorten the rows! And they kept getting shorter and shorter, until they were only 30cm (12in) long and 30cm (12in) wide – a small square planting area that would hold four plants per square if each plant was 15cm (6in) apart.

In summary, if plants should be thinned to 30cm (12in) apart, plant one per square. If plants should be 15cm (6in) apart, plant four per square. If plants should be 10cm (4in) apart then you can grow nine within the space of that one square. If plants are thinned to 8cm (3in) apart, you can grow sixteen in that same square. Doesn't it all make sense and seem easy enough?

I also realised that if each square could be planted with a different crop containing either one, four, nine or sixteen plants, all properly spaced, it wouldn't be necessary to plant a whole row of just one crop. If you're farming for commercial purposes, you want everything to ripen at once so it can be harvested together and taken to market. But with home gardening, you want to stagger harvesting your produce so you can pick little-and-often throughout the season with fresh pickings each day or so.

WHAT IS SQUARE-METRE GARDENING?

Square-metre gardening (SMG) is a simple, foolproof method of growing your own delicious vegetables and herbs, no matter how small your growing space

After perfecting my sowing and planting experiments, my rows got shorter and shorter until I eventually hit upon the idea of growing in 1-metre (3-ft) box frames, edged with timber boards to create raised beds. These are, in turn, divided with a lattice of wooden laths that form a planting grid of nine squares, each measuring 33 x 33 cm (13 x 13in). In practice, due to the width of the lath, a planting square of 30 x 30cm (12 x 12in).

Into these squares I plant, or sow, different numbers of crops depending on their size at maturity. If plants need to be spaced 30cm (12in) apart, e.g. cauliflower, I grow one plant in each square; if they need to be spaced 15cm (6in) apart, e.g. lettuce, I grow four plants in each square; if 10cm (4in) apart, e.g. parsley, I grow nine; and if 8cm (3in) apart, e.g. carrots, I grow 16. What could be simpler?

Here is a 1-metre (3-ft) square box frame with nine different crops growing. The grid gives each crop its own 30 x 30cm (12 x 12in) square and the number of plants in each depends on the vigour of the crop.

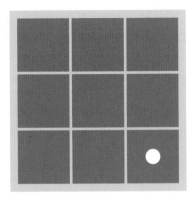

For plants spaced 30cm (12in) apart, e.g. aubergine, plant one per square

Plants spaced 15cm (6in) apart, e.g. lettuce, are planted four per square

Plants spaced 10cm (4in) apart, e.g. spinach have nine plants per square

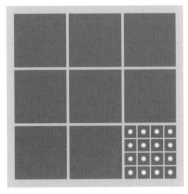

For plants spaced 8cm (3in) apart, e.g. radish, plant 16 per square

In order to create the perfect growing conditions within these squares I devised a specially formulated growing medium made up of ⅓ each, by volume, of: moss peat, vermiculite and blended compost. This mix is moisture-retentive and contains all the nutrients plants need without ever having to apply additional fertiliser. It also enables you to start growing straight away and avoids going through the years of soil improvements required by traditional digging methods.

Adding my mix to the SMG box creates a compact and easily managed patch for growing produce that will fit into the smallest garden, or even onto a patio or a roof terrace. My method is ideal for growing a wide variety of crops, even flowers, in a small space and for staggering your plantings. so you have a steady supply of produce through the season rather than a huge surplus that will end up being composted. But that's enough of the theory; let's get down to the practice...

SITES AND SIZES

One of the biggest problems of veg plots with single rows is their size. They're big! They take up so much room that they are usually located at the end of the garden. That usually meant it was out of sight, resulting in out of mind. It became less and less tended as the year went on. But guess what still grew? Weeds! And these pesky plants can quickly inundate and choke out your crops. Without your attention they'll take over the garden.

CLOSE TO THE HOUSE

All that has been changed for the better. SMG takes only 20 percent of the space of a single-row garden. That means it can be located much closer to the house where it will get more attention and care, resulting in a better-looking garden and a more usable harvest. You will now be able to reduce the size of your SMG so much that you can locate it close to your house for better care and more enjoyment. You'll never have to dig up your existing soil anymore as you now build your new garden on top of it. No more hard work or heavy-duty tools needed. All you'll need is 15-cm (6-in) deep layer of a perfect soil mix from three common ingredients available

The SMG method allows so many crops to be grown in such a small area that you can install a box to one side of a sunny patio. Having the box near the house makes growing and harvesting crops easier and quicker.

everywhere. This mix never needs changing and no additional fertiliser is needed using this method.

You'll use one or more bottomless box frames made from ordinary outdoor timber, laid out and then separated by paths and each box will have a permanent grid for that unique SMG look and use. You'll use a minimum of seeds, so you won't have to buy new packets every year. Best of all, some of your boxes can have bottoms so you can move them or place them at tabletop or railing height for easier care and to suit your garden.

MULTIPLE SITES

In addition, your productive growing area doesn't have to be all in one place. You no longer have to cultivate or water one big garden area all at once. You can split up your SMG so that a box frame or two are located next to the kitchen door, while more boxes can be located elsewhere in the garden. Small, individual garden boxes allow you much more flexibility in determining location. Now your garden can be located near where you walk and sit, or where you can view it from the house. It can even be located in a patio or entertaining area, where you relax. Your SMG becomes a feature rather than a burden.

ADDING FLOWERS AS A BONUS

Once your box frames are incorporated into your garden near the house and on view, then it is worth planning to keep them not only productive but attractive too. Adding some annual flowers to empty squares is the easiest way to do this but you can also look out for crop varieties with different coloured foliage too. Some ornamental plants just have pretty flowers, others can be cut for the house or they help attract beneficial insects, some flowers are even edible. For some ideas of flowers to grow in your boxes, see the Flower Directory on page 234.

SOIL PROBLEMS SOLVED

The question I hear most, all around the world, is, "What can we do about our local soil? It is so hard to work and garden in." Why do we really need to improve our existing soil if it's so bad? Couldn't we just start with a perfect soil mix above ground and eliminate the need to ever dig up or improve our existing soil? You probably could if your garden wasn't so big . . . but hey, SMG isn't big. So, if we could find a perfect soil mix, there would be no more digging and no more cultivating. Just think of the implications if you forget about trying to

The key to the success of the SMG method is to fill the box with a growing medium made up to my recipe (Mel's Mix) rather than rely on variable local soils. My mix has everything crops need so there is no need to provide extra feed.

improve your existing soil. It no longer matters what kind of soil you have; if you start with a perfect soil mix, it will save a lot of time. You don't have to have your soil analysed anymore, and you don't have to have a pH test . . . you don't even have to know what pH is! Hey, gardening can be fun now!

MEL'S MIX

So if you are not going to use your existing soil but instead use a perfect soil mix, what is it and how and where do you get it? There are three characteristics of a perfect growing mix. First of all, it's lightweight, so it is easy to work with and easy for plants to grow in. Next, it is nutrient-rich and has all the minerals and trace elements that plants need without adding extra fertilisers. Finally, it holds moisture, yet drains well.

After many experiments, I found that three of my favourite ingredients made the perfect mix when combined in equal portions by volume:
- ⅓ Peat Moss
- ⅓ Vermiculite
- ⅓ Garden Compost or bags of Blended Compost

Garden centres will have these products in large bags, although you might need to order the vermiculite as it is usually just sold in small bags for seed raising. Better still, try to use your own home-made garden compost as the third ingredient. If you don't have your own compost heap then start one as soon as possible (see page 66). For more details of Mel's mix, see page 70.

My mix drains well, so there are no puddles that can kill plant roots by waterlogging; but the mix can also hold large amounts of moisture so the plants will grow well. This mix is a pleasure to work with, has a light fluffy texture and smells good. The first two ingredients have no nutrients, but the last – garden compost – is loaded with all the nutrients and minerals that you could imagine. Garden compost is the most important ingredient of the three, and making your own is good for both the environment and the garden. This is about as organic as you can get.

BUILD UP, DON'T GO DOWN

For years, experts said your garden soil had to be improved to at least 30cm (12in) deep; some even said 45cm (18in) deep. But my experiments were proving otherwise, especially when I used good homemade garden compost as one-third of the mix. I asked myself, "If 15cm (6in) of perfect soil is good enough for window boxes and commercial greenhouse benches, why not in gardens?" And why dilute it by adding the mix to poor existing soil? Why not use this perfect soil mix in your garden and forget all about the soil underneath? Well, the experts still pooh-poohed the idea. But guess what? It works! Of course, everyone realises that you couldn't do that in a huge, old-fashioned, single-row garden or even in raised-bed gardening, but it can be done in a Square Metre Garden!

Can you really grow vegetables and flowers in only 15cm (6in) of soil regardless of how good it is? I've been doing it for decades in my display and home garden, and it really works. The usual question is, "How can you grow long carrots or potatoes in just a depth of 15cm (6in) of soil?" It's a good question, so we developed a special feature of SMG where you build a 30-cm (12-in) deep box for some crops.

NO FERTILISER REQUIRED

Square Metre Gardening needs no fertiliser. How can that be? After all, the gardening industry is built on using fertiliser. My own experiments of not improving the existing soil but rather of starting with a perfect soil mix was working so well that I began to consider another new idea – that you don't need to add fertiliser. The compost was providing all of the nutrients and trace elements the plants needed. Well, again, all the experts pooh-poohed the idea and still do, but guess what? It works! I haven't used any kind of fertiliser in my home, display or demonstration gardens for decades. If you go to ur website (for details, see page 37), you'll see how bountiful and beautiful the gardens look. And this is not just gardening the first year but year after year after year. Just think – no more digging and weeding and no more fertiliser! The only thing we ever add to our soil is a little more garden compost. Now all we need is some way to hold or contain our above ground 15cm (6in) of perfect soil mix. So how about a box?

ADJUSTING THE SIZE OF THE BOX

I think having your garden contained in a box frame adds uniformity and structure, not only to your garden but to your life. Once limits are placed on almost anything, you will find it much easier to take care of and therefore you will be more comfortable with it.

The basic 1 x 1m (3 x 3ft) bottomless boxes are easy to build out of ordinary timber, bricks, blocks, or you can even buy kits made of timber, plastic or metal ready cut that you slot together. These small boxes, filled with the perfect soil mix, will grow five times as much

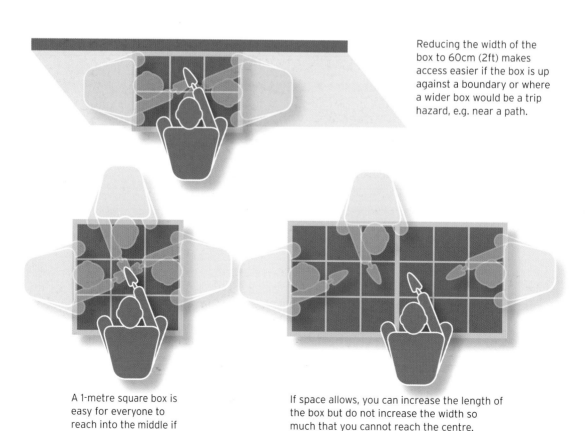

Reducing the width of the box to 60cm (2ft) makes access easier if the box is up against a boundary or where a wider box would be a trip hazard, e.g. near a path.

A 1-metre square box is easy for everyone to reach into the middle if there is access on three or more sides.

If space allows, you can increase the length of the box but do not increase the width so much that you cannot reach the centre.

as the same space in a single-row garden. So you don't need many of the boxes. There are no weeds to hoe or soil to cultivate. If you place the box on top of the existing ground, you eliminate all of the usual gardening concerns and work of improving your existing soil. The 1 x 1m (3 x 3ft) boxes have been chosen because it's a size you can walk around and easily reach into to tend your plants; this eliminates the need for stepping on the growing soil and packing it down, which then eliminates the need to dig or loosen it. See how everything in SMG is interrelated and works so well together?

For bigger gardens, you can always put some of the boxes end to end to create a 1 x 2m (3 x 7ft) or a 1 x 3m (3 x 10ft) garden box that you will still be able to walk around, yet reach in. If your boxes are located next to a wall, fence or building on one side, and on the other there is a main route through the garden, you can restrict the box depth to 60cm (2ft). That way you can reach all the way to the back and the boxes will not get in the way of passers-by. The boxes can be any length and made from any type of wood. The best is free wood that is found at a construction site. Just ask the foreman of the project if you can have the scrap 5 x 15cm (2 x 6in) boards. If you are going to buy your timber, boxes can be made from softwood such as pine or fir for the least cost, or hardwood such as cedar or oak for longer lasting use.

Hardwoods are naturally resistant to rot but softwoods are usually pretreated before sale to prolong their life. The timber is usually pressure-impregnated with preservative, so the chemicals are bonded deep within the timber. The chemicals used now are less toxic than years ago but if you are concerned, either try to source untreated wood or line the edges with polythene so the mix is not in contact with the timber. Ornamental paints and stains can be applied to the outside of the box; water-based ones are the least toxic but they have little protection against rot.

THE RIGHT PATH

The width of your paths is an important consideration for your own comfort and safety when tending the boxes but also from an aesthetic point of view. To find out just how far someone could reach in to maintain a garden without walking all over the soil, I got a little old lady and a big husky man and measured how far they could easily reach. I found that both could comfortably reach in 60cm (2ft) without losing balance. Now, the only soil that needs to be dug up, improved, watered and fertilised is in the SMG area and not all the paths. That reduced the actual growing area in the garden by 80

Once you know how much space you have and how many boxes you want, play around with some ideas on paper. Try out different layouts but aim to keep path widths greater than a width of 60cm (2ft) if possible.

percent. And an added benefit is the growing mix in the SMG area is never compacted by your feet, so you don't have to hoe or dig up the ground to keep loosening the planting soil.

So what is the ideal path width? In my original book, I had 30-cm (12-in) boards for paths as that was the most efficient use of space. But you need good balance to cope with 30-cm (12-in) paths and it isn't so easy for a wheelbarrow. So I now recommend you go a bit wider. Even a width of 60cm (2ft) is a little tight, so ideally I recommend a minimum of 1m (3ft) between your boxes. But, of course, you need to take into account the size of your particular site. In fact, if your garden has several boxes, you can vary the path width. Play around with some ideas on paper – then once your boxes are built (and before you fill them with Mel's mix), you can move them about until you get them just right. Think of it as arranging garden furniture in your patio.

Beds cut out of a lawn can have the paths left as grass but there will be mowing and trimming of the edges.

Bark chips or shredded shrub prunings over a weed-proof membrane will keep muddy paths dry and weed-free.

A hard-landscaped path, such as paving, looks smart and will give you clean access to your SMG in all weathers.

PATH MATERIALS

If you place your beds on a grassed area, the path space between your boxes can be left as grass but this means you will have to mow it and trim the edges. Or you can just remove any weeds or grass, level the ground and then lay down weed-proof membrane and cover it with loose materials such as gravel or bark chips. Or if your boxes are going to be set in an area that is seen from the rest of the garden, you might want to make a feature of the whole growing area, in which using paving or bricks on the path will link the growing area to the whole garden design.

GRIDS, SOWING AND SPACING

When we show people how a 1 x 1m (3 x 3ft) box frame looks without a grid and ask them, "How many plants could you plant there? How many different crops?" They draw a blank because it looks like a small area that isn't going to contain very much. As soon as we lay down the grid, they suddenly light up and say, "Aha! I see! Nine spaces, so it'll take nine different crops! Later, as soon as one square is harvested, I can add a trowel full of garden compost and replant that square with a different crop without disturbing anything else around it." Bingo! They see the light.

There are many interrelated reasons for the "different crop in every square" rule, and you will see and understand these as we go along. They deal with nutrients used, limiting over-ambitious planting, staggered harvests, weed and pest control, beauty of the garden, companion planting, simplification of crop rotation, cutting planting time in half, and many more factors that result in a very unusual and innovative gardening system. When you have no grid, your garden has no character. If you're having visitors over, they may not even notice your garden if it's laid out in plain beds. But if it's a Square Metre Garden with very prominent and visible grids, they will say, "Hey, what's that? It looks great!"

If I could condense thirty years of experience into my current advice, it would be this: don't use string or any other floppy material to make a grid. A rigid, prominent and visual grid permanently laid on every one of your boxes will make all the difference in the world as others see it but mostly in how you use and enjoy your garden. With a very visible grid, your garden takes on a unique character. You'll be able to immediately visualise your planting squares. Without a grid, your garden is not a SMG!

BETTER WAYS TO SOW

When I first started gardening, I found the traditional method of using an entire packet of seeds along a single row was so wasteful that I couldn't believe that's the way we've always done it. Why would anyone tell us to waste a whole packet of seeds along a single row, especially knowing that we would have to go back and thin out 95 percent of the seedlings in order to leave only one plant every few inches. How about just a few seeds in each hole, i.e. just a pinch of seeds? After testing this idea with many people and checking their ability to pick up just a pinch, this seemed to be the answer.

When direct-sown seeds germinate, use fine scissors to snip out all but the strongest to leave the correct number in the square.

A SNIP, NOT A TUG

I am against thinning – that's when you pull out all the seedlings except the one plant you want to grow to maturity. Thinning is a lot of work and also disturbs the roots of the remaining plants, and that's not good. If you plant just a few seeds, that is a pinch, in each hole and several seedlings come up, you just take a pair of scissors and snip off all but the strongest one. That eliminates any root disturbance of the plant you want to keep, and you're not tempted to replant the others. The only thing you need to do is just muster the courage to make that initial snip.

MAKE THEM PORTABLE

Now that we no longer need to improve our existing soil we need only a depth of 15cm (6in) of lightweight growing mix; we can build a 1 x 1m (3 x 3ft) box frame, and add a plywood bottom drilled with drainage holes. This means you can carry it to any location you want, even moving it to suit weather, climate, an event, a situation or even a person's needs, abilities or disabilities. If the size or weight seems too much for you to handle, think about using a 60 x 60cm (2 x 2ft), or even a 60 x 120cm (2 x 4ft) box for ease of moving.

Smaller-sized SMG boxes can become wonderful patio boxes, and it's even possible to plant several so there is always one or two with flowers in full bloom or salad crops ready for harvest. The rest can be kept somewhere less visible. With a system of rotation, there will always be a few garden boxes ready to bring out to show off. There's nothing like the visual impact of a beautifully planted box filled with vegetables, flowers and herbs. If you're giving a talk or doing a presentation on gardening, the "seeing is believing" technique will impress your audience. And just think, you won't have to answer the usual question about SMG, like "How on earth can you grow a garden in only 15 cm (6in) of soil?" Or, "How can you grow without fertiliser?" Now, you just point and smile!

I think Square Metre Gardening's best feature is that it now makes gardening available to just about anyone you can think of, regardless of their age, circumstance, location, ability or disability – anyone, anywhere, can now garden!

> ANNE WRITES...
>
> *Your method has given me the confidence to try growing veggies again after a few feeble attempts.*

Plan your garden

You can usually adapt the Square Metre Gardening method to suit your outdoor space. In this chapter, I highlight the key factors you need to consider and lead you through the options. A bit of time spent on planning will be time saved in the long run when you are caring and harvesting your crops.

Plan ahead so you have a variety of different crops from early summer onwards.

The basic components of SMG

Here I look in detail at the basic components of SMG: the size and number of boxes, where to put them and the final design. The aim is a neat layout that is practical to use.

BOX FRAME MATERIALS

Your SMG garden will be laid out in square or rectangular box frames separated by access paths. Build your box frames yourself from materials such as timber, bricks or blocks; alternatively, buy a raised-bed kit where the sides are pre-cut and fixings are supplied. Kits are available in: timber, plastic and metal. If you don't like the idea of softwood timber, which will eventually rot, use a more expensive hardwood such as cedar or oak. You can even use some of the man-made composite "wood" or recycled plastic or vinyl. The wood I like best is free wood. You can usually get it from any construction site, but always ask the foreman first.

If you decide to buy the timber, most home improvement or DIY stores will cut it to length for you at little or no cost.

> Should you first design the layout for your boxes, then try to find a spot where it will fit? Or first find the best spot for a garden, then design a layout that will fit into that spot?

HOW MUCH IS ENOUGH?

One Square Metre Garden box frame (with nine squares, each 30 x 30cm/1 x 1ft) will supply enough produce to make a salad for one person every day of the growing season. One more box frame will supply supper vegetables for that person every day. An optional extra box frame will supply extra of everything for preserving or sharing with others. So each person needs one, two or three box frames of 1 x 1m (3 x 3ft), depending on how much they will eat.

OPTIONS FOR USING THREE BOX FRAMES
If you only had room for three SQM box frames, this could provide salads, veg and preserves for one person – or salads for a family of three.

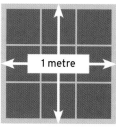

1 metre

Salad

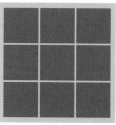

Vegetables

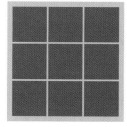

Preserving

Different sizes of box frame can make the garden look interesting and more personable, but you need to stick to a grid of 30 x 30cm (1 x 1ft) squares. The 1 x 1m (3 x 3ft) box frame can be stacked later on, on top of a 2 x 1m (6 x 3ft) box frame to start a pyramid garden – but more about designing your garden later.

YOUR FAMILY – YOUR GARDEN

An average kitchen garden is 40 square metres (430 square feet). To grow the same amount, a Square Metre Garden will need only 20 percent or one-fifth of that growing space to equal eight 1 x 1m (3 x 3ft) box frames. That's quite a difference isn't it?

CUTTING IT DOWN TO SIZE

Whenever I'm giving a lecture I like to illustrate the difference between a conventional garden and a Square Metre Garden. I'll walk down the middle of whatever room we're in and, standing in the centre, stretch out my arms sideways, as I say, "If this whole room were our garden, when you switch to Square Metre Gardening, you'll no longer need everything on this

Space to feed an average family

For a typical family of two adults and two children you will need:

9 squares salad + 9 squares vegetables = 18 squares per person

4 people x 18 squares = 72 squares

These 72 squares would fit into eight box frames (1 x 1m/3 x 3ft) or, alternatively to save making so many 1 metre square box frames, you could increase the size to 2 x 1m (6 x3ft), which would require just four rectangular box frames or a combination of both sizes whichever suits the size of your garden. If you want surplus produce for preserving, you can add extra boxes up to a maximum of one extra box frame per person. Remember you can start with box frames for salads and veg and add extra boxes later, it is best to start small. You can calculate how many squares you need for your family by creating a simple chart as shown below.

How many squares does your family need?

Family member	Number of 30-cm (1-ft) squares			
	Salad	Vegetables	Extra	Total
Mum	9	9	0	18
Dad	9	9	0	18
Grandpa or Grandma				
Child 1	9	9	0	18
Child 2	9	9	0	18
Child 3				
Other				
			Total squares	72

72 squares ÷ by 9 (the number of squares in a box) = 8 boxes

CALCULATING THE NUMBER OF BOX FRAMES TO MAKE

For each family member, estimate the number of squares required and once you have a family total convert that into box frames.

side." That cuts the room in half. Then I turn to the side that remains, cut it in half with my arms again, and say, "Everything on that side we don't need." That cuts that half in half again. And then I add, "That's still too much room. We can still cut down this remaining corner even more so we end up with only 20 percent of the total room. We can grow as much in this size of a SMG as we previously could in this entire room."

Try it in the room you're in right now and see if you aren't impressed. You suddenly begin to think of the reduced amount of work, equipment, supplies and fencing. Then you begin to see many of the advantages of being able to locate the garden where you wish and all the possibilities. Visualising the great difference of space needed for a Square Metre Garden is really the first step in learning and appreciating the entire system. Then you can begin to take advantage of all the other attributes you will discover with SMG.

ALL THAT IN ONE BOX

How much salad could you pick every day from this little garden? More than you can imagine. So as an illustration, I've listed opposite examples of what you can harvest from just one 1 x 1m (3 x 3ft) box in early summer after one spring season.

START SMALL

Once you decide on the final size and layout of your garden, keep in mind you don't have to build the entire garden right at the start. Try a three-phase plan instead.

If you build and plant just one-third of your ultimate garden boxes and grow for one season – for example, the spring season— you can then see how much you'll harvest and see if you've correctly judged the amount you really need. Then you can go into phase two, or the summer crop, and build more boxes according to your layout or master plan. At the end of the summer crop, move on to phase three, building more boxes if you still need them, to prepare for planting an autumn crop.

Yes, it's okay to lay out the whole area and to design it for the ultimate, depending on how big your family is and how much you think you want to harvest. Just don't do everything the first season. I've seen so many people start out too ambitiously, and they become overwhelmed because they underestimate how much they can actually grow in such a small area. Their gardens are actually larger than they need so there is more to take care of – and all while they're learning a new system. Take it easy and start small.

BOX SQUARE NUMBER

ONE BOX FROM A SPRING SOWING

By early summer, there will be lots of fresh salads and baby veg to enjoy. Some crops you can pick little and often, others just once. Remember to replant any empty squares.

FIRST HARVEST FROM EACH SQUARE

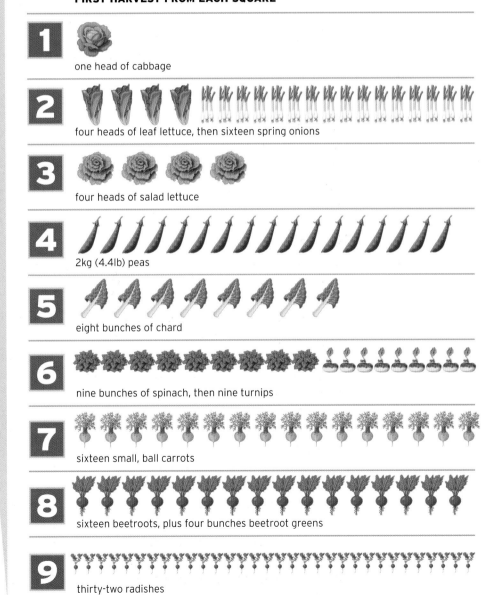

1 one head of cabbage

2 four heads of leaf lettuce, then sixteen spring onions

3 four heads of salad lettuce

4 2kg (4.4lb) peas

5 eight bunches of chard

6 nine bunches of spinach, then nine turnips

7 sixteen small, ball carrots

8 sixteen beetroots, plus four bunches beetroot greens

9 thirty-two radishes

If you have a single-row garden and don't really want to give it up yet, I suggest taking one small corner of your old-fashioned garden and planting it in just one or two of my box frames. Use the correct Mel's mix (don't just shovel your existing soil into the boxes no matter how good you think it is), put down the grid and try planting this way. Next year, I'll bet you'll probably be ready to convert your entire garden into a SMG.

OVERALL SIZE OF THE BOXES

Once you decide on the overall size and number of box frames, the next step is to determine the dimension of the paths. We'll cover this in more detail later, but for now you can figure on a 60 to 90-cm (2 to 3-ft) wide path between all boxes. You could also decide now if you want to join several boxes together end to end to create a rectangular box frame of 1 x 2m (3 x 6ft) or 1 x 3m (3 x10ft). This will save a lot of space but you may not like the look of it or you may find walking around a long box inconvenient. I would never make a box longer than 12m (16ft) or you'll end up trying to cross it in the middle and then – whoops! – there you are, stepping in your garden. I hope no one saw you! If you are going to be putting some boxes against a fence or wall check, you can reach into the centre; if not then consider making them 60cm (2ft) wide.

I always remember this old nursery rhyme

One for the blackbird.
One for the mouse.
One for the rabbit.
And one for the house.

So they're suggesting you plant four times as much as what you really want or need. Well, that's cute, but what a waste of resources and energy.

DON'T FORGET THE PATHS

The whole idea of Square Metre Gardening is to walk around your garden boxes and reach in to tend your plants. This way, the soil never gets packed down and you eliminate digging it up to loosen it again. In fact, the only tool you really need once you fill your boxes with Mel's mix is a small hand trowel. It doesn't have to be the strong, expensive kind; a basic model works just fine and can last a lifetime.

So how wide should your paths be? It depends a lot on how much room you have and what kind of a look you want for your garden. If you're going to have many boxes – remember, we suggest you begin using only a small number because you can always add more later – you may want to have, for example, a central path that is at least

75cm (2ft 6in) wide so you can easily get in with a garden cart or wheelbarrow. If wheelchair access is required, the minimum width is 1m (3ft), and the surface needs to be level and solid, i.e. not covered in loose material such as gravel or bark chips.

If possible, your paths should be 75 to 90cm (2ft 6in to 3ft) wide. I would caution against 60-cm (2-ft) wide paths because once the plants grow, some cascade over the sides or get bushy. Those 60-cm (2-ft) paths begin to shrink down to maybe just 45cm (18in) or even 30cm (12in) of useable access. At the beginning, when nothing is planted or growing, it's hard to imagine what it will look like in midsummer with everything growing like crazy. Pretty soon you're sorry that you made the path so narrow. But by then, it's too late to move the boxes. Since SMG takes up so little room, why crowd all your boxes together? The more spacious your Square Metre Garden is, the more time you are likely to spend there enjoying it.

> ALEJIENDRA WRITES...
>
> *Gardening has always seemed too overwhelming. Now with your method, I can't wait to start.*

DRAW IT UP

Once you get a rough idea of how much space you'll need, make a quick sketch more or less to scale. You don't need graph paper (unless you're a designer or want to use it); just draw the paths slightly smaller than the box frames. Now you're ready to tour your grounds looking for nice open areas near the house. Later in this chapter we'll discuss design in more detail.

LOCATION

There are five major things to look for when touring your grounds for a SMG location. Use these as a test for the area you're considering for your Square Metre Garden. Remember, convenience is king so make sure you follow Rule 1.

1. Place it close to the house for convenience.
2. Pick an area that gets six to eight hours of sunshine daily.
3. Avoid siting near overhanging trees and shrubs as roots and shade may interfere or, if there is no other site, take precautions to stop the roots invading the box.
4. The area should not puddle after heavy rain.
5. The existing soil is not really important, since you won't be using it.

1. Close to the House

With the Square Metre Gardening method, you have so many more places to put your garden than ever before.

Keep in mind foot traffic and sites where you will often notice and enjoy your garden. If your SMG is near well-used paths, you'll walk by the garden more often, hence take better care of it (remember – no need to change into gardening clothes, or run and get some tools).

This means your SMG will always look nice and the end result will be that you'll enjoy it more as will every other member of the family.

I Can See Clearly Now When you think about observing your garden, consider where you can frequently see it – especially from inside the house. What room are you in the most? Can you see the garden from there? The reason is not only for your pleasure but for protection. If it is close, you will see problems (such as wilting plants, a neighbour's dog or cat) when they begin rather than hours later after all the damage has been done.

Remember the Square Metre Garden way is to treat your plants just like you treat your children or grandchildren, and you know you would be glancing out the window at them. I believe that every plant out there is constantly seeking your attention by saying, "Look

> **The best location is where you can see your garden more often from more directions. Things like sunlight and avoiding trees and shrubs are merely precautions to help make your garden more successful. So walk around your garden and think about the best place to locate and enjoy your garden.**

HOW MUCH SUN WILL YOUR BOXES GET?
The numbered boxes represent potential locations around a garden. As the sun rises in the east and sets in the west, the boxes are shaded to various degrees by the house and tree. So box 7 is in the sun all day, while box 2 is in shade for much of the day.

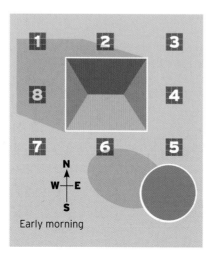

Early morning

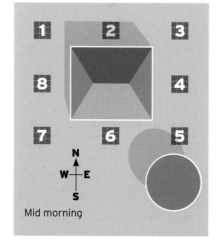

Mid morning

at me, look at my new blossom, look how big I'm getting." Isn't that just like children?

Placement of your Square Metre Garden opens up so many opportunities to the way you care for, enjoy, appreciate and harvest it. Plus you'll show it off more often and get the whole family involved. It's even possible to split up your garden and place some of your boxes in different locations.

2. Sunlight

The next thing to consider in selecting a location is sunlight. Growing plants need sunlight. How much they need depends on the type of plant. In general, large-flowering or fruiting plants need a lot – at least eight hours a day. These types of plants are referred to as sun lovers and include most of the favourite things that people grow, such as tomatoes, peppers, squash, basil and sunflowers.

In determining the amount of sunlight an area receives, keep in mind that it changes throughout the year with the seasons. In early spring and again in late autumn the sun is lower in the sky than in the summertime. And of course, there are not as many hours of light in the day in the spring and autumn as there are in the summer.

If You Only Have Shade If you have shady conditions and no other place to locate your garden, you can still have a thriving garden but you'll have a limited selection of crops to grow. So, obviously, you'd stay away from the tomatoes, peppers and squash and instead plant the root and leaf crops like radishes, spinach and lettuce. Of course, there are many flowers and herbs that love shade; check the plant directory to find out what your favourite crops need.

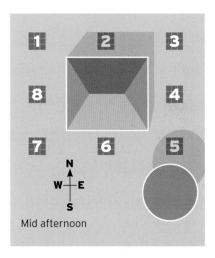

Mid afternoon

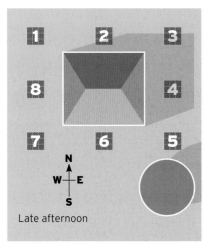

Late afternoon

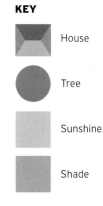

KEY

House

Tree

Sunshine

Shade

Too Much Sun Sometimes you might have a location that gets full sun all day long, from sunup to sundown. That could actually be too much for some of the leafy crops, and at the very least would mean more watering. Of course, with a big, huge garden there's not much you can do. But with a Square Metre Garden, it's very easy to provide shade by building a simple support and covering the box with some shade cloth. For more on crop covers, see page 55.

3. Coping with Trees and Shrubs

If the only location you have is near trees, shrubs or hedging, then you need to take precautions to stop their roots coming into the mix in the box. One way is to attach a plywood bottom to your boxes; another is to raise up the boxes off the ground. You can raise them up by just putting a brick under each corner and one in the centre. Or you can use a cement block, or even two blocks and build little piers and have it as a garden you sit down beside to harvest. Then, of course, the tree's roots won't even know that the garden is there. This is a nice way to have a shade garden right under a tree along with a bench or a few lawn chairs. An alternative is to place the box on hard landscaping such as a patio or paved area.

Keep in mind, too, that as trees and shrubs grow, their shade will increasingly cover a larger area so be prepared to prune or trim them.

4. No Puddles, Please

Roots will drown in accumulated and stagnant water, so you don't want to locate your SMG in an area that holds water after rain. The materials in Mel's mix, though they drain well and hold a lot of moisture, will soak up all the water in a standing puddle and your plant roots will be harmed. Areas that puddle also promise muddy paths and that makes gardening less fun.

Where a box will sit on hard landscaping or on wet ground, you can raise each side of the box up slightly to allow for better drainage before lining the box.

If you have no other place and can't drain the area, then of course you could fill in the low area with sand or grit to raise your box slightly and/or you could again put a bottom on it and raise it up with stones, bricks, blocks or something similar.

5. Existing Soil – Who Cares?

When you're choosing a location, it doesn't really matter about the condition of your existing soil. Many of the other gardening books tell you how to go around the garden and dig test holes and see what kind of soil you have. Sometimes you're even supposed to make a drainage test, in which you have to dig a hole, fill it with water, see how long it takes to drain, blah, blah, blah . . . . Or how about all the unnecessary advice on how to take a soil test and what the results mean? Forget about all that now. You don't have to know about it because we're not going to use your existing soil. We're going to build bottomless box frames above the ground. You can even put your boxes on a patio and it won't make any difference.

Once you choose the right spot in your garden, you'll love Square Metre Gardening for so many reasons. It's simple and easy to understand. It's quick and practical to do. SMG has every benefit you can think of. It fits anywhere in an existing or planned landscape; anyone can do it regardless of their abilities. SMG costs very little. It requires very few tools and equipment. And the best part of all is that you don't have to be an expert gardener!

DESIGN

Now that you've determined how many boxes you'll have and strolled around your garden to find the best spot(s), it's time to think about design. You can lay out your boxes so they turn corners, even intersect each other, but keep in mind foot traffic and how people move around the garden. Don't make dead ends or narrow places. Keep paths as generous as possible, perhaps even leave extra generous areas for chairs and entrances. Here is a fun idea: explain to the entire family the basic size and layout, then let each member draw up ideas and plans. Maybe everyone could have an area to design, build and plant. Wouldn't that be a great family project? Then take a picture and send it to our website so we can share your designs with others.

LINE THEM UP

You can probably guess that, being a former army officer, I am going to want all the box frames lined up neatly and precisely, even perhaps having them in a row (oh, what an unfortunate word) – excuse me – in a line. I might want the entire area to be a square or at the very least a rectangle...but that's just me. How about you – do you want a U-shape or an L-shape? Do whatever appeals to you.

Here's another idea – no matter the season, you can build a SMG box with a plywood bottom and place it on your patio or picnic tabletop near your back door. You may want to use smaller SMG boxes on the patio or deck such as 60 x 60cm (2 x 2ft) or 60 x 120cm (2 x 4ft).

Raised-bed kits

There's now a wide range of raised-bed kits and by choosing those with the correct dimensions, you can easily adapt them to the SMG system by adding a grid.

A basic timber kit where the sides slot into grooves in the corner posts.

It is easy to increase the depth on these recycled plastic boards using the holding rods supplied.

A kit with an extra capping on the top of the box frame makes an attractive feature for a patio.

If your SMG will sit on bare ground under trees or hedging, it is worth building a box with a plywood base to prevent neighbouring roots invading the box. Remember to drill some drainage holes.

BE CREATIVE

You don't have to be a landscape architect to measure and draw up what you imagine. The design is just as important as the size. You're going to be spending a lot of your time in your Square Metre Garden – not working or weeding, but just enjoying and relaxing. Be sure to make room for some chairs, a bench, a water fountain or a birdbath. One of the advantages of a SMG is that you have options in how you put it together so that it's perfect for you.

Seeing a picture is so helpful. If you want to see what others have done in their garden with Square Metre Gardening, go to <www.squaremetregardening.com> and click on "Neighbourhood Gardens." Everyone likes to see what others have done, so take the garden tour and see which one you like the best. And then let your imagination help you create the SMG that is perfect for you.

Building boxes and structures

If you like to build things, you are going to love this chapter. A Square Metre Garden can be a lot like working with Lego®. Since SMG grows so much in so little space and is made with readily available materials, the basic box frame projects outlined in this chapter won't take all your time, space or money.

Why boxes?

Growing your own crops is a lot of work if you follow traditional methods. Luckily my observations and experiments on sowing and planting in garden situations show there is a better way.

Just as a reminder, there are several reasons we build box frames for our Square Metre Gardens.

1. Looks neat and tidy.
2. Organises and simplifies your gardening chores.
3. The box frames hold a special soil mix above ground.
4. It's easy to add protective crop covers.

If your garden is "boxed in", it has already-established limits for you. And if you make sure to add a grid, it establishes not only a pattern but a formula for success.

Box frames also hold your perfect soil mix so that it doesn't spill out or wash away in heavy rain. When garden beds have no borders between plant-growing soil and walkways, there's a greater chance that someone will step into the growing soil – a big no-no for this SMG method.

Let's start with the basic 1 x 1m (3 x 3ft) SMG box frame. Materials that can be used include:

■ Natural wood
■ Man-made wood
■ Recycled plastic
■ Metal
■ Or any other man-made material available in timber lengths

Recommended Material Size

■ 2.5 x 15-cm (1 x 6-in) timber for the most economical, low traffic garden; or
■ 5 x 15-cm (2 x 6-in) timber for sturdier boxes or heavy foot traffic garden areas.

ROTATE CORNERS

When constructing your SMG box frame, cut all four pieces of your wood sides to the same length, and then rotate the corners to ensure you end up with a square box. If you want a different look than the rotated corners, measure the thickness of the timber and subtract

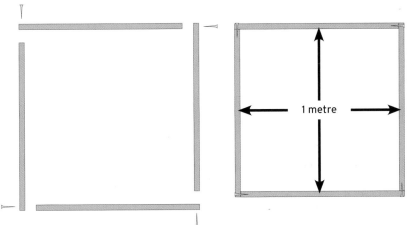

KEY

Board

Decking screws

HOW TO ROTATE THE BOX CORNERS
Each board is only pre-drilled and screwed in place at one end; the other end is held in place by the screw ends of the adjacent board.

that from two of the sides and add it to the other two sides so you still end up with a square box. It is not critical that your garden box frame be exactly 1m (3ft) either inside or outside, but it should be square so each planting square is the same size.

Attach the corners of your box together with coarse-thread decking screws that are twice as long as the thickness of the timber. Use three screws per corner. Pre-drill your holes in the first piece of the two pieces you're connecting; the threads will embed themselves into the second.

CONSTRUCTION DETAILS
Work on a hard surface – such as a drive, pavement or path – and keep your frame flat so it won't end up crooked or twisted. When your frame is screwed together, carry it to the garden area, lay it down and see how it looks. If you want to preserve the appearance of the wood, you could use linseed oil. It's also possible to paint or stain the outside and top, using a water-based stain but leave the inside unpainted.

OTHER BOX MATERIALS
SMG box frames can also be constructed with brick, cement blocks or prefabricated stone. Stone for your SMG box can be man-made preformed sizes or natural slate or any other type of decorative stone that is easy to place and forms an interesting border. If it is not possible to attach the planting grid to the tops of the border frame, then simply lay the grid on the surface of the planting mix.

Thrifty tip

My idea of the best kind of wood is free wood. Go to any construction site, tell the foreman you are building a Square Metre Garden, and ask if they have any scrap timber. Chances are they will be throwing out just what you need. They may even cut it to length for you if you ask nicely. Then your box frames are free.

Building a basic box frame

Materials

Gather the materials. Four boards 1m (3ft) long, 15cm (6in) wide, 25mm (1in) thick. Four 1-m (3-ft) wood lath boards, weedproof membrane (woven polypropylene), large decking screws, smaller screws for the grid, a power drill with relevant screw heads and a pencil.

Preparation

Stack your four boards, mark where to drill and pre-drill three holes in one end of each board. Slide the board back to expose the next one for drilling.

Assembly

Use a drill to screw three large, coarse-thread decking screws through the pre-drilled holes. Attach the boards end-to-end, remembering to rotate the corners until you have a complete frame.

Installing a basic box frame

Preparing the box

Here the box is being installed on a paved surface. If installing direct on the ground, remove the grass (including the roots) or weeds first, and cover that spot with weed-proof membrane.

Use the box frame as a template to cut off sufficient membrane to line the box; it should come up to a half to a third of the box sides.

Place the box in its final location (here on paving) and fit the membrane, pushing it into the corners.

Filling the box

Fill the box with Mel's mix (see page 70) until it covers the base of the box and then water. Repeat this process three times until your box is full of moist mix.

Once the box frame has been filled with mix, the next step is to make a planting grid and to start planting!

Plywood Bases

If you decide to create a base for your SMG box frames, use plywood sheeting and drill 7-mm (¼-in) drainage holes, one per square plus an extra hole in each corner. You attach this base by putting it on top of the assembled box sides, screwing it down, then flipping it over so the box sides are sitting on top of the plywood base.

The thickness of the plywood required depends on the size of the box. A 60 x 60-cm (2 x 2-ft) or 60 x 100-cm (2 x 3-ft) box (anything spanning less than 1m/3 ft) needs 13-mm (½-in) plywood. Any 1 x 1-m (3 x 3-ft) boxes need 15-mm (⅝-in) or even 20-mm (¾-in plywood bases. Use the 20-mm (¾-in) thick plywood if you are going to move the box often. If the box is going to rest on sawhorses or cement blocks and span a large, unsupported distance, it requires thicker plywood. I use regular plywood although some like to spend extra on the longer lasting, but much more expensive, marine or waterproof plywood.

SPECIAL STRUCTURES

For out-of-season gardening, you can create spring, summer, autumn and/or winter box frames. These are just 1 x 1-m (3 x 3-ft) garden boxes or smaller 60 x 120-cm (2 x 4-ft) size that can be modified for special uses. Depending on the time of year, boxes can be equipped with double decks, extensions, covers, or special modifications to allow a longer growing season. Usually these modifications are weather-related items such as crop covers to shade tender seedlings in the summer or a frost protector either in spring or autumn. You will need to determine the best modifications, depending on your particular area and the weather each year.

Balcony Boxes

If you have flat wooden railings, it is easy to set a box right on top of it. For stability and safety, it should be securely bolted to the wood railing. If you can't bolt your boxes down and you're higher than the first floor, I would place the boxes on the floor. Consider the strength and size of your railing and the surrounding environment, and make sure your balcony boxes aren't too big.

Balcony boxes make a very decorative addition to a garden, particularly if you add trailing types of plants that add some colour and character. There are various holders sold at home improvement stores that snap onto your railings to accommodate standard-sized boxes. Hang the box over the outside edge, and it won't take up any of your valuable deck space, and, should it drip when you're

Buy or make extra deep boxes (30 x 30 x 30cm/ 1 x 1 x 1ft) for patio crops such as chillies, peppers or aubergines. Then you can move them around to the warmest, sunny places such as these steps. Deep boxes are also good for long roots and tuber crops.

watering, the water will bypass the deck below. However, if your box is on the inside of the railing, it would be much safer.

Pyramid Boxes

Be creative and make your SMG uniquely yours. Why not get fancy and stack a smaller one on top of another to create pyramids? Why would you do that? Because they're spectacular, and they will be the highlight and focal point of your entire garden. Construction is very simple with just a few braces for stability.

Stepping Up a Level

The next fancy garden layout would be to make a 1-m (3-ft) wide by any length box but every 60cm (2ft) or 1m (3 ft) step up by one level. There are many arrangements you could design, and they would be

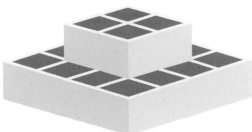

DEEPER BOXES
Pyramid boxes allow you to grow crops such as long carrots, potatoes and chard in the top section and salads or flowers around the perimeter – an all in one space-efficient structure.

limited only by your imagination. Build them the same way as the corner pyramid with an inside brace for every 1-m (3-ft) section.

Extra Deep Boxes

I know I've told you that a depth of 15cm (6in) of Mel's mix is enough for all plants, but your garden becomes more dramatic when the container is extra tall. If you decide to build such a box, just use 20-cm (8-in), 25-cm (10-cm) or 30-cm (12-in) timber instead of the normal 15cm (6 in). The only drawback is cost. But no matter – if you're after that particular look. Since the plants don't need more than 15cm (6in) of Mel's mix, don't spend your money on filling the entire depth with mix. Instead use sand or grit (cheap and available at any home improvement centre) for the bottom layer. "I'll just use my existing garden soil," someone says "and save even more money." Don't! Most soils don't drain well and have weed seeds. Remember weeds? We don't have them anymore in SMG, so if you're going to have multiple layers for your garden boxes, fill any space below 15cm (6in) with just ordinary sand or grit.

An Alternative to Digging Down

There is one last item that you might want to construct – high-rise boxes for long carrots, leeks and potatoes. These crops need deep soil so instead of digging down as in most gardening methods, we take the easy way and build up. Build a 30 x 30-cm (1 x 1-ft) box either 15cm (6in), 23cm (9in) or 30cm (12in) tall out of plywood or any thin type of timber. You can also buy square containers in a range of materials from plastic to fibreglass to polystyrene.

GRIDS AND MATERIALS

Grids are a must. Every box frame should have its own permanent and prominent grid. I'm so adamant about having a grid on every box I tell people that if your SMG doesn't have a grid, it is not a Square Metre Garden. But with a grid, it's an attractive, unusual and unique garden. It tells the story of SMG in one glance. In addition, it has many unseen benefits, so stick with me on this one and build a grid for all of your boxes.

Wood Lath

Wood lath is inexpensive thin timber sold in home improvement centres and DIY stores. Sometimes the laths are a little crooked, filled with knots or break easily, so sort through them. But they're very, very inexpensive. Once you lay them out and drill holes at the

Make a grid

Preparation

Measure the wood lath so it will fit right across the box frame for easy attachment, then cut the laths to length with a saw.

Stack up the lengths of lath and pre-drill. Measure out and mark on the edge of the box where the laths will be fitted.

Assembly

Attach the lath to the box edge with screws, repeat until the four laths form a grid of nine squares.

At each grid intersection, drill a pilot hole (4) and then secure the grid with screws (5).

Once you have made and fixed the grid onto your box frame you can see how to use the SMG to sow and plant nine different types of crops. If you build a box frame from a kit made of plastic or metal or use bricks or pavers, it might be difficult to screw the grid to the edges, so simply lay the grid over the surface of the mix.

30-cm (12-in) intersections, they're very easy to connect together with a nut and bolt or some other type of fastener. Because the wood lath is rigid, it can span from one side of the box to the other side in case your Mel's mix is not level with the top of the box. Otherwise, it can just lie on top of the mix. If your grid spans across the box sides, keep the grid from moving about by drilling a hole in the ends of the two centre slats and screwing them to your wooden box. Some people like to take the wood lath grid up for the winter so it doesn't get wet and rot as easily. Unscrew the four screws, fold the grid and hang it on the garage wall. Put the screws in a plastic bag and hang it up with the grid to keep the screws safe and dry over the winter.

Grids need to remain in place during the entire growing season. Remember you're harvesting and replanting each square throughout the season. Besides that, you want to make sure everyone notices you have an authentic SMG.

Budget Grids

Old Venetian or slat blinds can be used to make a grid. They come in many widths and lengths, and if you visit a local charity shop you can usually find a used set at a great price. Find one that's at least 1m (3ft) wide. Cut off the strings and lay out the strips. Trim the ends with a pair of scissors so they fit your box, drill holes at the half and quarter points, and attach them together with some sort of screw, nail or snap-fastener. The one problem I've found with blinds is their weight. When you first start your garden in the spring, it's usually windy. Sometimes the blinds blow around a little just because the garden is empty and they have no protection from the wind. One solution is to attach them to the soil with a long galvanized nail at every 30-cm (12-in) intersection. This helps hold them down so they don't blow away.

Fun Ideas for Children

The wood or blind grids can be painted, which kids love to do, creating fancy combinations of colours. For the best visual effect, I think plain white is best. (Kids will say, "Blah!") You can also write on them. (Kids will say, "Cool!") Some people like to record what they've planted. It's fun to have visitors sign your grid, especially children and grandchildren. Let them pick out which square they like best, and tell them it can be theirs. When they call, you can tell them how their plants are doing. I bet they'll call more often.

PROTECTING YOUR SMG

To protect one or more squares next to each other from weather or pests, the first step is to make a wire U-frame cage to fit over those squares. You may want to make several U-frames of different sizes that can be used for each size of box you have. Basically, you want to make a wire cage that will fit over the top of each of these areas. Later you can attach a covering made from any number of materials to protect those squares from a variety of hazards. I've found that the easiest cage is made from plastic-coated wire fencing. This can be cut with wire pliers and easily bent over a straight edge to almost any shape. You can make a four-sided wire box from two U-frames or just a two-sided one. There is quite a variety of wire to choose from, so first check out what is available in your area. The wire comes in rolls of different widths and lengths as well as different openings and wire thicknesses.

Chicken Wire

Another common material I like to use is chicken wire. It comes in smaller 2.5-cm (1-in) openings or larger 5-cm (2-in) openings. The 2.5-cm (1-in) size is much stronger but will cost a little more. It also takes a little longer to bend into shape but will keep out more pests than the 5-cm (2-in) size. Chicken wire can be cut with pliers or cutting shears. It's sharp, so be sure to wear gloves. You can buy a whole roll of it, 1m (3ft) or 1.2m (4 ft) wide. In many hardware stores you can buy whatever length you want from their roll, and they will cut it for you.

Building a wire cage

Materials

To build a protective barrier for a 1 x 1-m (3 x 3-ft) box frame you will need: four 25 x 50-mm (1 x 2-in) boards 1m (3ft) long, roll of chicken wire (the stiffer kind found in agricultural stores), plastic cable ties, wire cutters, decking screws, heavy-duty stapler (optional) and a power drill.

Preparation

Double-check the measurements before cutting the timber for the cage as it is important the cage sits squarely on top of the box frame. Mark the width of the box boards on the ends of the cage timber (2). Pre-drill holes (3) in the timber (as shown previously for making the box frame).

Assembly

Screw the frame together using decking screws. *See* page 55 for more on the cage construction.

Roll out the wire and place the frame close to the centre, cut to the required length. This cage is 1m (3ft) high so is three times the length of the box.

Brace the frame with your foot, bend the chicken wire up. Then do this again for the other side. Remember to wear gloves! Repeat steps 5 and 6 so you have two U-shapes of wire. When joined together there will be a double layer of wire on the top of the cage, which makes it more rigid.

Set your wire frame over the wood frame and connect the wire with the plastic ties (or use a heavy-duty stapler). Take the time to secure so as not to leave any sharp wire edges.

Once the wire is bent on all sides, remove the frame and connect the four corners at three locations using the plastic ties.

Once the cage has been made it becomes more rigid and it is then easy to move on and off the box frame by holding the cage at the top.

The Benefits of a Wire Cage

A chicken wire cage over the entire box frame makes it fairly easy to protect your crops against rabbit damage, birds that pull up onion and garlic sets or cats that like to dig in the soil. You can cover the cage with shade netting to protect seedlings from too much sun. The cage will also shelter young plants from strong winds. Build your wire cage high enough to fit the plants' mature sizes as once plants start growing through the wire, it is very difficult to take the cage off. Grab the cage wire with your fingers and lift the whole thing off, tend to the plants and then put it back down. A full cage needs a wooden-frame bottom for support, but it then fits nicely on your wooden garden box frame. See how everything in SMG fits together so nicely.

Construction

To make a wooden base for a wire cage, attach four pieces of 25 x 50mm (1 x 2in) timber 1m (3ft) long in a box shape with two deck screws at each corner. Then cut and shape your chicken wire or fencing wire to the box to create any height you want. Staple the wire to the wood frame using 9mm (3/8-inch) staples, and then wire or tie the vertical corners together or wherever the wire forms a corner. If you are using chicken wire or any wire that has sharp edges, you may want to cover the sharp points – including where the wire is stapled to the wood – with something like duct tape to prevent getting scratched while you're moving your cover. Another way is to attach the wire to the inside of the frame. It's a little more work to staple the wire to the inside, but there won't be any sharp points to scratch you.

If you have a couple of these cages made up ahead of time – one or two that are 30cm (12in) high, another couple 45cm (18in) high and a few at 100cm (3ft) high – they will be available at the right time they're needed for your garden. Don't forget you can use them as a framework for crop covers: for spring protection from cold, cats or crows. They can be summer protection from sun, wind and rain, and autumn protection from rabbits, frosts and snow. They can be stacked on the ground in a pile or hung on the garage or fence wall.

CROP COVERS AND THEIR SUPPORTS

Materials used for covering the wire cages can changed to suit the season and the weather. Clear polythene or garden fleece will warm the soil and protect plants from wind or cold weather and snow, sleet or heavy rain. Later on in the season they are best replaced with fine mesh nets that keep above-ground insects out but remember to allow for easy ventilation and watering.

Clothes Pegs and Clips

A cover can be easily held in place with clothes pegs or clips. The cover can be open on some sides to allow air to circulate or it can be completely enclosed. One consideration, of course, is whether too much heat will build up inside the cage, and that depends on the season and the amount of sunlight your garden receives in your area. When there is too much sunlight for newly planted subjects, just put a shade cloth over the top of your cage. If you have several newly planted squares among other well-established plant squares, you can attach shade patches over just those young plants that need a little shade.

Dome Support

A dome support is so easy to make if you have some bendy pipe (see opposite). Think of it as the structural framework for a greenhouse – in the early spring it can be covered with clear plastic, in the late spring with fine mesh net to keep out flying insects, and in the summer with shade netting to provide a little shade for tender young plants. You can provide protection for autumn crops too.

Covered Tunnel

Another neat looking PVC frame is one in the shape of a covered tunnel. It requires a bit more material, but it gives a lot more headroom for more plants and is much easier to use when you have a cover over the frame. See page 58 for step-by-step instructions. It requires the two 3-m (10-ft) long PVC pipes, but they're arched over each end of your box. Then you need an extra 1-m (3-ft) long piece of pipe that becomes the strut holding the two arches from collapsing. Tying the intersection will not work in this design, so you have to drill holes in the centre of the arches and in each end of the strut, so that a bolt will connect the central strut to the top centre of each arch. Use a bolt and nut that won't tear the plastic or net covering. Now you can see the shape is much more conducive to lifting one side to work inside, and it makes it easier to throw a blanket over the entire box on a cold night.

For those that don't want such a high frame – for example, if you are just going to grow salads – you can cut the 3-m (10-ft) PCV pipes down to 2m (7ft) and you'll have a much lower tunnel top.

Making a dome support

Preparation

1

2

Just bend a 3-m (10-ft) length of 12mm (1/2)-inch PVC pipe from one corner to the opposite corner of your box frame.

Then another from the opposite corners. The pipe should stay in place, but if it keeps popping out you can secure it with a screw into the side of the box.

Assembly

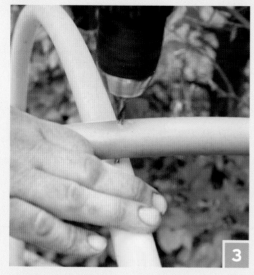

3

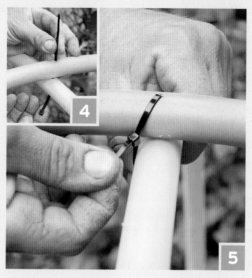

4

5

Find the centre where the pipes cross over and drill a hole through both pipes.

Use a long cable tie (4) to join the intersection at the top (5). You now have a dome that can support any type of loose crop cover.

Making a covered tunnel

Preparation

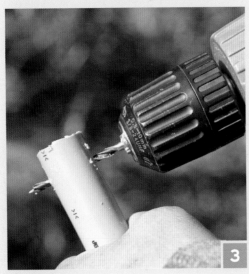

First take the long 3-m (10-ft) pipes and drill one hole in the centre of each pipe. Then bend each pipe into the corners of a box frame as shown. These pipes form the ends of the tunnel.

Assembly

Drill holes in the ends of a 1-m (3-ft) PVC pipe. It will form the supporting strut.

Insert a plastic cable tie through the holes or use a nut and a bolt to keep it in place.

The finished tunnel framework with the strut secured in place. This framework allows for more head height for plants growing in the outer squares than the dome-shaped support. Frameworks can be left in place through the growing season and used to support a range of different crop covers.

PLANT SUPPORTS

How do you support heavy fruiting plants such as tomatoes, peppers and aubergines? One way is to stake the plants and tie them in; another way is to make or buy a permanent cage that the plants can grow through. The cage's height depends on the height of the mature plants. This could be for one square, two, four or for the whole nine squares; it all depends on what is planted in each square. The cage can be self-supporting with sides that stick into the mix just like the wire U-frame previously mentioned, or, if you are making a support for the entire box frame, it is very easy to put a stake of some sort in each corner – either wood or metal – and then suspend the wire horizontally between these four corners.

Even better, if you are supporting the entire box, put in the four corner stakes and then horizontally tie on some nylon pea and bean netting. This netting is available at most garden centres and is particularly good because it is soft and cushiony and won't cut the plants when they rub against it in the wind. It also has large openings you can reach in to and the plants can grow through. It won't bother any of the shorter plants either. It is very easy material to work with and well-suited for SMG. Corner posts must be very strong and firmly held so the horizontal wire or netting won't sag. Posts can be constructed of wood and driven into the ground or attached with decking screws to the inside or outside corner of the wood frame. You can also use PVC pipe or even metal pipe or fence posts. The many options available show how flexible Square Metre Gardening can be.

> *SMG is great for the family. Each person can have his or her own plot.*

Hold Me Up

Tall ornamental plants such as dahlias and sunflowers may also need extra support as they mature and grow in height. Sunflower seeds will need temporary protection when first planted to prevent birds or rabbits from digging up the seeds and to prevent other birds from eating the young seedlings. Temporarily covering your garden with a lid of chicken wire 15cm (6in) high over the box will provide protection until the plants get that tall. Then after the plants reach a height of about 1m (3ft), it is time to put in four corner posts – strong steel fence posts and nylon netting horizontally at several different levels. Start the first at 1m (3ft) and the last should be as high as the fence posts. This will support plants through to maturity and keep them from falling over in strong wind and heavy rain.

Sweetcorn Protection

The easiest way to grow and protect sweetcorn is to grow it in its own box frame (1 x 1m/3 x 3ft is a minimum, 2 x 1m/6 x 3ft would be better) with tall 1.5 to 2-m (5 to 6-ft) steel posts at each corner. Stretch pea and bean netting horizontally across the bed, about 60cm (2ft) or so off the ground and attach to the posts. The plants will then grow through this and be supported. Once the cobs mature, birds and mammals are attracted to the sweet kernels, so you can then wrap chicken wire netting around the whole bed, with a chicken wire top if necessary.

VERTICAL FRAMES FOR VINE CROPS

When I first invented the Square Metre Gardening method, I knew one of the real challenges was going to be some of the big sprawling vine crops like tomatoes. Without a doubt, tomatoes are a favourite crop for home gardeners. However, most varieties can take up a lot

Pea and bean netting can be stretched taut across a box frame and held in place by four metal posts. Plants will then grow up through the netting and be supported.

of room and can become unsightly by season's end if they are allowed to grow without proper care. Also, if left to sprawl over the ground, tomatoes can attract additional pests, and many get damaged or ruined from foot traffic. The whole idea of growing tomatoes this way seemed very non-productive.

I was determined to find a better way to grow tomatoes and what I devised turned out to be not only good for tomatoes, but for all other vine crops too. Every plant that has a vine that sprawls all over the ground – even pumpkins and melons – can be grown vertically as long as you have a strong enough support; the result is a spectacular sight with very little wasted ground space.

Nature Supports

Through the years I experimented with all different types of materials and frames. Finally, I settled upon one that was so simple, easy and inexpensive to use that it was almost ridiculous. Then I began growing all different types of plants vertically. I originally

Building a vertical support for at least one or two of your box frames will allow you to train crops vertically in your SMG. For example, climbing beans and peas, plus vine crops such as tomatoes and cucumbers can be added without them sprawling over neighbouring squares.

thought I would need to design some special way to hold up and accommodate heavier fruits such as winter squash and pumpkins, but as it turned out, these plant vines seemed to understand the situation; the stem supporting the heavy fruit grows thicker and heavier as the fruit becomes larger. If you have a framework and support that will hold the plant, the plant will hold the fruit.

Best Material

I use the strongest material I can find, which is steel. Fortunately, steel comes in tubular pipes used for electrical conduit. It is very strong and turns out to be very inexpensive. Couplings are also available so you can connect two pieces together. I designed an attractive frame that fits right onto a square metre box frame, and it can be attached with clamps that can be bought at any store. Or steel reinforcing rods (rebars) driven into the existing ground outside your box provide a very steady and strong base; then the electrical conduit slips snugly over the bars. It's very simple and inexpensive to assemble. Anyone can do it! To prevent vertically grown plants from shading other parts of the garden, I recommend that tall, vertical frames be constructed on the north side of the garden. To fit it into a square metre box, I designed a frame that measured 1m (3ft) wide and almost 2m (6ft) tall.

Tie It Tight

Vertically growing plants need to be tied to their supports. Nylon netting won't rot in the sun and weather, and I use it exclusively now for both vertical frames and horizontal plant supports. It is very strong, almost unbreakable and lasts for years. It is a wonderful material and the 13-cm (5-in) mesh type sold as pea and bean netting is widely available at garden centres, online and in mail-order catalogues. I actually prefer the 18-cm (7-in) mesh type for tomatoes and larger vine crops as it is easier to get your hands through but this size is hard to find, so plan ahead (for specialist suppliers, *see* page 272). The nylon netting is also durable enough to grow the heavier vine crops on vertical frames, including melons, pumpkins, winter and summer squashes, and tomatoes. Because the netting is loose, it can flop around unless you tie it very tightly to the frame. You will see in Chapter 7, how easy it is to train plants to grow vertically and how productive this can be in a small space such as a SMG box frame.

Winter Storage

At the end of the season the vertical frames can be left up or they can be slipped off the steel rebars and hung on a garage wall. Although the conduit is galvanized and endures many years of service, it eventually will rust – especially at the bottom where it comes in contact with the ground. If you do hang up your metal frames in the winter, for safety reasons make sure you cover or clearly mark the steel rebar that is left sticking out of the ground. You can flag it with brightly covered tape, paint it, or find caps that can be screwed on to prevent someone from tripping over.

COMPOST BINS

One of the key components of Mel's mix is garden compost. This is produced from your own garden waste and it is worth making one or more bins to contain your compost heaps. A composting operation can be as simple as a pile of leaves, weeds and kitchen scraps.

Mother Nature does it all the time. Go to any forest or field and you'll see she gets the job done without any structures. But people are different. We like to conserve space, keep things in their place; and we usually want to build a container or enclosure for our compost materials, which speeds up the operation by creating bulk, which then allows the pile to heat up and decompose faster.

What can we buy or build? There are many compost containers on the market mostly made from plastic or from timber. All work well and are reasonably priced. There are even plastic or metal 'composters' that tumble or turn, speeding up the process, but they cost more and worst of all – you still have to turn them. It's fun at first but it gets old very fast.

Make Your Own

We need a structure that will hold a pile of material in either a round or square shape. Wire fencing works well for round and even square structures if you use four fence posts. Make wire cylinders at least 1 to 1.2m (3 to 4ft) in diameter. The exact length of fencing you'll need isn't critical. I am just going to tell everyone to buy a 3 or 4.5-m (10 or 15-ft) roll of fencing and shape it into a cylinder by attaching the ends together by bending the cut wire ends.

So, if you want a 1-m (3-ft) diameter compost bin, buy 3m (10ft) of fencing. If you want a 1.2-m (4-ft) diameter, buy 4.5m (15ft) of fencing and have enough for a door. And if you don't like round compost bins, buy four 2-m (6-ft) long steel fence posts, drive them in each corner of your composting area, bend the wire around those, and you'll have a square compost bin, much more suited to SMG. Find the best location for your compost bin and fill as explained in Chapter 4. When full or ready to turn, just lift up the wire cylinder, place it next to the pile, and use a garden fork to fill the cylinder in its new location – there you've just turned the compost heap!

Easier Access

It can be difficult to lift off the wire cylinder, particularly if the compost heap is high. An alternative structure, where the compost is easier to remove, is a square bin where one side is made into a hinged gate that can be opened and the compost can then be forked out. You will need an extra post and an S-hook latch.

Thrifty tip: Recycle pallets

Find four wood pallets of similar size and appearance. The place to find them is behind the stores and shops; just ask first to make sure they are being thrown out. A brick or stone under each corner helps keep the wood off the ground to keep it from rotting; corners are tied with rope, cord or chain. It doesn't have to be nailed or screwed together, and it doesn't have to be really tight. You may want to have the pallet boards face outside to look nice, and you can make them all run either horizontally or vertically - whatever looks best.

An even better alternative is to build a square bin, where one side is made up of removable horizontal slats. These slot into posts with grooves in them. Simply add the slats as the compost heap grows and then remove them so you can access the compost more easily. You can make your own bin with removable slats or buy a ready-to-assemble kit.

If you don't have a compost heap yet, start one now. It's essential to the Square Metre Gardening method.

A Series of Bins

In a large garden, it is worth having a series of bins lined up together. You can have one, two or up to six bins. When and why would you need more than one? If you grow veg and have borders and a lawn and you are serious about composting, you may be able to produce enough material to fill up more than one bin. Then for mixing (as explained in Chapter 4), you could just move the material from a full bin to an empty one right next to it. It is also efficient to separate material just added for composting, from material that has been fully composted and is ready to use. The nice thing about a series of bins is you only need three sides of timber for each additional bin.

I could include directions for other materials to use like bricks or cement blocks, landscape timbers or logs, but unless you have these

Making a compost bin

Here's how to make a basic timber bin with slatted sides for easier filling and emptying. It is worth having more than one bin, one to fill and another with rotted-down compost ready for use.

MATERIALS
All timber was rough-sawn and tanalised.
Six boards 1m (3ft) by 150 x 25mm (6 x 1in) for the back panel
Twelve boards 1025mm (3ft 1in) by 150 x 25mm (6 x 1in) for side panels
Six boards 850mm (2ft 10in) of 150 x 25mm (6 x 1in) for the slats
Four lengths 1m by 25 x 20mm (1 x ¾in) to form the slots
Four posts 1m (3ft) by 75 x 75mm (3 x 3in)

Plus decking screws, a drill, pencil and a saw.

Mark the width of the posts on the panels (2) and drill pilot holes for the screws (1).

Screw the 1-m (3-ft) length back boards to the two rear corner posts. Then screw the side boards to one of the front posts, again flat on the ground and repeat for the other side.

Screw the 1025-mm (3-ft 1-in) side panels to the back posts creating a three sided box. Using longer timber for the side panels means you can overlap at the back edge making a neater job.

Attach the 25 x 20-mm (1 x ¾-in) timber to the front posts making a slot slightly wider than 25mm (1in). The slats can be easily inserted and removed (6) to access the compost.

materials spare already they would be too expensive and inefficient. They may look good in books but not in our system because they are just not practical.

Of course, no one says you have to have an enclosure or a bin, but if you're a Square Metre Gardener and you have nice square boxes for all of your garden, why would you want just a heap for your garden compost?

PATHS

"Put your best foot forward" is the saying, but what are you going to put it on? Grass, brick, bark chips, gravel or just plain soil? Most people put their boxes on their lawn and leave the grass for their paths. This helps keep a natural look. One word of warning – do remove any grass under the box before you start as pests will feed on the dead grass, then move to your crops. If you want to leave natural soil in your paths, use a Dutch hoe or your favourite long-handled weeder once a week.

Mulch Paths

If you don't want grass paths, lay down a mulch. Here again, you want to first dig out any weeds or grass; then to prevent weeds from growing back without using chemicals, you can put down a sheet mulch. There are many on the market today. They come in 1-m or 1.2-m (3- or 4-ft wide rolls) and do quite a good job. Don't use regular black plastic – it won't drain and it's slippery. Then just cover the sheet mulch with at least 2.5 to 5cm (1 to 2in) depth of loose mulch.

You can use gravel, which comes in all different kinds and sizes, colours and shapes, or you can use bark chips or wood chippings; I've even seen people use straw, hay or even autumn leaves. As you walk, these materials break up and gradually decompose, creating something you can add later to your compost heap.

You can also build walkways out of pavers, wood planks or paving stones. Again, take out any weeds and put down a sheet mulch first. You can create some very interesting patterns with bricks and paving blocks. Keep the joints fairly tight so the surface doesn't shift.

Smart Paths

Brick paths or pavers look neat and it is possible to lay them simply without any mortar or cement. It is important to use bricks suitable for outdoor use (i.e. frost-proof or engineering bricks). I use many layers of newspaper or a single layer of weed-proof membrane followed by a 2.5-cm (1-in) deep layer of sand and then start laying

Frost-resistant bricks or pavers make smart paths. Bed them down on a sand bed and take time to tap each brick down as shown so it is even and level with the other bricks.

bricks on that sand base. Just fill in the tight joints with loose sand and tap the bricks down so they are even. Brick (or any well-designed hard landscaped) paths can really smarten up the area and they can be laid out in a range of different patterns.

One Last Idea

How would you like to carpet your garden . . . wall to wall? Well, you can. Buy new or used artificial grass but, don't worry, you won't have to mow it!

LET'S REVIEW

When building a SMG, start with the basic building block – a 1 x 1-m (3 x 3-ft) bottomless timber box frame. Then depending on the situation, add special features to solve any gardening problem or to protect your garden from any hazard. Some of the simple additions you can add to your SMG boxes:

- A wire bottom to keep out moles
- A weed-proof membrane to suppress weeds
- A chicken wire top to keep out cats, dogs and rabbits

A PVC top frame plus suitable crop covers will give you:

- Clear plastic to create a miniature greenhouse
- Bird or rabbit netting
- A blanket to protect plants from frosts
- Fine mesh covers to protect from insects

After all this talk about building all these different things for protecting your garden, I don't want you to become worried, thinking that you have to spend a lot of time creating complex structures for your SMG. It's not so! For the most part, your plants will just sit there quietly growing, looking better and better every day. So relax and enjoy watching the plants grow!

COMMONSENSE CARE

Remember, protecting your garden is a lot like protecting your children – if it's cold, add garden fleece (a sweater); if sleet and hail are predicted, add clear plastic (a raincoat); and if it's windy, add a windbreak (jacket). Since you wouldn't let your kids play out in the cold winter without warm clothing for protection, do the same for your plants. Keeping this in mind, you'll be able to come up with easy and practical solutions for protecting your garden from the worst of conditions. That makes it very rewarding because then you can enjoy your garden much longer every year.

Thrifty tip: Kill weeds for free

Some gardeners use double sheets of newspaper or heavy-duty cardboard from flattened large boxes to kill grass or weeds. This is a good way to smother and kill grass or weeds in the paths without any digging but you need to be patient. However, it needs to be weighted down and looks a bit scruffy unless you cover it with bark chips. Old carpet is no longer recommended as a mulch due to concerns about the chemicals, such as the glues, particularly in cheaper foam-backed carpets leaching into the soil.

4

Mel's mix

My special growing mix is the backbone of the entire Square Metre Gardening method! It is the reason all the other improvements are possible. So, please, pay careful attention to everything in this chapter so you can give your plants the best possible start and reap the benefits for years to come.

Making up a special mix to fill the boxes is a crucial part of my SMG method.

Mel's mix, the Essential Ingredient

Now, with my SMG method, you'll never have to do all the time-consuming, back-breaking labour of improving your garden soil every spring. Your Mel's mix is ready to go whenever you are. It never has to be replaced and you don't have to do any soil cultivation except plant your crops.

Mel's mix may be the most costly part of SMG, yet at the same time it is the most cost effective. How can it be both? The answer: if you try to skimp on this item, you'll be disappointed in all the rest. But if you do it right, all the other advantages of SMG will fall into place and you will be the richest gardener in your area. Sorry to be so adamant, but this is really what makes SMG so different and successful. We have never had a failure of SMG except when someone decided to skimp on the ingredients to save money.

Let's review what this perfect soil will do for your garden, then the why and how so you fully understand the nature of the mix.

We'll go through each of the three ingredients indicated: garden compost, peat moss and vermiculite. Then what each one is, why you need it and where to obtain it all. Then I'll discuss how to mix, moisten and place it in your boxes. If you do it right, you'll have the most enjoyable gardening experience of your life. That wonderful feeling will be repeated every time you plant and replant every single square. Your hand will just slip through the loose, easily worked, earthy-smelling soil, and you will sigh with happiness and smile every time. But enough talk and teasing, let's get started!

SO SIMPLE

Square Metre Gardening is so simple you don't have to learn all the intricate details of soil structure, texture and drainage. You don't even have to know what pH means, how to pronounce it, or which letter is a capital and which is lower case (or why people are always getting that mixed up). Why, you may ask? Because I've designed a perfect growing mix that is suitable for just about all plants. For those of you who crave more information: the well-rotted garden

Things You Have To Know	
Garden soil for traditional cultivation:	**Mel's mix for Square Metre Gardening:**
■ Structure	■ The Formula
■ Drainage	
■ Texture	
■ Organic content	
■ pH	
■ Fertiliser	
■ Digging	
■ Weeding	

compost (or the alternative of five blended soil improvers) balances out the acidity in the peat moss. In addition, since we don't use your existing soil (remember we only need a 15-cm/6-in depth of pure Mel's mix), you won't be concerned with what type of soil it is or what the pH is. You won't have to buy a pH soil test kit or take soil samples.

NO FERTILISER, NO WORRY

Mel's mix has all the nutrients, minerals and trace elements that plants need. So you can forget all about adding extra fertiliser. Isn't that amazing? Not only do you not have to buy it, you don't even have to learn about it. After the inital set-up and filling of the boxes, in subsequent years you'll find there is no work to do; there is no going to the garden centre reading labels, lugging big bags or bales of soil improvers home, no working in lime, getting a rotovator working and trying to turn over that wet, mucky soil. Why, you don't even have to do the soil ball test in the palm of your hand only to find out you have to wait another week because your soil is too wet or still frozen. What's the soil ball test, you ask? I'm not going to tell you because you don't now need to know.

> **My Simple Formula**
>
> ⅓ **Garden Compost**
> ⅓ **Peat Moss**
> ⅓ **Vermiculite**
> *Mix equal parts of each, measured by volume not by weight.*

Your Mel's mix is always ready to plant no matter what the weather. It's always loose, friable (which the experts define as that which is easily worked, i.e. good and crumbly), and ready for the right time of year to plant. It drains and becomes unfrozen so much quicker than regular garden soil.

WHERE HAVE YOU BEEN?

Planting a garden will no longer depend on when the soil is ready but only on the right date to plant seeds and young plants. This is just one more simplification of gardening the Square Metre way. How does that all sound? Simple and easy, no work and no fuss. I have had people ask me, "Why weren't you born one hundred years ago so I could have started with Square Metre Gardening instead of having to do all the work of single-row gardening all my life?" Good question!

NO DIGGING

By using Mel's mix you completely eliminate all the hard work of digging and moving existing soil. All gardening in the past has been

MEL'S MIX IS MADE FROM...

One-third by volume garden compost

One-third by volume peat moss

One-third by volume vermiculite

based upon improving your existing soil. Now you don't have to know anything about soils. Just start with a perfect growing medium of ⅓ garden compost, ⅓ peat moss, and ⅓ vermiculite. All ingredients are measured by volume.

LIKE A SPONGE

Through many experiments, I came up with the very best ingredients for that perfect growing soil. Of course, I made sure they were inexpensive, readily available and able to hold just the right amount of moisture for plants while not becoming too soggy for roots, which would be fatal for your plants. I created a formula that holds moisture, yet drains well.

At first this seemed like an impossible task, but then I thought about sponges. When you take a dry sponge and slowly add water to it, the sponge just keeps soaking up water until it's finally saturated. At that point, any extra water just drains out the bottom. Well, it turns out that two of our ingredients, peat moss and vermiculite, do exactly that same thing. It may take a while to wet them and keep them moist so you have to keep adding water, but finally, when they become saturated, any excess water just drains right out the bottom. Peat moss and vermiculite are sold at garden centres, DIY stores and from online horticultural suppliers (*see* page 272).

The biggest problem turns out to be arithmetic, not the materials. All three ingredients in Mel's mix are sold in different-sized bags or bales, and this may make it harder to figure out how much of each you need. But don't worry, I'm going to give you some examples so you won't even have to think about the maths.

1 GARDEN COMPOST

The best kind is home-made compost that you make in your own garden. As this will take several months to break down into a useable ingredient, you should start a compost heap straightaway so you have garden compost ready for spring planting. If it is already spring and you are keen to get growing straightaway, you can substitute with bags of a good quality brand of potting or multi-purpose compost or buy several brands of soil improver and blend them. It is still worth starting a compost heap as garden compost is added each time you replant a square. Garden compost is absolutely the best material in which to grow your plants. It has all the nutrients needed for plant growth, it is loose and friable so easy to plant. Finally, garden compost holds lots of moisture, yet drains well. It's easy to make, yet hard to find.

Home-made garden compost is free and makes up a third of Mel's mix. So it is well worth filling a compost bin with all the plant waste material from your garden. This material will then get broken down by Mother Nature to form a crumbly mixture.

Good and Bad

Composting can appear to be a confusing subject because the word "compost" is both a noun and a verb. As a noun, compost is described as a rich, crumbly, soil-like material used in gardening. As a verb, composting is the process of breaking down plant material that is no longer growing through a decomposition process. There are actually two types of processes: aerobic, with air; and anaerobic, without air. Both are natural processes but the aerobic process has no odour, heats up and does its job, so this is done by, what I call, "good bugs". The anaerobic process smells of bad eggs, is messy, and is very objectionable. The more common name for this is rotting.

I don't have to tell you that I call the microbes that work anaerobically the "bad bugs".

What to Use

Any plant material is perfect for adding to your compost heap as long as it's not hosting a major plant disease, plant virus or pest. When the ingredients are heaped together and if they have enough bulk, they will decompose organically by the aerobic process all by themselves. But it takes time; Mother Nature can't be hurried. Some people say, "I can't wait for a year or two. How can I speed up this process?"

The Importance of Mass

Using the right ingredients and mixing, mashing, moistening and moving them will help speed the composting. But there is one more ideal condition, and that is mass. The more bulk you have in your heap the faster it will compost or decompose. If your heap is higher than 1.2 to 1.5m (4 to 5ft), you'll have a hard time adding new ingredients. If the area is larger than 1.2 x 1.2m (4 x 4ft), the air will have trouble getting into the centre where all the action is and the good bugs will be overcome by the bad bugs and the heap will start to decompose anaerobically (without air) and start to smell. If you don't have enough bulk, i.e. smaller than 1 x 1m

Most plant material can be added to a compost bin, apart from badly diseased or pest-infested plants and weeds with seed heads.

Tips for Successful Composting

	Do	Don't
Ingredients	Add plant material such as spent top growth, prunings and roots	Do not add any animal parts such as bones or synthetic materials
Bin size	About 1 x 1m (3 x 3ft)	A lot smaller or larger than 1 x 1m (3 x 3ft)
Moisture	Moist	Too dry or too wet
Mixing	As often as you can	Never mix ingredients

Garden compost that is dark, crumbly and ready to use. If there are a few large bits that have not broken down, simply add them back into the compost bin.

(3 x 3ft), your heap will just sit there and do nothing except cry out, "I'm going to wait for Mother Nature."

We keep calling it a heap, and you may wonder if it will be ugly and messy. But the heap can be contained very nicely with a home-made or store-bought container called a compost bin. Oh no! Another name! So now, I'm going to be composting my garden compost in my compost bin. You've got it! See, that wasn't so bad.

Compost Heap Ingredients

What you need to remember about the ingredients is that animal by-products are not good for your compost heap. Eggshells are okay; just crush and sprinkle around. Manure is okay from plant-eating animals, such as horses, but no manure from meat-eating animals, such as pigs.

KAREN WRITES...

I had always been a little afraid of composting, but Mel's advice makes everything so logical and easy to understand

CHOP, CHOP, CHOP

If you are in a real hurry, there are expensive, but effective, rotating drum compost makers you can buy. You just turn a handle, flip a container or push a barrel around, and the contents are mixed and moved.

I've also heard of, but never tried, the closed, black-plastic-bag-of-ingredients-left-in-the-garage-over-the-winter method. Be careful when you open the bag because, as you can guess, that method uses the no air: an anaerobic process that smells. Some gardeners have tried using plastic dustbins. You have to drill or poke holes in them so the air can get in, but if the lid is tight-fitting, you could roll it around every day.

I've found from my own experimenting that no matter what method you use, the sooner you mix and move and the more you mash (cut or chop), the sooner and faster you'll start the composting action going. Just add compost ingredients by mixing them in with the top of the existing heap. Each time you add a lot or just a little, stir it into the top of the pile and mix it in well. But don't just add

Detailed list of ingredients

Yes	Caution - Limited Amounts	No
Each item should be under 20 percent of total by volume	*Each item should be under 10 percent of total by volume*	*These items should not be added to a compost bin*
Straw	Sweetcorn cobs	Seriously diseased or pest-infested materials
Hay	Shredded twigs	
Leaves	Shredded bark	Meat or bones
Grass clippings (dried)	Pine needles	Grease
Old turf	Hedge trimmings	Whole eggs
Reject or spoiled garden produce	Wood shavings	Cheese
Vegetable and fruit peels	Sawdust	Seeds and fruit pits
Newspaper (shredded)	Coffee grounds	Cat or dog manure
Eggshells (crushed)	Nut shells	Bakery products
Stable or poultry manure		Dairy products
Tea bags		Supper plate scrapings or kitchen scraps

Large quantities of autumn leaves are best kept separate from compost heaps. Instead, put the leaves in their own container where fungi will rot them down into leaf mould. A simple wire enclosure is sufficient as the fungi do not generate or need heat to do the job.

one type of material, such as grass clippings, in thick layers; it is better to mix them up, with shredded newspapers or prunings.

PRACTICAL COMPOSTING TIPS
Mow those Leaves
Save some of your leaves from autumn to add to the compost heap next year rather than all at once. After you rake them up, run the lawnmower over them to chop them up and then stuff into plastic bags (make sure they are not too wet) or, if you prefer, store them in a wire enclosure.

Dry that Grass
Others like to save their grass clippings the same way, but you have to be very careful. If piled up, fresh green grass will quickly turn into

an anaerobic operation that's a stinking, slimy, gooey mess. Grass clippings have to be dried before adding them to the heap or stored for later addition. It does seem like an oxymoron to dry the grass clippings only to moisten them in the compost heap, but now I'm sure you can see why we do it that way.

I compare it to my mother's meatloaf. She would dry bread and then crumble it to make breadcrumbs. She would then add milk to moisten everything. If she had just added moist, fresh bread, it would have become clumpy and gooey. The garden compost is similar. If material is put in wet, it packs down in clumps, preventing air from entering the heap, and then it smells.

So spread your grass clippings out on a tarpaulin or on the driveway, turn them a few times with a rake or flip your tarpaulin before storing them or adding them to your compost heap. How long? Until the grass is brownish and dry to the touch. It depends on the sun, humidity and rain, as well as the climate of your location.

Thrifty tip

Your home compost heap should include every different thing you can think of and you can bulk it out with other materials. Go to the grocery store and ask for the produce manager. Many shops throw out tons of spoiled vegetables and fruits they can't sell. These are from all over the world, so just think of the different soils and climates all that has grown in and what different vitamins, minerals, and trace elements they contain. Simply chop them up and mix them in the compost heap.

Mix and Turn

This is a good time to remind you that the centre of the heap is where most of the action is. It will be the hottest (up to 65° C or 150°F), the moistest, and where the microbes will be decomposing the ingredients. Knowing all that, when you turn the contents of one compost bin into another, you will be putting the top of A into the bottom of B – assuming you have two bins or heaps side-by-side – then you make sure you put the outside material of A into the inside of B. Get it? It's just like the theory that opposites attract. Mix in (at the same time) opposite colours, wetness, size – everything opposite for the fastest operation. In other words, brown with green, wet with dry, coarse with fine. That's all easy to remember.

Coffee grounds and free buckets

Any place people gather, there will be waste thrown out. Check out farmer's markets, local fairs or street carnivals, flea markets, even places like Starbucks (guess what they would have for you there?). In addition to compost material, many of these restaurant-type places have big buckets used for pickles, mayonnaise or oil that make great water buckets - all these items are free for the asking.

How to speed up composting

When will the compost be ready? So much depends on the volume of material, the temperature inside the bin and the individual ingredients but, as a guide, allow three to six months depending on the weather conditions. Here's how to give it a helping hand.

Remove any material that is not composting as fast as the rest of the heap; this material is usually at the edges of the bin where it is cooler.

Mix the uncomposted material together on the ground; you can chop up any large pieces such as fibrous stems or roots with a spade.

After mixing and chopping the uncomposted material, return it to the bin and push it down into the centre where conditions are warmer.

Cover the compost with a waterproof cover during heavy rain. Once the material has fully broken down, it is ready to be used around the garden.

GO BIG TIME

If you are really into this, you can brainstorm to think of places that throw out organic or plant material. There are all kinds of places where you can collect ingredients for your compost heap. And, you know, the nice thing is that you'll find the same situation the world

Peat is a natural material formed millions of years ago from decomposing moss. It is extracted and processed for use in horticulture but as it is non-renewable and its extraction can damage rare habitats, use it responsibly or use a peat-free alternative.

over. When I'm visiting foreign countries, my hosts say, "We are poor here, and we have nothing to compost." I take them on a tour and find all of these places have things that could be composted. It's always things people are throwing out. I've done that in India, Haiti, Argentina, Nepal, Thailand, Ghana, and even in London, Paris, Amsterdam and New York City, so look and you'll find it.

ALTERNATIVES TO GARDEN COMPOST

You may not make enough garden compost for all the boxes you want to fill, or you might want to get growing straightaway. Instead, you can substitute bags of potting or multi-purpose compost from garden centres. These are a blend of different materials, mostly peat or a peat-free alternative together with other ingredients, such as sand, perlite, lime (to bring the pH to neutral) and fertilisers. A cheaper alternative is to buy bagged soil improvers. But don't buy all of one kind of soil improver. Don't let the salesperson sell you the "best and most popular", especially if it's loose and not bagged. Here's why. All commercial compost is a by-product from one industry. It might be the wood, cattle, mushroom industry that has a waste product and they have to get rid of it. They said, "What if we take our waste product (sawdust, manure, mushroom compost) and compost it, people will pay us and take it away." Everyone laughed but, by golly, it happened just that way. Now every industry with a waste product is finding ways to get rid of it at a profit, all the while protecting the environment. What a good deal. The only setback for gardeners is most bags of soil improver come from a single product and have only one ingredient. What's the solution? Buy a variety of composts and mix them together. Now you are more likely to get a better mixture.

2 PEAT MOSS

The second ingredient in Mel's mix is peat moss. It's a natural material occurring on the earth that has been made after millions of years from decomposing plant material. There are plenty of debates about the use of peat moss because it's a non-renewable resource. Because there is a limit to this valuable material I'd like to guide you in using it responsibly while maximising its benefits.

Only a Little

You add peat moss once and only once when you first create your Mel's mix. Thereafter, you'll never need to add peat moss to the garden. (What you will add is garden compost, which is renewable.)

Most peat moss comes from Ireland and the Baltic States where it is still readily available but some of it in the UK is extracted from sensitive habitats. Because it's such a valuable resource, SMG says let's not waste it. Let's be conservative and sensible and use what we have, a beneficial, natural material, but make it longer lasting. If you do not want to use peat moss at all, then experiment with replacing it with a peat-free substitute such as coir or composted bark.

3 VERMICULITE

Vermiculite, the third and final ingredient in Mel's mix, is also a natural material and is obtainable all over the world. It's mica rock mined out of the ground. Once the rock is collected, it is then ground up into small particles and heated until it explodes just like popcorn, forming small pieces from as large as the tip of your little finger down to almost a powder. However, this material is filled with nooks and crannies and these hold a tremendous amount of water and yet can breathe, making the soil extremely friable and loose. The moisture is always there for the roots to absorb. Remember that roots don't grow through soil; they grow around soil particles. That's why plants do better in a loose, friable soil because the roots have an easy time growing.

Different Grades

Vermiculite is graded into several sizes – fine, medium and coarse – and is also tested and qualified for different types of uses. The coarse agricultural grade holds the most moisture while at the same time giving the most friability to the soil mix. You may find that many garden centres do not stock vermiculite.

Locating it can be difficult, so plan ahead and research horticulture wholesalers or agriculture sundries (*see* page 272). Ideally, you want 100 litre bags of coarse vermiculite but you might have to settle for medium grade. There is one caution when you mix it, and it is the same caution with peat moss. Both materials can be dusty when dry right out of the bag, so wear gloves and a painting mask. Mix outdoors, on a calm day.

Perlite versus Vermiculite

Perlite is another natural material mined out of the earth and used in agriculture for the same purpose as vermiculite, to break up and loosen poor soils and to retain moisture. I personally don't like or use perlite, and here's why. It is hard as a rock, rather coarse and gritty, and I don't like the feel of it in the soil mix. It doesn't hold moisture like vermiculite. In addition, it floats to the top of the soil mix as you water your garden and because it's white, it looks rather unsightly and unnatural. And it makes me sneeze! Many people do use perlite instead of vermiculite and, in fact, most of the commercial mixes are made with perlite because it's cheaper. It's a matter of preference and availability.

BUYING WHAT YOU NEED

If you found the maths about area difficult in previous chapters, don't even bother with volume. Get the kids to do the maths for you.

Why concern yourself with volume? Because you need to know the quantity of the three ingredients for Mel's mix necessary to fill your boxes. The good news is bags of compost, peat moss and vermiculite are usually sold by volume (in litres).

So, let's review how to figure volume. Volume is merely: area x depth = cubic metres. In other words, square metres (the area) times the depth equals cubic metres.

Our 1 x 1-metre box is 1 square metre in area. If it were 1 metre deep, the volume would be: 1 (the area) times 1 (the depth) equals 1 cubic metre. But it's not 1 metre deep, it's only 0.15m (15cm) so we need only one to two-tenths for our 1 x 1-m box. The maths looks like this: 1 times 1 divided by 5 equals 0.2 cubic litres. Or to show it mathematically, $(1 \times 1) \div 5 = 0.2$ cubic litres. (Now don't laugh, kids; some of the parents will be thankful for this kind of help).

Peat Moss

Peat moss is milled to be light and fluffy but as it is bulky to transport, quantities above 150 litres are compressed, then wrapped in bales. A full bale is equivalent to 300 litres, a half bale is equivalent to 150 litres.

Vermiculite

Don't buy the small-sized bags if you can help it, insist on the 100 litre bags. Call ahead to locate. The coarse grade is preferable but medium (standard) will do better than fine.

WORKING OUT VOLUME

Now here's the tricky part. Since all the products for Mel's mix come in different volumes, you'll have to purchase them already knowing how much you'll need to mix correctly and fill your boxes completely. Let's use a hypothetical example. So if we had four boxes to fill, we would need 4 x 0.2 = 0.8 cubic litres of mix. (Four boxes times 200 litres for each box equals 800 litres of mix.) One-third of the total for each ingredient equates to about 250 to 300 litres of each. We don't have to be too exact, we aren't mixing a cake.

Shopping List for Four Boxes
- **Peat Moss**: One bale compressed
- **Vermiculite**: three 100 litre bags
- **Compost**: Whatever it takes to get 250 to 300 litres (bags are usually 60 litres, but are often sold as buy two get one free)

More Shopping Lists for Different Sized Batches
If you had three 1 x 1-m boxes, you would need 600 litres:
- two 100 litre bags of vermiculite.
- three to four 60 litre bags peat moss
- three to four 60 litre bags (different brands) of compost

You often need to buy more than you think you actually need because the volume stated on the pack is the volume when packed; it often reduces by the time it gets to you as the bags are piled on top of each other. Remember any surplus can be stored and used later on. For online sources of ingredients, *see page 272.*

HOW TO MIX

This is where making your Mel's mix and filling your boxes starts to get fun. Mix it all at once if possible (storing any excess in recycled bags). But if it's too big a batch to handle, split it into smaller batches. Here's a suggestion: use a pair of scissors to cut open your bags carefully along the top so you can reuse them, e.g. for measuring out garden compost.

For small quanties, for one or two beds, use a large wheelbarrow so you can mix, then tip straight in. The alternative for large quantities is to get a large tarpaulin, at least 4.5 x 4.5m (15 x 15ft), and open it near your garden where you have all your boxes built and located. Make sure you have them in their final resting place.

The peat moss and vermiculite (or perlite) might be dusty when dry, so do this when there is no wind. Don't do it in the garage, or you'll get dust all over your nice new car or workshop. Wear a painter's mask and have a hose ready with a very fine spray. Don't forget to have a mixing tools ready, e.g. a shovel, a hoe or a spade.

Count out the bags and boxes, do the maths one more time and start opening the bags and pouring the contents out on the tarpaulin without walking on the ingredients. Roughly mix the three ingredients as best you can as you pour it.

Quick guide to making Mel's mix

A large tarpaulin can be used to mix all the ingredients. If you are using soil improvers instead of garden compost, empty out the first bag of soil improver into the centre of the tarpaulin.

Tip the other soil improvers into the centre, these will be mixed together before you add the peat moss and vermiculite.

To mix, each person takes two corners of the tarpaulin and drags it over and rolls the ingredients together.

Once the soil improvers are well mixed you can add the vermiculite: pour out gently. If you are using garden compost instead of soil improvers simply put the garden compost down, then follow with the vermiculite.

Next add the peat moss or a peat-free alternative (coir, composted bark, bagged compost or extra garden compost).

If the ingredients are dry and dusty, you can water them lightly before mixing or wear a protective mask.

The finished Mel's mix should look similar to this with the ingredients well distributed.

Using a wheelbarrow

You can mix up enough Mel's mix in a large capacity wheelbarrow to fill a SMG box frame. Add equal quantities of garden compost, vermiculite and peat moss (or alternative) to the wheelbarrow.

Use a garden spade or shovel to carefully mix all the ingredients together. If all the ingredients are very dry, you can lightly water them. Then tip the mix into the centre of the box.

Fill the box with the mix, spreading it out evenly and making sure the corners and edges are filled. The mix can settle overnight, so if you have any excess, top it up and keep in an empty bag.

Then drag two corners of the tarpaulin to the opposite two corners. You'll see the material roll over, mixing itself. When you've pulled the tarpaulin so that the mixture is almost to the edge, move 90 degrees and pull those two corners over. You just work your way around the tarpaulin and repeat, pulling corners together until your Mel's mix is uniformly mixed. It's finished when you don't see any single material or one colour.

Use the hose with a fine mist or spray to wet down any dust, but don't spray so much you make puddles or wet the ingredients so the mixture becomes too heavy to move easily. Don't let the kids play in the mixture, or they will crush the large particles of vermiculite. (By the way, I'd save a small plastic bag of vermiculite for seed starting. We'll get to seed starting in the next chapter.)

The next step is to fill the boxes, wetting down the mixed-in layers if they are dry as you fill it. Once the box is full, push it into the corners and level off the top, but don't pack it down as it will settle just right all by itself.

If you have any leftover Mel's mix, put it back in the empty bags you set aside for reuse. That extra Mel's mix will come in handy for sowing and planting as well as extra to top off the boxes when the soil level settles. Turn the bags inside out if you want a plain look, label with a marker and put them aside. Since you don't really water the mix until it's in the box, your stored mix will be fairly dry and lightweight to carry.

To fill other boxes, work with someone else to drag the tarpaulin close to the new boxes. Don't try to carry shovelfuls of mix to the box as it will spill and be wasted. This is precious stuff.

> Don't wet the mix any more than is absolutely necessary; use a fine spray to reduce any dust. The mix becomes very heavy when wet, and it would be difficult to drag the tarpaulin around your garden.

That's also why we don't water the Mel's mix in the tarpaulin, but as you are adding it to the box; that way the remaining material in the tarpaulin doesn't get so heavy that it is hard to drag. As soon as you add your grid to each box, you are ready to plant.

You have now completed the most important and rewarding step in SMG. If you followed the formula correctly, and didn't add any of your existing soil, it will stay loose and friable as long as you need it.

AN AFTERTHOUGHT

I want to make doubly sure you got the message of this chapter, so I'd like to summarise the critical facts about compost. If you use bagged compost or soil improver with only one or two ingredients, mix several different types of compost together. Most commercial composts have only one or two ingredients because they are merely leftover waste materials or by-products from an industrial or commercial operation. By themselves, they do not make a good ingredient in Mel's mix.

However, the good news is, if you can find at least four of these individual composted materials you can mix them together to make a well-rounded blended compost ingredient for your Mel's mix.

And if you did your job and got a blended compost made from at least five major ingredients, you will be blessed with the most wonderful garden you could ever imagine. And no more work ever.

How to plant your Square Metre Garden

This chapter covers choosing which crops to grow and how to visualise your harvest to avoid gluts. Here are my tried-and-tested ways to get started with growing your crops from sowing seeds to planting out. Proper spacing is key to the success of the Square Metre Gardening method.

The grid that divides up the box frame will guide you to the correct spacing when sowing and planting.

Planting square by square

Now we're getting to the interesting and fun part. You've picked the size and shape of the boxes and planned the layout. You've built the boxes, put in the Mel's mix and added the grids. Now it's time to sow and plant your crops!

Here you'll find out an easy way to work out exactly how many seeds or plants to put in each square and how to space them out evenly – just by using your fingers.

VISUALISE THE HARVEST

In SMG, begin by visualising what you want to harvest. This simple step prevents you from planting too much. Picture a large plant like a head of cabbage. That single cabbage will take up a whole square so you can only plant one per square. It's the same with broccoli and cauliflower. Let's go to the opposite end of the spectrum and think of the small plants like radishes. Sixteen can fit into a single square. It's the same for spring onions and carrots, sixteen per square. Yet that's an 8-cm (3-in) spacing between plants, which is exactly the same spacing the seed packet recommends as it says "thin to 8cm (3in) apart."

Plants by Size

Think of these plants as if they were international shirt sizes. Shirts come in all four sizes: small, medium, large and extra large and so do our plants (there is actually a fifth shirt size twice extra large but let's forget about that for now). It's that simple.

The extra large, of course, are those that take up the entire square plants such as cabbages, peppers, broccoli and cauliflower. Next are the large plants, those that can be planted four to a square, which equals 15cm (6in) apart. Large plants include lettuce, French marigolds, chard and parsley.

Some crops can be planted one per square if you let the plant grow to its full size or the crop can be planted four per square if you harvest the outer leaves throughout the season. This category includes parsley, basil and even the larger heads of leaf lettuce and chard. Using the Square Metre Gardening method, you simply use your scissors to snip and constantly harvest the outer leaves of edible greens, so they don't take up as much space as in a conventional garden.

PLANT SPACING
Square-metre beds can be used to grow a wide variety of edible crops, spaced in the planting grid according to their cropping size.

EXTRA LARGE
1 Plant
Placed 30cm (12in) apart:
Broccoli
Cabbage

LARGE
4 Plants
Placed 15cm (6in) apart:
Lettuce

MEDIUM
9 Plants
Placed 10cm (4in) apart:
Beetroot
Spinach
Bush Bean

SMALL
16 Plants
Placed 8cm (3in) apart:
Carrot
Radish
Onion (spring onion)

Medium plants come next. They fit nine to every square, which equals 10cm (4in) apart. Medium plants include bush beans, beetroot and large turnips.

To help keep up with this, you may want to copy this chart so you always have it handy. Some people even have it laminated so they can take it outdoors without worrying about the weather destroying it. Another way to get the proper spacing and number per square is to be a little more scientific and do a little arithmetic as shown below. You can see that one, four, nine or sixteen plants should be spaced an equivalent number of centimetres or inches apart. This is the same distance the seed packet will say "thin to". Of course we don't have to "thin to" because we don't plant a whole packet of

Dividing up your squares

Each 30 x 30-cm (1 x 1-ft) square can grow either one extra large plant or four large plants or nine medium plants or sixteen small plants. Here's how to mark out the space for each size of plant.

Extra large plants need to be sown or planted right in the middle of the square. This will mean the plant is less likely to grow into neighbouring squares.

For large crops grown four into a square, divide the space into four sections and poke a hole in the middle of each one.

To grow nine medium plants in a square, divide the square into nine sections using two fingers spread apart to draw two lines horizontally and vertically.

To grow sixteen small plants in a square, first divide the square into quarters. Then, using your index and middle fingers, make four holes in each quarter.

seeds anymore. So if you're planting seeds, or even putting in young plants that you purchased or grew from seed, just find the seed packet or planting directions to see what the distance is for thinning. This distance then determines whether you're going to plant one, four, nine or sixteen plants.

Just because we're talking about measuring in centimetres or inches doesn't mean you have to get out your ruler or tape measure, and you don't have to do any complicated measuring or figuring either. This is when the grid becomes handy. When your square is defined by a grid, it's much easier to think one, four, nine or sixteen plants in each square.

All you do is draw lines in the soil with your fingers! For one plant per square just poke a hole in the middle of the square with your finger. For four per square, draw a vertical and horizontal line dividing the square in half each way. The plants go right in the centre of these four smaller squares.

HOW MUCH TO PLANT

I recommend, especially at the beginning, that you plant only what you want to eat. Occasionally try something new, of course, but especially at first only grow those vegetables and herbs that you normally eat.

Remember, plant each adjoining square with a different crop. Why? Here are several reasons:

1. It prevents you from overplanting any one particular item.

2. It allows you to stagger your harvest by planting one square this week and another of the same crop in two weeks or so.

3. It automatically helps to improve your growing mix three times a year in very easy, small steps. Remember the saying, "Square by square, you'll soon be there."

4. Besides all of the above, it looks pretty.

Just like a patchwork quilt, the different colours, leaf textures, plant densities, shapes and heights, plus the visible grid, will give you a very distinctive garden feature.

Some people ask, "Why can't we plant all sixteen squares with leaf lettuce or spinach or Swiss chard or whatever we want to plant?" Oh, that's going right back to the single-row mentality. Square Metre Gardening begins with visualising the harvest. It's very difficult to put in four tiny plants of chard and think that's going to be enough for the whole family, but one square of red and one square of green chard usually is more than most families eat. Proof

Sowing and planting the squares

Sowing seeds

Use your fingers to divide each square into sections (here into quarters for large plants) and poke down in the centre of each quarter to make a hole.

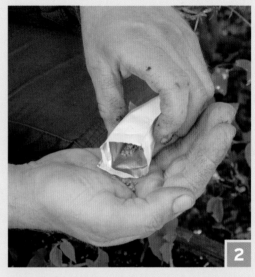

Tip out some seed into the palm of your left hand (if you are right-handed); using your right index finger and thumb take two or three seeds (or a pinch if the seed is tiny).

Drop the seed into the hole, taking into account the sowing depth on the seed packet as fine seed should not be sown too deep. Move the mix over to cover the seed to the correct depth.

Water the square, if the mix is dry, using a watering can fitted with a fine rose. The watering should mimic light rain: if the water flows too fast the seed could be dislodged.

Planting young plants

Mark out the planting positions in the usual way. Water the plant plugs or potted plants and allow the water to drain; this will reduce stress to the roots.

To remove plug plants, insert a pencil into the drainage hole or squeeze the base of the container. For pot plants, you can just knock the pot, upend the plant and take the pot off.

Settle the plant into its planting hole, most plants should be planted at the same depth as they were in the previous container. Push the mix around the base of the plants and firm in gently.

Planting asparagus

Asparagus is a perennial plant that will crop again and again over many years so I suggest you plant a whole box just with asparagus, using these bare roots.

Divide the square into quarters; in the centre of each quarter make a little mound 8cm (3in) high to take each bare-root plant.

Position the plant at the top of the mound and let the roots hang down, spread them out and then push in place.

Add more Mel's mix to cover the roots to an extra depth of 5cm (2in) or so. It can take a couple of years before they crop.

of the pudding . . . how many bunches of chard did you buy last week or even last month? The stores have it, it's fresh and it looks good, so why didn't you buy any more than you did? Well, it's the same answer as to why you shouldn't plant too much of one thing.

It's worth repeating here that the biggest problem for single-row gardeners has always been, "I planted too much. I can't take care of it. It's too much work and I'm sorry now." All that has changed with SMG and you now have boundaries (the grid) and the opportunity to ask yourself, "For every single square I plant, is that enough? Do I really want more? Would it be better to plant another square of the same thing in a week or two or three?"

TIME OF YEAR

Keep in mind that you can build a Square Metre Garden any time of the year: spring, summer, autumn and even winter. In most areas, you could start planting something in any season other than winter. What time of the year is it right now for you and where are you in the sequence of a yearly gardening cycle? Think of it like a visit to the cinema before the main feature. You're all settled in with your popcorn, ready to devote your full attention to the film. In the gardening year, this is usually the equivalent of springtime. What if you came in the middle of the picture? For gardening that would be summertime. You can still plant a crop such as pak choi even if you missed the spring crop. If it's now autumn, you can still start your SMG with some garlic or kale plants and get some valuable experience before next spring. Start whenever you get the urge to plant.

For convenience, we'll start with the beginning of the garden year for most of the country – springtime.

How To Select Plants

Looking through a seed catalogue (or the online version) is not the best way to decide what to grow. They make it all look so good and sound so exciting that you can easily get carried away. I recommend you review your shopping list from last week and last month. That eliminates the "Oh, I'd like to grow that!" or "Wouldn't it be fun to grow okra?" Start simple and easy with the foods you already eat regularly. Expand and experiment later on. Don't ruin a lifetime hobby by starting off too big.

Seasonal Plants

You can get at least three crops a year in every square of your SMG. Every choice is going to be fun, exciting and tasty. Of course, your selection depends on the time of year, and what you and your family need and want. There are two types of crops when you consider weather. The first are hardy crops that are not sensitive to frosts. The second group is the tender crops that are very sensitive to frost so cannot be planted out before or after the last frost date in your area.

HARDINESS AND PROTECTION

SMG's size makes it very easy to protect your new plantings from an extra early or late frost. There's a lot more information about frosts and freezes in Chapter 8, especially if you are interested in extending the season, as well as ways to protect your plants so you can get more from your garden.

Plants aren't all the same, of course. They are just like people. Some can stand the heat, cold or humidity better than others. We classify these as hardy, and those that can't handle it as non-hardy or tender. Each of the four seasons has three time periods—the early season, midseason and late season. If you're thinking about a spring crop, for example, there may be some vegetables that can only grow in the mid-part of the spring while others can tolerate a little more cold in the beginning of the season, but can't stand any heat at all near the late part of the season. It takes a little while to get used to which is which, and how best they fit in with your planting schedule.

Though the weather is never exactly the same every year, it helps to know a plant's hardiness. Don't worry – you'll learn it in time. This is not an exact science so relax if you're a beginner and just enjoy the ride. Don't expect to find a perfect list because how well plants

A crop cover such as a double layer of garden fleece will help protect your plants from early or late frosts. Fleece is quick and easy to drape over a dome support and secure at the base with some bricks or stones.

thrive differs in different parts of the country and, of course, different years, some times for no explainable reason. If you lose a few squares of something one year it's no big deal. It doesn't mean you're not going to be a great gardener.

Plants Don't Read Calendars

Although people like to celebrate the first day of spring (March 20th) according to the calendar, plants don't give a hoot about our calendar – they respond to weather. In the spring we need to know the usual date of the last frost in our area. That will help us determine when to plant. Each different crop, whether hardy or tender, will need to be planted so many weeks before or after that last day of frost.

For plants, the autumn-growing season begins not with the first calendar day of autumn (September 23rd), but with the first frost and continues until the first freeze of the autumn. The average dates of your first and last frost dates depend on where you live in the country and the regional and local variations of weather. All we can do is go by the past and hope it will be similar this year. To help, national weather stations collect dates for your area and calculate the average date from the past 100 years or so. Of course, this average is only a guide to what to expect.

Local Frost Dates

How do you find your local frost dates? The Internet is the best resource for detailed information. You can also check national and regional weather reports on TV and radio. Local knowledge from nurseryman, professional gardeners or keen gardening neighbours about weather and what varieties do well is also useful.

You can access your frost dates on any number of websites, by entering "frost dates" in the search engine. The best weather forecasting website for the UK is <www.netweather.tv>. Here you can get detailed information for specific areas by postcode over different time periods.

SEQUENCE OF GROWTH

Did you know that plants grow and bloom everywhere in the same sequence? In other words, throughout the country, daffodils bloom in the springtime, then a little later tulips bloom, then it's time for the lilacs to bloom. Did I leave out dandelions? Start noticing the sequence of flowering in your location. It would include trees, shrubs, flowers, even weeds.

If you know what kinds of plants are tender (mostly the most popular and well-known fruiting veg), it's easy to remember that everything else is hardy. Tender crops include most beans, peppers, aubergines, tomatoes and squash. If you plant these out when it's too early or cool, they'll either die or their growth will most likely be stunted and so they will not fruit well.

CHARTS TO GUIDE YOU

I've designed charts for Square Metre Gardening so you'll know when to plant and in what order. I've included calendar charts that show, based upon area frost dates, how soon before or after a frost you can plant a given crop. You'll find that some plants are very frost-hardy and can be planted much earlier than those that are just on the borderline. Turn to page 260 to see the charts.

CARRY ON PLANTING

As soon as you harvest a summer crop, fill the gap by planting a hardy crop for the upcoming autumn These crops are frost-hardy, meaning that both young and mature plants withstand frost. The seeds you plant at the end of summer will germinate quickly since the soil is still warm. Young plants can begin outdoors and grow much faster than the same crop planted in the spring. The autumn crop gains an extra advantage from late summer weather. The problem with hardy plants planted out in the spring is not always cold weather early in the year but also warm weather at harvest time. A plant's purpose in life is to produce seed, and the rising temperatures of an approaching summer makes this happen sooner. As it does so, the plant's whole character changes. Many people don't realise that plants like lettuce put up a flower stalk, which then goes to seed. If you wait too long to harvest lettuce, the stalk will shoot up, and the same thing happens to other crops like cabbage. The head splits open, a stalk shoots up, develops flowers and then turns to seed. It's nature's way of allowing the plant to reproduce, but the plant changes taste when this happens. All the energy goes towards the seed, and the plant itself; as far as taste is concerned it becomes rather tough, coarse and bitter.

In cooler weather, this process is delayed. The plant feels no urgency to complete the growing cycle. So in the autumn, the plant

> **JEFF WRITES...**
> *Fantastic! It very much appeals to my innate sense of organisation and efficiency.*

slows its maturation process, allowing it to maintain flavour for a longer length of time as temperatures continue to grow cooler and cooler. If it's frost-hardy, it doesn't matter if it is the middle of autumn and you start getting frost. Some plants can endure some freezing and still provide a crop for harvesting. Autumn is a great time to plant if you put in the right crops.

SOIL TEMPERATURE

Soil temperatures vastly influence germination times. For example, if you sow carrot seeds in the summertime when the temperature of the soil is 16°C (60°F), the seeds will germinate in less than a week. But if you plant the same seeds in early spring when the ground temperature is perhaps 5°C (40°F) , they will take a month and a half to sprout. Just a bit warmer and they will germinate in a little over two weeks. When the soil is cold and freezing, no seeds will germinate. When the soil warms up to 5°C (40°F), only half of them will germinate; but as soon as it gets to 10°C (50°F), suddenly almost all of them will germinate and will continue right through the warmer temperatures of summer and autumn.

What happens to seeds when they don't germinate because the ground is cold and wet? They could rot, or bacteria or fungi could attack them. Seeds can break their dormancy and then go dry. They could be attacked by insects, or dug up by animals or birds. So the quicker you can get them to germinate, the better off they will be.

SPRING, SUMMER AND AUTUMN CROPS

Some crops, like members of the cabbage family, take so long to grow that there isn't enough time to plant seeds directly in the garden and wait for the harvest. So instead you need to buy plants or raise your own young plants indoors ahead of time.

The same situation applies to the tender summer-fruiting crops, such as tomatoes, peppers and aubergines. They take so long to mature that you must plant your box with young plants.

The autumn crop is better for raising your own young plants because you will be able to start the seeds in the summertime, raise the young plants outdoors in your garden, and then move them into their permanent spot in the early autumn for a later harvest.

STARTING SEEDS AND YOUNG PLANTS

There are plenty of advantages to growing your own young plants from seed and storing the remaining seeds in their packet until next year. First, seeds cost pence, while young plants cost £s. There are many more varieties offered in seed catalogues than as young plants at garden centres. The only drawback is time because growing your own from seed depends on the time you can spare. If you're a brand new gardener, however, you may want to wait until next year to start your own from seed. Like everything else in life, we tend to go overboard and do too much and then it becomes a chore. Don't let it happen to you!

Saving Spare Seeds

If your surplus seeds are stored properly, they will last for many years. Contrary to what the gardening industry would like you to believe, it is not necessary to buy fresh seeds every year or to pour out that whole packet of seeds all at once. SMG teaches you to plant just a pinch of seeds. Then store the rest. By planting just a pinch of seeds instead of a whole packet, you can save a lot of money by saving the excess seeds for next year's crop, and the next year's and so on. Some seeds will last up to five years. Seed companies guarantee that a certain percentage will germinate; this number is always very high, usually up into the nineties. Of course the seed industry wants you to buy a fresh packet of seeds every year so they can stay in business. There's nothing wrong with that! But there's also nothing wrong with saving money with a more efficient system.

Instead of starting from scratch each year by buying all new packets of seed, get into the habit of storing your surplus seed from one year to the next.

How to Store Seeds

What is the ideal storage condition for seeds? It is just the opposite of the moisture and warmth that make them germinate. You'll want to store them in a cool, dry place, i.e. the driest, coldest place in your home. Some people freeze their seeds. But I find they get moisture even if they are in a ziplock bag because it never seems to be totally airtight. I prefer refrigerating them in a wide-mouth jar with a screw lid. Label your containers and store them in the refrigerator on a back shelf. In each jar place a desiccant packet (from a medicine vial, shoe box or box with electronic equipment in), or add a little powdered milk wrapped in a tissue to soak up any excess moisture in the jar.

Germination Rates

What happens to seeds that are in storage? As they grow older, their germination rate (the percentage that sprouts under ideal conditions) gradually diminishes. But the solution is very simple. Plant a pinch of seeds, just two to three, instead of only one to ensure that at least one will germinate. If your seeds are many years old, test the germination rate yourself or just sow three or five or however many seeds, depending on how well they germinated the year before. If you marked the germination rate on the packet, you can reasonably estimate how many to plant the next year.

WHAT DID I DO WRONG?

Knowing that roots germinate first before the shoot emerges will help your seeds successfully grow. Here's why. Traditionally, gardeners made a seed drill with a draw hoe, planted a row of seeds, covered the row with soil, watered and then walked away from their garden hoping for the best. If nothing grew, single-row gardeners thought the worst: "Maybe they were bad seeds. Or worse, maybe I'm a terrible gardener!" What all of these gardeners did not realise was that the seed might have already germinated, perhaps after a week or two, and the root was heading down before the top could come up and break the surface. If the gardener gave up and quit watering, it is possible that their seed did die. Why? Because if the soil dries below the seed in the root zone, only 2.5 to 5cm (1 to 2in) below the surface, the root will wither and die from lack of moisture. But if the gardener had kept the soil surface moist, then the seeds would have had a good chance to put the root down to support the plant and its new shoot.

DROP A PINCH

We have learned about seed storage and germination. The next thing is to practise sowing. You can do this indoors in the winter before you start your garden. Take different kinds of seeds from the tiniest to the largest and practise picking up and dropping a pinch of seeds onto a piece of white paper to count your results.

This can be fun but there is a very practical reason for doing this. When I tell people to just plant a pinch of seeds, i.e. just two or three, I think I have given them all the instructions they need. But I always find so much variation in how many seeds they end up planting. It all depends on your finger dexterity, and you may need a little practice. If you are having trouble, you may even want to use a spoon for picking up that pinch of seeds. A white plastic spoon usually works great, especially if you're using darker coloured seeds. If you scoop up too many, you can just shake a few back into the palm of your hand.

HOW DEEP?

How deep should you plant a seed? This depends on the size of the seed and the soil you plant it in. Generally speaking, a seed's sowing depth is two to four times the thickness of the seed. It's important to place your seeds below a moist surface to prevent it from drying out. Too close to the surface and it can dry out from the hot sun. Once a seed receives moisture and begins germinating (known as "breaking dormancy"), it will die if it dries out so don't forget to water regularly.

A Helping Hand for Seeds

You don't have to worry too much about placing your seed too deep, in part because your Mel's mix is loose and friable. If the seed is planted too deep for the kind of seed it is, as soon as it begins to receive moisture, nature will tell it, "Get going, buddy, put some roots down and start growing." That sprout can push right up through Mel's mix because there are a lot of nooks and crannies and the soil is very easy to move. This is one of the hidden advantages of starting with perfect soil. It almost guarantees that all of your seeds will grow into plants.

TIME TO GERMINATE

How long does it take to germinate seeds? In addition, what percentage can you expect to emerge? The germination times vary with the crop and the soil temperature. But most vegetable seed should germinate within a week or two. Keep the sowing mix moist;

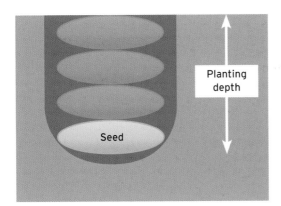

HOW DEEP TO PLANT YOUR SEEDS
Big seeds are planted deeper than small seeds, as a rule of thumb, seeds should be two to four times as deep as the seed size. Seed packets usually state sowing depth required.

if nothing happens then re-sow. Most vegetable seed has a high percentage germination, flower seed is more variable.

PRE-SOAKING SEEDS

If the seeds are viable you should not need to soak them; they will break dormancy naturally when they comes into contact with a moist mix. But you can pre-soak seeds before sowing, if you wish to speed up germination, e.g. when the weather is not ideal. While some can be soaked overnight, some fall apart after only an hour; it depends on the seed. Big seeds should be soaked for only about a half hour to an hour. Bean and pea seeds, which might look shrivelled up, swell up and break in half if you soak them too long. Beware: water makes some seeds slippery. A plastic spoon can help you handle them.

INDOOR SOWING

The easiest way to start seeds indoors is to place them on a moist paper towel. Then put the paper towel and seeds in a very shallow tray or dish; keep it moist (a plastic bag would be handy to maintain moisture) and in a warm place in the house. Check daily; when you see roots, it's time to plant. Rather than handling the seed at this point, carefully cut the paper towel into little squares, and lift each one out with a knife. Now you're ready to take it outside, plant it in your SMG filled with Mel's mix, cover it and give it a drink of water. You've just given your plant a head start – in about half the time. Instead of fourteen days, you may see a seed coming up in just six.

Starting off Young Plants

Now it's time to decide whether you want to start some seeds off and grow them on into young plants indoors, rather than sowing them direct outdoors. To raise your own young plants, you need a

Modular trays allow roots to develop in their own cell of growing medium. This means they don't get tangled up with neighbouring roots and so transplanting young plants is easier and there is less of a check to growth.

little bit of paraphernalia: a few pots, modular trays and seed trays, plus a thermometer. You can also start your seeds in a recycled food container of vermiculite and transplant them into modular trays filled with seed or multi-purpose compost after they begin growing.

Transplant Early

When you're sprouting seeds in a cup of vermiculite, I suggest you transplant them into modular trays as soon as the tops have sprouted and you see the first two leaves called the "seed" leaves. Most garden experts say to wait until you have two "true" leaves, but I have found that if you wait until the set of true leaves develops, the roots have already grown so long and tangled that it's almost too

Growing from seed

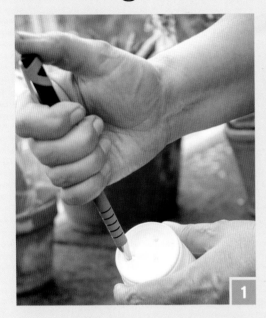

If you use "free" containers such as food containers make some drainage holes in the bottom first.

Fill a container with vermiculite and moisten with clean water until it darkens.

Pour some seeds into the palm of your left hand (if right-handed), take a pinch of seed and sow as evenly as possible on the surface of the vermiculite.

Cover the seed with a thin layer of vermiculite and check the seed packet to see what germination temperature is required.

late to transplant. The seed leaf comes first, and it's usually a fairly flat, large leaf that doesn't look like the plant's regular leaves. The first set of "true" leaves comes out next as the stem grows higher.

Pricking Out

When the seeds have seed leaves and you're ready to transplant into the modular trays, carefully lift the plant by holding on to one of the seed leaves between two fingers. Then with your pencil, dig in the vermiculite, loosen it up and lift the whole plant out – root and all – from the bottom while your other hand is holding the top of the plant by one of the seed leaves. Don't touch the plant stem, just the leaf. If the roots are very long, trim off the bottom third with a pair of scissors. Don't worry . . . you won't kill the plant. For every root you cut off, two new roots will sprout as it branches out, creating a much stronger plant.

To transplant a seedling, take your pencil and make a hole in one cell of your modular tray, or outdoors in a planting square. Then lower the plant root down into the hole. Make sure the hole is big enough to hold the whole root. Take the point of the pencil and push the Mel's mix around the plant. Plant it a little lower than when it sprouted. Give it some water, either from above for outdoors or from below for indoors in modular trays, and then keep it out of direct sunlight but somewhere that there is light. As the plant starts to grow and the leaves develop, you can gradually introduce the plants to full sunlight.

Check the Roots

When you place young plants into the garden, take a look at the roots to see if they are root-bound, in other words, if they've grown in a circle. My solution for a root-bound plant is to take that same pair of scissors and just cut off the bottom roots. Yes, the whole thing – the mass of roots at the base and the soil. Then all the ends of the roots, wherever they are, will branch and send out little feeder roots. Lower the whole plant into the hole at the proper spacing in your SMG box and firm in gently.

Water Well

One caution: the root should be wet before you transplant into your SMG. Take your modular tray and let it float in a bucket of warm water until it sinks and there are no more bubbles coming up. That's when you know the rootballs are totally saturated with water. Then take it out, pop each plant out of its container, cut the root bottoms

This is a good example of a rootbound container plant. You'll want to trim the matted roots at the base before planting. Don't worry: it's better for the plants anyway.

Gently push the mix around the young plants to form a slight saucer shape in the mix. Because of the saucer shape, water will be directed straight down to the roots.

off (if necessary) and plant it. The Mel's mix you are planting into should be moist, so you're not putting a wet plant into dry conditions. Dry ground will suck the moisture right out of the roots.

Target the Watering

Next, push the mix back around the plant to form a slight saucer shape in the soil. Make sure you plant at the level of the mix, factoring in the slight depression of the saucer. Because of the saucer shape, water goes straight down to the roots. We don't want to water the rest of the square if we don't have to. How's that for conserving water?

OUTDOOR SOWING

The procedure for outdoor seed germinating, transplanting, watering and then planting into the garden is all the same, just in much nicer weather. Late afternoon on a cloudy day is the best time, unless there are lots of slugs about, then morning is best as slugs usually feed at night.

Hardening Off

Hardening off is the process of getting the plant adjusted to a new environment, from the warm, still indoors to the cooler, windy outdoors. It's important that your plants are acclimatised gradually so they can get used to their new location and different weather conditions. This requires some effort because you don't want them out at night when it's cold or freezing and you also don't want them out in the burning hot sun in the daytime.

Regulate their Temperature

To help harden off plants, you need to regulate the sun exposure. If it's hot out, place your plants out in the sunlight in the morning, but at noontime provide some shade. Let them receive direct sunlight in the early morning, shade at midday and, perhaps, when the sun starts down, a little more direct light in the afternoon. Now that's really pampering your garden plants. And don't forget the little drinks of water every now and then. Likewise, if cold spells, unseasonal frosts or strong winds threaten you need to protect the plants; gradually, over seven to ten days, they will become tough enough. Crop covers whether shade material or fleece for frost protection can help here. Also remember, slugs and snails love young plants so protect your plants with your preferred method of control.

SPECIAL CASES

The majority vegetable crops are planted as seeds or young plants but there are exceptions. For example, asparagus is a perennial vegetable that is planted as dry crowns and will then stay *in situ* and crop for ten years or more. I've found it can be grown in a SMG system but it needs a box on its own and a dry crown is planted in a mound of Mel's mix (*see* page 74 for more details). Potatoes are another exception, as sprouted tubers rather than seeds are planted; you can also plant onion sets, garlic cloves and so on. Herbs that are perennial such as thyme, tarragon, sage and rosemary will be purchased as small plants and planted out rather than raised from seed. For details see the individual plant entries in Chapter 10.

SPACING

How many plants will fit into a square? The numbers are so simple and easy to remember: 1, 4, 9 or 16. If you like maths, and who doesn't, you will recognise right away that these numbers happen to be the squares of 1, 2, 3 and 4. Square Metre Gardening is as simple as one, two, three, four. The number of plants you grow in a square depends on a plant's size when it's fully grown. You can also figure it out very easily from the "thin to", directions on a seed packet. Now, every time you read "thin to", you will think of me and say to yourself, "Why do the seed packets tell me to plant so many seeds, only to go back and thin to just one plant?"

A TYPICAL GARDEN

Let's plant one 1 x 1-m (3 x 3-ft) box frame and see how much we will grow in those nine squares.

We'll start with a quick-growing box providing salads and baby veg. Three of the taller plants on the north side of the box could include bush beans, chard and beetroot.

Carrots require little care until they're harvested. So let's plant a square of carrots in the middle row, then some spinach and a square of baby turnips (or 16 radishes).

Then we'll plant two or three varieties of leaf lettuce in the front row, perhaps either side of a square of four parsley plants. This front row will provide a continual harvest as we cut as required.

An alternative, SMG box could be for tender fruiting crops such as tomatoes and peppers and could contain more colour by adding either some edible flowers such as nasturtium or violas, or even conventional bedding plants.

A newly planted bed of quick growing salad crops, all correctly spaced so the plants can grow away without too much competition.

If you are planting something that may need a plant support later as it gets fully grown, you might consider other plants that could share the same support and plant them in adjacent squares.

A SMG box could also be used to lay out a chequerboard herb garden using woody herbs such as sage, rosemary, tarragon and thyme that would remain in place for a couple of years.

TO PLAN OR NOT?

Remember I mentioned that some people feel a desire to think ahead and draw up a list of everything to be planted in their garden and assign those plants to spaces ahead of time. So it means drawing a chart and assigning those particular crops to each square. Despite being an engineer, who loves charts and diagrams, I don't usually do that. I just like to plant as I see fit. It's very easy to stand in the garden and as the square becomes vacant you just look around and decide it's time to plant another square of radishes. Or maybe you'd like to have some more beans, but this time you'll put in the yellow variety instead of green. It's also very easy to spot and plant where you'd like some colour. I find it very easy to just bring home a pack of seasonal flowering plants I liked at the garden centre and decide by looking at the garden where they would look best. But remember it's your Square Metre Garden, and you should do whatever makes you happy.

REPLANTING

Keep in mind that, as soon as you harvest one crop, it won't be a big deal to replant because you're going to do it one square at a time. Once your newly planted garden starts maturing in the spring, for example, that square of radishes will be ready to harvest in four weeks or so you'll be ready to replant just that one square. After there is no more danger of frost, you can plant out tender crops. So your choices have increased and also most of the fruiting crops are fairly long-lived and will be in that spot through the whole summer season. As you replant, keep the same criteria in mind, put taller plants on the north side to keep them from shading other plants, working your way to perhaps some trailing flowers on the front corners to look pretty. Place plants that don't need much attention and only occasional harvesting, like peppers on the inside, and shorter plants and those that need constant care or harvest, to the outside just to make them easier to tend.

WEEDING

This could be the shortest paragraph in the entire book. To start with, your Mel's mix has very few weed seeds in it, and any weeds that do appear are easily observed and removed because they're not in the proper space and they look different from the plants that are there. Because the soil is so soft and friable weeds come out easily, root and all. You have to weed about once a month. End of paragraph; end of story.

HARVESTING

Keep in mind that we harvest many of the crops continuously, if possible. For example, a leaf lettuce is not allowed to wait until it forms a large, mature head, but with a pair of scissors and a salad bowl you can continuously trim the leaves from such things as lettuce, chives, beetroot, chard, spinach, parsley and even onion tops. As long as you don't take too much at one time, the plant will easily survive and thrive. Filling your salad bowl each day should not diminish the garden in any way. In fact, right after you harvest you'll find it hard to notice where you got everything as the leaves grow to fill the space.

YOU'VE LEARNED THE BASICS

You've now learned all the basics of Square Metre Gardening. You have learned how many and what kind of plants fit into a square by memorising, calculating or by looking it up on the chart. You've learned how to mark out with your finger to get the proper and exact spacing, then start planting your seeds and young plants. Are we having any fun yet? Next chapter we're going to discuss how to maintain and harvest your SMG.

Growing and harvesting

This is going to be a fairly short chapter because Square Metre Gardening requires so little maintenance once your garden is prepared and planted. You'll experience a continuous cycle of nurturing, harvesting and replanting each year with no soil preparation and no major weeding.

A fresh harvest from a quick salad and baby veg box frame in early to midsummer.

Plant care and cropping

Apart from providing support for vine or climbing plants, a bit of weeding and pest and disease control, the main care is to water when required. Spend the time saved observing your garden's growth; every square is different so there's plenty to enjoy.

All growing plants, particularly annuals, need to be checked regularly but with my method any "maintenance" is quick, lightweight work and fun. Cropping plants grow quickly so you want to harvest them at their peak so it pays to check their progress daily.

AFTERCARE

When asked to name the greatest advantage of the Square Metre Gardening, most people say it's tending their garden from paths and never stepping on their soil. Like many others, I always wondered why we were taught to loosen soil with a rotavator, spade, fork and hoe, only to walk all over it again packing it down.

So why are the experts still teaching us to do this? I say, just stop walking on your growing soil. It's that simple.

- ◼ **Don't walk on your growing mix**
- ◼ **Only three tools needed**
- ◼ **Support your plants**
- ◼ **Weeds and other pests are not a big problem**
- ◼ **Water the right way**

KEEP IT LOOSE

Let's think of some of the advantages of not packing your soil down. The plant roots need air and moisture, just like people. If you pack the soil down, it becomes more and more compressed (this is called "compaction") and it becomes harder and harder for air spaces to be retained within the soil, making it more difficult for roots to grow. The roots may not die, but they certainly won't grow well. So why not provide them with nice, loose, friable soil like Mel's mix? This way, water can percolate down through the air spaces separating the solid particles.

JUST A FEW TOOLS

Another big advantage of SMG is that the number and cost of tools are reduced to almost nothing. You don't even need a spade or rake or any of those special digging tools that have been invented to dig up the tough soil. Gardening "experts" will tell you to go out and buy

These are the only tools you need to care for your SMG. A trowel, a pencil and scissors – plus a bucket and cup for watering.

the best tools you can find because they will last longer, but they also cost more. With SMG, you no longer need lots of soil cultivation tools – in fact, they're suddenly obsolete.

A TROWEL, A PENCIL AND SCISSORS

The first tool you need is a trowel. I've found that a budget one is really the best buy as they have all the features of an expensive trowel. So instead of just one, now you can afford four trowels. You can have one in every box just sitting there waiting so that you don't have to go looking for a tool when you walk by and see a square that is ready for replanting. Of course, if you see an occasional weed, your big, strong weeding tools are your own thumb and forefinger!

Look for a transplanting trowel as these have a narrower blade than a standard trowel and are easier to use in a confined space. The trowel is for planting, for mixing in an added trowel full of compost when you replant each square, and for loosening up and turning over the Mel's mix in an individual square or even an entire 1 x 1-m (3 x 3-ft) box. In the spring, you won't believe how perfect the soil will be

Thrifty tip

I like to buy children's pointed scissors in August when you can find back-to-school sales. Usually I can purchase them for an affordable price that allows for several pair around the garden.

if you follow the Mel's mix formula and start with a perfect soil.

You'll need a pencil (yes, that's a tool) for poking holes and lifting out young seedlings for transplanting, and a pair of scissors for harvesting leaves of beetroot, lettuce or chard leaves and cutting off dead blossoms, and snipping off extra seedlings if more than one seed sprouts in a hole. Because SMG tools are so simple and inexpensive, I love to splurge and keep one of each at every box. That way, I never have to look for a tool.

It would be fun to list all the tools that you no longer need if you have a SMG. In fact, you could probably just go into your garage or tool shed and see them all right there. Poor, lonely tools – maybe you have some old-fashioned, single-row gardening friends who just can't give up all that hard work and could use some extra heavy-duty tools?

Thrifty tip

You can make your own kneeling pad out of scrap carpeting. If you have some leftover indoor/outdoor carpeting, it won't matter if it gets wet; it dries quickly and folds up nicely to make a great kneeling pad. It wouldn't hurt to have a few of these pads scattered throughout your SMG. They are available as scrap or samples at any place where carpeting is sold.

OPTIONAL ACCESSORY

You might want to invest in a kneeling pad. Unless your boxes are placed on tabletops, your most frequent position while gardening will be kneeling. You can buy an inexpensive kneeling pad that is comfortable and durable. There's no need to buy the fancy ones that strap to your knees. They're terribly uncomfortable and will end up hanging in your tool shed along with the other lonely tools.

WEEDS

SMG has few or no weeds. But how? Weeds plague every garden, right? First, there are no weed seeds in peat moss or vermiculite. Next, most seeds that were in the ingredients you added to the compost heap should get cooked and killed as the material heats up, although there will always be a few. If you prepare the bed properly and line the bottom of the box with landscape fabric, weeds will not get through from the bottom. Since we are not using our ground soil, which is filled with weed seeds, the only other possible weed seeds in our SMG might have blown in, and as soon as they sprout, you will see them because they are out of place. Your two fingers will do the rest, pulling out the weed, roots and all. Compare that to what you've experienced with your existing soil. Anytime the existing soil anywhere in the country is left alone, it sprouts weeds. Which system would you like to have in your garden?

Remove the grass and roots under the box frame before laying down the membrane. Wireworms that feed on decaying grass can multiple and then move on to root crops growing in the box.

Weeds can easily be removed by hand if you catch them when they are seedlings or young plants. Simply pull out with your finger and thumb before their roots establish.

Weed Spotting

How can you tell if a new seedling is a weed? First, it's not in the proper space among your little plants . Remember one, four, nine and sixteen.

If it is out of place (and I'll bet you were careful to make sure your spaces were correct in that square), you'll pull it out of that soft Mel's mix without a problem.

PESTS AND PLANT PROBLEMS

The only way to answer correctly the questions we get about pests and plant problems requires knowing the weather, growing conditions, history and present gardening condition in an area. If the question came from my local area, I'd give a great answer. But when it comes from across the country or anywhere in the world, it's difficult to give an accurate answer as pests and diseases vary.

You will have local experts, perhaps lecturers at nearby horticultural colleges or staff at nurseries or head gardeners at public gardens, who can advise. There are also garden clubs with expert home gardeners who can advise on slug control, etc. The only issue I have with local experts is that they are not the best source for answers to SMG questions. You'll have to come to us for those questions (for how to get in touch, *see* page 259).

To summarise pests and problems, try not to worry about them. Enjoy your garden. If one square gets devastated, pull it up and replant it with something else. If you didn't use the protective structures of Chapter 3, try them out next season to help eliminate your problems or take specific preventative action against prolific pests in your area. For example, if slugs and snails are a problem then you will need to look at protective barriers and controls available for seedlings and young plants.

WHICH PLANT VARIETIES?

Quite often people will ask questions like, "Which are the best varieties of potatoes or carrots to grow?" These questions can only be answered by your local experts. They will be up-to-date on all the new varieties and what grows best in your area, but seed catalogues often indicate which varieties are particularly compact or dwarf and so suit container growing or growing in small spaces.

SUPPORT TALLER PLANTS

Some plants, such as root crops and low-growing salad crops, need no support, so there is nothing to do for them. The taller crops might need a little help, however, depending on whether they are a leaf or head crop such as some bassicas (members of the cabbage family). If a heavy wind and rain or hailstorms knock them over, simply straighten them up and push a little extra Mel's mix around the stem and firm in.

Too Top Heavy

The plants that usually need a little support are the summer-fruiting crops such as peppers, okra, aubergine, sweetcorn and tomatoes. Most of these can easily be supported by using a U-shaped wire support cage or horizontal fencing or netting suspended across the entire 1 x 1-m (3 x 3-ft) box, held tight by four corner posts. The same support technique will also work for tall flowers like gladioli, sunflowers and tall dahlias. One of the reasons we provide plant support is the soil mix is so loose and friable that the tall plants need a little help.

WATERING

Plants need water just like people do. Everyone asks, "How do you water and how much?" My ideal way to water is ladling out a cup of sun-warmed water from a bucket that can be left in the sun next to your garden. Gently lift the bottom leaves of the plant and, with your other hand, ladle a cup of that water into the depression around the plant. With a saucer-shaped depression in the soil, the water will

Notice how easily climbing plants use the support netting all by themselves. Other crops, such as tomatoes, need a little help from you each week.

soak right down to the roots instead of rolling away from the plant into other parts of the garden.

We do get a few people who say, "Oh, that would take too long." But they've failed to think about the fact that, first, their garden is only a fraction of the size that it used to be. That means 80 percent of the watering you used to do is no longer needed and was actually wasted. Next, you're not watering the tops of the plants or the leaves, so you're not encouraging fungal diseases and other problems. You're keeping the water where it will do the most good—

If you don't have a watering can or a hose, keep a bucket of water and a cup near your SMG and then you can quickly water each square that needs it as you notice it is drying out.

Use a small cup so you can water each square gently and steadily as required; direct the water at the mix near the plant roots, rather than pour the water over the plants.

around the base of the plant where it can travel down to the root system. The soil consistency of your Mel's mix is already 100 percent of materials that hold moisture. When you water, it goes right into the growing media around the root system and stays there. The root system is going to be able to drink up the water when and in the amount needed. This is a very efficient method of using water.

And why sun-warmed water? One answer is that it's for the same reason people don't like to take a cold shower. The more scientific reason is plants can absorb nutrients in the soil much faster and grow better if the soil and water temperature are warmer. In spring and late autumn, sun-warmed water helps warm the Mel's mix. The warmer the growing media, the faster seeds will germinate and grow and the quicker you'll harvest. That's why people have greenhouses. If you build a structure to form a miniature greenhouse around your SMG, the radiant heat from the sun will warm the soil from the surface down. But simply pouring warm (not hot) water into the soil means the warmth tends to go a little deeper – and even quicker – than the sun baking the surface of the soil.

Don't Drown Me

Invariably gardeners water plants too much, perhaps out of kindness or fear that they will fail. So they think, "Oh, I'll give it a little extra. It won't hurt." Usually it did hurt with local soil that didn't drain well, but it won't if you have a Square Metre Garden where the Mel's mix absorbs excess water. Most people don't realise that plant roots need air as well as moisture. Mel's mix is formulated to be loose and friable so there is plenty of air particles.

With Mel's mix it's hard to overwater. Remember the sponge? Each little piece can hold moisture so a plant root can grow around that piece and take out the moisture when needed. When that little sponge gets saturated, the rest of the water drains right out through the bottom. That's how my mix works, and that's why you never have to worry about giving your plants too much water.

But because your soil mix drains readily when saturated, it also has a tendency to dry out quicker than most garden soils. Regular soils stay saturated, so single-row gardeners may be used to turning on the hose or flooding the garden twice a week and that's it. Your Square Metre Garden is different. You have to water a little more often and pay more attention to watering.

The secret, of course, is looking at the plants. After a while you'll be able to walk by your garden box and immediately spot any square that needs water. Perhaps the plants will be slightly wilted. Maybe they'll be just a little droopy or their colour will be a little off. You merely water those squares right then and there because your bucket of warm water is always right next to your garden. And because you're dipping a cup in the bucket you're not going to get yourself all wet and dirty.

> **With Mel's mix it's hard to overwater as it acts like a sponge and the plant roots take moisture when needed.**

Think of your plants in your garden the same as you do your children. If they've been out in the hot sun and playing hard and one of them looks a little droopy and wilted, you know right away to inspect the child a little closer to make sure he or she is properly hydrated. Get used to observing your plants in the same way.

Nurture Your Plants

I suggest watering by hand because it allows you the time to nurture your plants. You're able to stop and notice how your plants are growing. You can appreciate their beauty and colour, notice their blossoms and fruit. It tells you when the plant is going to be ready for harvest. It's a satisfying feeling to work in your garden with each plant. You're not standing off in the distance with a hose, which is very impersonal. You're not opening a tap and letting the sprinkler system take over. Even an automatic drip irrigation system is impersonal, although I must admit a system correctly set up is efficient if you have a lot of box frames and containers.

Water Conservation

Existing watering systems give all different types and sizes of plants the same amount of water at the same time. This is not only very impersonal; it's also very inefficient. If our farmers did that we'd have water shortages all around the country. Hey, wait a minute, we do have water shortages all around the country!

Learning the Signs

In conclusion, only water as much as each plant needs. And the best way to tell is from experience, the same way you know your child needs a drink. Yes, it does take a little bit of experience to raise a family, but gaining this experience brings a lot of pleasure.

ALTERNATIVE WATERING METHODS
A Watering Can

A watering can is a halfway house between applying a cup of water to a square and getting the hose out. Just like the bucket of water, keep a full watering can nearby to warm up in the sun and then water each square. Watering cans are very versatile for watering; you can water growing plants using the spout to direct water onto the mix or fit a "rose " at the end that will mimic gentle raindrops, useful for watering seedlings.

A Hose

For those who want to use a more traditional method, there is always the hose. Yes, it's a nuisance to get out or put away, and in row gardening it always seemed to be knocking plants down as it has to be dragged around the garden. Another advantage to SMG box frames is the hose won't do that anymore as the box corners keep the hose from crushing the plants.

If you do use a hose, make sure you have one of those shut-off valves right at the end of the hose so you have complete control of the force and amount of the water. There are many short and long extension watering lances that come with a spray nozzle. This also allows you to water directly under your plants, and the nozzle on the end of the lance can be poked down and worked around the lower leaves of the plant so that most of the plant remains dry.

Leave an extra length of hose coiled in the sun to help warm the water up a little, maybe just to take the chill off tap water, but you

A watering can with a detachable rose fitted at the end of the spout is a gentle way to water young plants.

Using a hose fitted with a watering lance or spray gun is a quick way to water plants when you have lots of boxes.

A SMG box frame fitted with automatic drip irrigation is efficient but you still need to check the plants.

have to be careful at the start if it's hot out and a hose full of water has been laying in the sun for some time. You don't want the water to be too hot. Do what you do when giving the baby a bottle, first test the water on your wrist.

Drip Irrigation

A very efficient way to water your SMG is with a drip irrigation system. I know it was designed for row gardeners, but it can be adapted for SMG just as easily. The only problem I have is it sort of takes away the nurturing and close attention paid to your plants. If you just turn a tap or worse yet, an automatic timer turns the water on and off, you never get close to your plants and they will miss you. But I must admit the watering gets done very efficiently and effectively. Try running small soaker tubes spaced every 15cm (6in) the length of your box for complete coverage of every square.

HARVEST

Harvesting your crop is the culmination of the gardening experience. The harvest should be a joyful and exciting time because, after all, this is why you're growing all these plants in the first place.

Too Much

The problem with traditional gardening is that there is too much to harvest all at once. If you plant an entire row of something all at once, it's all going to be ready to harvest all at once, and it becomes an overwhelming task. Not so great for the home gardener who just wants dinner tonight, not a month's worth of lettuce in one day.

Controlled Planting

Everything is different with a SMG. Now, every time you begin to plant something in your box frame, look the item up in Chapters 10 to 11, to find how many to plant per square. Prepare the soil, smooth it out and mark the spacing. Now, select the varieties you want from your seeds, pour some into the palm of one hand and plant a pinch in each hole. As you smooth the soil over the seeds, water with a fine spray. Then ask yourself, "Do I want any more than sixteen radishes all at once? They'll be ready in four weeks and they'll all come to harvest within one week." Usually the answer is "No. I really don't want any more than this. I'll wait a week or two to plant another square of radishes somewhere else." Right then and there you can see one of the huge advantages of your grid establishing boundaries and SMG giving you automatic control in a simple and easy way.

Remember that the SMG theory is to visualise the harvest. Ask yourself, "How much do I need for one or two weeks?" Then only plant that much. It takes about a minute.

Pick and Mix

You don't have to wait for the plant to mature to its maximum size. Go out at harvest time (which might be half an hour before lunch or dinner) with your pair of scissors and a small basket or salad bowl, and cut off a few outer leaves, perhaps one from each plant.
To harvest a mixed salad, just take four lettuce leaves, parsley leaves from another and perhaps beetroot leaves from another. Each square may contain a different variety and colour of lettuce. You might pull one radish and one carrot, even though they've only grown to half size, wash them off in your bucket of sun-warmed water, put the tops in the compost bin, and then continue around your Square Metre Garden taking just a little bit here and a little bit there of this and that. Soon your harvest basket is full and you look at your garden and cannot even see that anything is missing.

Snip, snip

Continually harvest any type of leafy vegetable such as leaf lettuce or chard by snipping a little here and a little there throughout the season. This technique is often called "cut-and-come again" and you will see in seed catalogues that many salad leaf and herb varieties are highlighted as being suitable for this treatment. This can't go on forever because the plant will eventually go to seed. When it sends up a seed stalk, the plant has completed its growing season and its use for harvesting. Take one last harvest, remove what's left over and

Some young salad crops can be cut down to a stump and they will re-grow and can be cut again. Look out for varieties sold as "cut-and-come-again" for lettuce and coriander.

prepare that square for replanting – unless you want the kids to see how a lettuce or radish plant produces seed.

HARVEST AND REPLANT

With Square Metre Gardening, you're only dealing with one square at a time. With SMG, our saying is going to be "square by square, you'll soon be there". As soon as you finish harvesting one square, it's time to prepare the soil and plant a new crop. Just take out any debris like dead leaves, stems or roots and then place these in your compost bin. Then add a trowel-full of garden compost (hopefully it's home-made) to the square, turn the soil over with the trowel, smooth it over and you're ready to replant. It's so quick, you can do all of that in 60 seconds!

Replanting

Now it's getting more interesting and fun because you will be able to choose what you want to replant in every single square all through the garden season. Remember, you can get at least three crops a year

Harvesting and replanting

To make the most of your SMG box frames, as soon as you have harvested a square and the plants have finished producing, you need to be ready to replant with another crop.

Harvest the crop from the square. Here hearted lettuce, planted and grown from spring to early summer, is being cut.

Clear the remaining debris from the square, e.g. dead leaves, weeds and then dig out any lettuce roots left behind.

Add extra Mel's mix or garden compost to top up the square - just a trowel's worth will do. Then smooth over and level.

Replant the square with a new crop. Here a single pepper plant is being planted in early summer once there is no danger of frost.

in every square. So, multiply your number of squares by three and there are a lot of choices to make! Every choice is going to be fun, exciting and interesting. Of course, what you select depends a lot on what time of the year it is and what you can use.

GINA WRITES...

I've lived my life doing the backbreaking work of single row gardening – this is so much better!

A LITTLE NOW

Whether you're planting, harvesting, maintaining or watering you don't need hours and hours to enjoy your garden. Because you can do a little bit here and a little bit there, you can do it anytime of the day even on your way out the door! If you see a few tiny weeds growing, pluck them out; give a drink of water to any plants that appear a little droopy or wilted (remember your bucket of sun-warmed water is right there and so is your trowel if you need to loosen the soil). It's like straightening a crooked picture as you walk down the hall, jotting a note to someone who will be coming home soon or putting something away in the refrigerator. These are things you can do right then and there. And they're fun things to do. No heavy work. No getting all dirty and sweaty.

EXTRA BENEFITS

If your SMG garden is close to the back door or kitchen door, you'll probably use it much more, but remember most edible crops need a sunny place so if it is shady outside your kitchen door then pick another site and walk a bit further. You'll enjoy the fresh greens and salad more often, eat more healthily and feel better. SMG could be part of a weight-loss plan, if you ask me! On top of all that, you'll have fun doing it! Don't forget to share the fun with your spouse children, or grandchildren because the wonder of growth and harvest is priceless. Harvest a few small plants with a child, and that child will remember the experience forever.

ON WITH THE NEXT CROP

When the summer is finished, you're ready to plant an autumn crop, using hardy plants. Go through the whole quick process of picking out any debris, adding a trowel full of garden compost, mixing it in, smoothing it over and deciding what's next. There goes another minute out of your busy life. How about spinach? Check the spacing, get the seeds out, soak them for a little while, pop them in the ground, smooth them over, water and you're all finished. Another minute gone, but you are creating life. You've now planted three crops in one square in only one year. You started with a root crop, replaced it with a fruiting crop and finally, in the autumn, added a leaf crop. In addition, you practiced soil improvement three times in one year, square by square.

ROTATION NOT CRITICAL

The nice thing about SMG is you are also practising crop rotation without even knowing it. Crop rotation is very important in traditional gardening when dealing with existing soils that have very few nutrients in them, nutrients that can quickly be depleted by planting and replanting the same crop year after year in the same soil. When you begin gardening with a healthy, rich soil like Mel's mix, crop rotation is really not critical. Mel's mix gives you a growing medium that is 33 percent garden compost, which has all the nutrients and trace elements that plants need. But crop rotation is still a good idea for soil-borne pest and disease control in addition to soil nutrients. If you grow the same thing continuously in the same place, eventually pests or diseases may take over since they have lived and played in that spot for so long. But if you replant every square three times a year, SMG is going to be no picnic for them.

ADD COLOUR

One more thing. Now that you've become an accomplished gardener one square at a time, you've improved the look and landscape of your garden and perhaps even your patio. When you decide you need a little colour over here or there, you may put in a summer crop of flowers, perhaps pink cosmos or petunias, and you become a designer. Just think – you're enjoying a painting in progress when you garden the Square Metre Gardening way!

Summer flowers will not only add colour to your box frame but many, such as this cosmos, will attract beneficial insects too. Chapter 11 has some suggestions for flowering subjects for spare squares.

7

Vertical gardening

If you like to grow climbing fruiting crops, such as beans, peas, tomatoes, cucumbers and winter squash, then this chapter is for you. I'll explain how to grow these crops efficiently within a Square Metre Gardening system, so they grow up to use the vertical space rather than sprawling all over the box.

Climbing pea plants growing up a vertical frame create a summer screen plus the pea pods are easier to pick.

Growing climbers and vine crops

Here you'll find a step-by-step guide to building and installing a vertical support for your SMG boxes based on my experiments. Plus there's plenty of tips on how to get the most out of vertical gardening.

It is perfectly possible to incorporate vigorous but productive climbing and vine crops into a SMG box frame but you need to train the plant up a vertical frame or support so they stay within bounds.

PICTURE THIS

Can you just picture a wall of green in your garden filled with vine crops? All the fruit just hanging there waiting to be picked! No sprawling plants all over the ground with their fruit lying on the soil getting all dirty and eaten by slugs. These walls of green can even be located so they hide any unsightly areas of the garden such as the garage. They can even give you some privacy to keep neighbours from peering over the fence to look at your SMG. It's not only a spectacular sight, but those plants will be up in the air getting better sunshine and air movement. They'll produce a more useable harvest for you with nothing wasted. To top all that off, each plant will only take one or two squares of a box frame and grow perfectly well in your 15-cm (6-in) depth of Mel's mix. Another big advantage is you can do all this standing up, which means no bending, kneeling or squatting down to tend your plants.

CHOOSING VERTICAL CROPS

Potential vertical cropping plants include tomatoes, cucumbers, climbing beans, climbing peas, melons and some types of squash but in practice not all of these will necessarily produce ripe fruit outdoors in your region – it depends on the length of the growing season so take this into account. In some areas, ripe fruits of tomatoes, cucumbers and melons are possible only when crops are grown under glass or in a polytunnel.

CONSTRUCTING SUPPORTS

I experimented through the years with all different types of materials and frames, and I finally settled upon one that was so simple, easy and inexpensive to use that it was almost ridiculous.

I found that electrical conduit is the cheapest, strongest and best material to use for the vertical supports. I do not like PVC pipe or wood because it eventually will bend and break and destroy your whole vertical garden. When you first build and plant a vertical frame out of just about anything, it looks sturdy and strong. But near the end of the growing season, when your plants have grown to the top and filled up all the open spaces, that frame acts like a sail on a boat. Just when your fruits are getting ripe and ready to pick, along comes a late summer storm with lots of wind and rain, and the next thing you know the whole thing is flat on the ground.

Using electrical conduit and a steel ground rod (rebar) will prevent this from happening. And the two posts and top are simple and inexpensive to buy and install. If you can find round metal conduit it is inexpensive and the staff at the DIY store will cut it to the required length. For the corners you can buy elbows, pre-bent rounded corners or bend your own if you have a conduit bender. It's kind of fun to bend the conduit, and once you get the knack of it, it comes out nice and smooth with good curves. The bent pipes can be connected with a simple metal coupling, which has two set screws that tighten each pipe together. If only PVC conduit is available, then instead opt for metal plant-support kits sold in garden centres or online; these come ready cut with their own fittings.

Why should you consider growing crops vertically?

■ **It saves space.**
■ **You grow better crops.**
■ **It adds a living screen to your SMG.**
■ **It costs less than you could imagine!**
■ **It lasts for years.**

Placing Vertical Supports

When you're deciding where to place your vertical frames, keep in mind that you don't want the vertically trained plants to shade the rest of the garden. So the frames work best when placed on the north side of each box. If you want more vertical crops than one vertical frame per box, you can make double or triple boxes and turn them east and west so the frames can go all along the north side. You could also devote a special-sized box just for vertical crops – just make a 60-cm (2-ft) deep box of any length with a vertical frame continuously on the north side. This could stand against a wall or fence. You could even plant the front squares with pretty flowers such as French marigolds or a fruiting crop such as chillies or aubergine plants that will look great and will hide the bottom stems of the vertical vines.

Installing a vertical frame

Materials

To install a vertical frame you will need: two 2-m (6-ft) lengths of 12–16mm diameter metal pipe, one 1m (3ft) length of 12–16mm diameter pipe, two ground rods, 60cm (2ft) long, connectors (two 90° elbows), nylon pea and bean netting with 13 x 13-cm (5 x 5-in) openings, 1m (3ft) wide, 1.5m (5ft) tall, fixings for trellis and a hammer.

— Hammer

— Nylon pea and bean netting

— 12–16mm diameter metal pipe
— Ground rod

— Fixings for netting and pipe connectors

Assembly

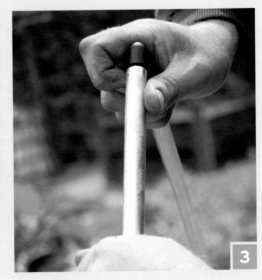

Insert the elbows joints so the top 1-m (3-ft) pipe is joined to the two support legs.

Installation of the frame and netting

Use the frame to measure the location for the two ground rods and hammer the rods halfway into the ground. Slip the support frame over the rods.

Attach the trellis along both sides and the top of the frame. Here plastic push-on fixings have been used but an alternative is to cut the netting so there is a long strand to tie in.

The netting should be tight. Once you are happy with its fit, trim the netting to the size of the frame.

INSTALLING THE VERTICAL FRAME

Ideally, your vertical frame should be installed outside the box frame, so it sits on the ground but if the ground is too hard to hammer the rods in, then insert them just inside the box. Aside from driving the concrete reinforcing bars (rebar) into the ground, and slipping the conduit over them, you could also attach the vertical frame to your box frame with pipe clamps to give them even more stability.

Securing Vertical Supports

To secure the vertical frame, pound two 12-mm (½-in) diameter pieces of concrete reinforcing bars (rebar) into the ground. These bars can be purchased already cut at any building supply store and should be anywhere between 45 to 60cm (18 to 24in) long depending on your soil. The looser (sandier) your soil is, then the longer the bar should be. Drive the rebar halfway into the ground, keeping it nice and straight; I suggest you wear gloves for this. The two supporting legs slip right over those rebars and are securely in place. We never pound on the support itself because the ends will bend and then they won't fit into the coupling or over the rebar.

As you get accustomed to bending plants, you'll get used to their resilience. The growing tips are very supply and easy to bend, but if you're trying to bend a stem closer to where it's planted, the stem will be hard and fairly rigid so stuff something under it such as a piece of folded up wadding. Once the stem has taken the new shape, the piece of wadding can be removed.

Adding Extra Strength

To make the vertical frame extra strong for melons and squash, drive a steel fence post into the ground first instead of the rebar. A fence post can be just the shortest 1-m (3-ft) tall size. Once the fence post is in the ground, then the conduit is attached to it with three pipe clamps. The whole frame then becomes so strong that it will hold up any weight no matter how high you go.

VERTICAL SUPPORTS ON SOLID SURFACES

Vertical supports can also be added to patio, balcony, roof garden or waist-high gardens. They are constructed in the same manner. However, we suggest that they be no taller than 1.2m (4ft). Instead of using rebar in the ground to secure them, they are fastened to the garden box using special clamps screwed into the sides of the box. Buy those when and where you buy your conduit and timber. In this situation, there's not a great strength with the vertical frame, so it would be necessary to put the struts from the top down to the sides of the box, and depending on how high, and your location, the wind and the plant growth, you might have to provide additional support on both sides.

How Many Squares?	
Plants per square	**Plants per 2 squares**
Tomato (cordon) 1	Melon 1
Cucumber 1 or 2	Courgette (vine) 1
Bean (climbing) 8	Winter Squash (vine) 1
Pea (climbing) 8	

NYLON NETTING

Once the vertical frame has been constructed, then add something for the plants to grow on. Nylon garden netting is now the only material I use for vertical gardening. It can't be broken, will last forever and is easy to work with. The netting is tied tightly and securely to the top and sides of the vertical frame, and the plants can then be gently woven in and out of the netting as they grow. The netting comes in 1-m (3-ft) and 1.5-m (5-ft) widths and various lengths and is available at most garden centres and online.

ARBOURS AND WALKWAYS

Think of all the various shapes, sizes and arrangements you can make with vertical frames. You can put two together in a straight line, turn a corner or even zigzag. You can put four together to form an arbour. You can put netting on two sides so it's a walk-through, on three sides so it's a sitting area, or on four sides with one little opening for the kids to play in. That would be a secret place, and you could put netting across the top or run two sets of vertical frames down a pathway, creating a wall. You could even create a whole maze with dead ends, turns and twists. All of the types of plants that would grow on it produce huge leaves, and make a very interesting visual pattern for your garden.

And don't forget flowering climbers, either annual climbers which are lightweight and are removed at the end of the season, or if you want something that blooms every year with little care required perhaps a patio clematis. If you had long walkways with the vertical frames down each side, you could build 60-cm (2-ft) by-any-length box frames and have them on the outside giving you plenty of walking room. You could also put them so that one square is inside the path, and one square is outside. I would plant the vine crops on the outside so they would climb up the netting, and plant flowers along the inside that will do well in the eventual shade of the pathway, perhaps something like begonias or violas.

Here a double length SMG box frame with a vertical support along all of one side has been planted with climbing beans, a tomato, squash plants, cardoon and an edging of parsley and sage plants.

PLANTS THAT GROW VERTICALLY

The seed companies are constantly changing and adding new varieties, and in order to find out the best ones that climb rather than bush out, I would suggest that you look carefully at the descriptions. Look for climbing peas rather than dwarf varieties and climbing beans rather than bush beans, cordon tomatoes rather than bush ones and so on. Few squash plants climb successfully as the heavy fruits tend to pull them down around harvest time but you might find winter squash varieties that yield lots of small fruit.

Planting Out

Remember, tomatoes are a vine crop that you cannot start as a seed directly in the garden. They take so long to grow into a sizeable plant that in most cases we have to grow or buy young plants to put into the garden as soon as the last frost of spring is over. The rest of the vine crops can often be started from seed directly in the garden, but so much depends on the growing season in your area so check seed packet instructions or take local advice as often it is worth starting off seed or young plants in small pots indoors, then planting out.

EASY CLIMBER CARE

One of the particularly desirable points of vertical gardening is that there's very little maintenance to do for the plants considering the yield you get from each plant. Aside from watering, it's a matter of once a week tucking the tops of the plant in through an opening in the netting, and back through another one, so they keep climbing up the netting. Some of the vertical crops, such as climbing beans and peas, will do all the climbing themselves, but tomatoes have to be helped through the openings and pointed to the top. The netting is so strong that it will easily hold up the plant and, in fact, after further studies I found out the netting will also hold up all the fruit, including small melons and some squash. Some of my winter squashes got so heavy I was afraid late summer storms would blow over the whole contraption. It depends on how strong the ground rods are and how firm the soil is to anchor the supports.

TOMATOES

One of the most popular home garden crops is tomatoes, and when you're vertical gardening the SMG way, there are a few things you can do to increase your yields.

Vines need a little direction from you from time to time. Gently weave a vine in and out of the trellis netting to help the plant clothe the support evenly.

The theory behind pruning cordon (indeterminate) varieties to one single stem is that all the energy goes straight up the main stalk, and you will have more tomatoes per square than if you allow the plant to put energy into branching out. That means you have to cut off the branches, and the best time to do it is when they're tiny. Unfortunately, most gardeners don't. The side-shoots look so small and cute, and as they grow bigger and bigger, they begin to take on the appearance of a productive plant and it becomes hard to cut them back. Get in the habit of inspecting and pruning your tomato plants once a week to a single stem, and remember to weave the top in and out of the netting.

Tomatoes on Top

What do you do when the tomato plant gets to the top of your support, and there is still a lot of growing season left? You have two choices, depending on how many tomatoes you've picked so far and how many green ones are coming. You can either cut the top right off, stop its growth and allow a good part of the energy to go into the existing tomatoes. Or you can let the top continue to grow, and let it hang over the side. It will keep growing until the end of the season,

To train cordon tomato plants against a vertical frame, just remember to weave the top growth in and out of the netting once a week. Also, remove any surplus side-shoots at the same time.

which for a tomato plant is the first frost. If you want to protect this plant from the first frost (and everyone does), the vertical frame is designed so all you have to do is gently lay a tarpaulin or blanket of garden fleece over it. Next morning take it off, fold it up and you're ready until the next threat of frost. This way you can keep your tomato plants growing and producing for several more weeks.

> MICHAEL WRITES...
> *I was surprised at how much I could get from such a small area*

PRUNING OTHER VINE CROPS

The other vine crops can have their side branches continue to grow until the whole plant takes up too much space. In general you want the plant to spread out to be approximately 30 to 60cm (1 to 2ft) wide on the vertical frame netting. If you plant one plant per square, it can fill that 30-cm (12-in) wide square, going right up the netting. If the spacing for that particular vegetable (e.g. cucumbers that are spaced two per square), you would trim the side branches back so that each one is from 15 to 23cm (6 to 9in) wide outside of its space. Squash is a little different because the leaves are so large that it's hard to judge where the stem is and how much room the entire plant is taking. That's why we give squash a lot more room (two squares per plant) in the vertical garden. Although most squash plants will grow on one central stalk, some do branch. Those with branches take longer to have fruit, so if you cut them off all the energy will go to the main stem and the flowers and fruit on that main stem. When the main stem grows to the top of the frame, let it hang down until it gets near the bottom, put it through the netting, turn it up and start all over again.

All the vining plants are very vigorous, energetic and sturdy, so there's not much you can do to deter their growth. But whenever you're bending a stem to poke it through the netting or over the top, hold it with two hands and be careful so it doesn't break.

SAFETY PRECAUTIONS

In a windy location, it is worth installing guy ropes to secure the vertical support right from the start. Even in sheltered areas, if your crops are growing thickly and have covered the frames, you might want to play it safe and put guy ropes in when you get near the end of the season. This requires tying something like fishing line or strong cord from the top bar down to the south side of the box. For the north side, you could always prop the top up with a 3.6-m (12-ft)

Installing guy ropes

Attach a length of strong cord to the corner of each support, tie with a knot that will tighten if pulled, such as a slip knot.

Secure other end of the cord using metal pegs or a stake of wood hammered in at an angle. The cord needs to be taut.

board cut out with a notch to fit into the top bar. That would hold the frame up from both directions.

STORING A VERTICAL FRAME

After the growing season is over, the frame can be removed intact and hung out of the way in the garage to wait for the next growing season. Some people leave their vertical frame up all winter, and during the holiday season, weave brightly coloured ribbon or even lights in and out of the netting to decorate for the holidays!

CONCLUSION

We have seen how beneficial and easy vertical gardening can be. Not only can you grow vining crops in less space, but harvesting becomes much easier and crops don't get soft and mushy from resting on the ground. The trained plants also create a screen, which can hide eye sores and add beauty to a garden. So we encourage you to add this innovative feature of Square Metre Gardening to your own garden. You will be so glad you did!

8

Extending the season

We gardeners like to bend reality a bit. Nature says, "You can't plant now, it's too cold." But we say, "Want to make a bet?" This chapter will show you how to get the most out of your garden each year by pushing the envelope on nature's conditions. With a variety of easy-to-make adaptations, your garden can grow 30 to 50 per cent more each year.

A SMG box with a fleece crop cover will be more productive.

Get more out of SMG

Would you like to be the one on your road to pick the first home-grown tomato? Would you like your own fresh herbs in winter? Your answer to these questions will help you determine how much work you want to put into extending the growing season.

Extending the growing season isn't necessarily a priority for the first-time gardener unless you've got a lot of time, a natural talent and a lot of confidence. Nature gives us our gardening cues as the seasons change. We're going to use those seasonal cycles as our framework for this chapter.

THE GROWING SEASON

Say the average growing season runs from May to October; okay you might not live somewhere quite like that but this is just an example. This means that most gardeners grow vegetables during an average of six months out of a possible twelve. When these six months are extended by an additional two months, the growing season is extended by 33 per cent. A three-month extension provides a 50 per cent increase, a worthwhile goal that can be achieved easily and inexpensively. Gardeners gain a great sense of accomplishment from these increased yields, and modern home gardeners and food preservers find it an absolute blessing.

Square Metre Gardeners don't have the negative experiences associated with doing all that hard work when they garden, so they look forward to more gardening and want to lengthen the growing season. For them, gardening isn't a test of endurance. It's a pleasant experience. They don't want to know how soon they can quit, but how long they can continue gardening!

Don't think you must extend the season to be an accomplished gardener. Sometimes it's just as good to sit back, relax and just "go dormant" for a while. Instead of gardening you could be satisfied and save time and work.

It's your decision. But if you think it's time to trick nature into feeding you year-round, then read on! The rest of the chapter will explain what to do each season to extend your harvest.

Earlier and Later

The obvious way to extend the gardening year is to start earlier than usual and keep the plants growing later. Hardy crops can be grown in two extra plantings for a longer season. The first planting is made in the early spring (or even the autumn before) and will mature by late spring. The second crop can be planted in late summer to mature in the late autumn.

Since early spring and late autumn can bring some rather severe weather, growing out of season is simply keeping the cold temperatures away from your plants. To do this, it's important to provide these crops with the extra protection they need from the elements and make sure this is well-secured.

By covering and protecting your crops, you are basically creating an artificial environment. After all, that is what a greenhouse does: it keeps the cold air out but lets the sunlight in. What more could a plant want?

In addition, many summer and tender crops can be started two to three weeks earlier than normal and they, too, can be extended up to a month beyond their normal season in the autumn. Sound like a lot of work? With Square Metre Gardening, it's easier than you think. It

Instead of sowing seeds outdoors, you can start them off earlier indoors on a windowsill or in a heated greenhouse, then transplant them into modular trays or pots and grow them on until planting out.

The whole box frame can be covered in clear polythene or garden fleece. If you make a frame to hold it, this will warm up the soil mix and the air temperature.

all depends on you providing protection from the sudden and harsh temperatures and weather.

Protective Structures

Since a Square Metre Garden takes up so little space, it is relatively easy to protect your crops. While special techniques that provide extra protection may vary with the season and the variety of vegetable, they are quickly learned and easily practised. Chapter 3 explains how to build a special box frame and the various kinds of protective structures that can support crop covers. These structures make it possible to moderate the climate in that box so you can stretch your growing season at both ends.

EARLY SPRING

A great time to extend the growing season is early spring before anyone else is out gardening. Begin by warming up the soil in your SMG box frames. Spread clear or black polythene over the top of the soil, and weigh it down with a brick in each corner. After a couple of sunny days, take the cover off, lift the grid out and mix up the soil with a trowel, so the warmer surface soil is moved down below and the colder, deeper soils are raised to the top. Then replace the covers. This is no big deal since your Mel's mix is loose and friable at all times of the year. Besides, the soil is only 15cm (6in) deep. How much work could that be?

Cloche styles, sizes and materials vary. Here the square Victorian-style lantern cloches are the right shape for a single square, while the long row cloches at the back could cover two or three squares for out-of-season salads.

JUMP-START YOUR SEEDS

If you want to get a quicker start and earlier growth, germinate your seeds indoors, and then transplant them into pots or modular trays when they are very young. Before the plants get too large, harden them off before planting them outdoors in your spring box.

SPRING PLANTING

For your first spring planting, set up a box frame with a PVC-type structure over the whole box or just put a suitable-sized cloche over any garden square where you'll be planting an early crop, so the sun will start warming the soil. Do this about four weeks before it's time to plant your seeds. For a double-quick soil warm-up, cover the soil with clear or black polythene, and then remove it before planting. When the weather is warm enough, transplant the plants you've grown into the open garden squares. They can also be left to grow where they were planted by removing the protective cage.

Climate Control

When you're using a crop cover on your early crops, remember that fresh air has to get in and you have to vent out the hot air that builds up on sunny days even if the weather is cold or freezing overnight. You still need to check up on your plants.

Heat builds up quickly in the box frames on sunny days. As the weather warms up, slide or lift the cover open a little farther each week until you can remove it entirely. A light frost won't hurt most hardy crops, but too much heat will cook them. It takes a little

You must check your spring plant boxes every day in sunny weather. If your plants begin to wilt or if the soil dries to a depth of 2 to 3cm (1in), it's time to water. Water each square with a cup of sun-warmed water.

experience to learn how to control the heat and moisture inside your frame. Keep in mind these precautions when trying to grow out of season.

Running to Seed

Lettuce, radishes and spinach can quickly run to seed in hot spells. Lettuce is also hard to germinate at high temperatures as this induces dormancy, but there are varieties of these crops that will do better in summer, look for words like "stands well", "slow to bolt" and "heat resistant" in the seed catalogues or packet descriptions.

SUMMER TIME

As the spring season progresses, it's time to give some summer vegetables, such as most beans, squash and cucumbers, a head start. For earlier harvests, try starting the seeds for these tender crops right in their permanent location under a protective cage with a double layer of garden fleece two weeks before the usual planting time. They will be much hardier and stronger than seedlings grown on the windowsill. When there is no danger of frost, gradually remove the covers.

There is an entire industry with all kinds of protective devices and products to help the gardener be successful in early gardening. Try some of these products and see what happens. I always like to place an unprotected plant right next to the protected one for comparison.

Provide Water

If you're the type of person who doesn't like hot, sticky weather, and you literally wilt in the sun, then the obvious solution is to move into the shade with a large pitcher of your favourite cold drink. Well, lettuce and radishes are no different. If you can provide shade for these spring crops (especially during the noon sun), along with some extra water, you will be able to harvest throughout most of the summer. Look for special hot-weather varieties of your favourite plants in seed catalogues.

Summer Lettuce

Did you ever notice that just when all of the good summer salad vegetables are ready, such as tomatoes, cucumbers and peppers, the lettuce and radishes are all gone? In the hot, long days of summer, these spring crops bolt and set seed, becoming bitter and coarse. However, there is a way to get around this and still "have your salad and eat it, too!"

1. Cover lettuce with shade netting.

2. Give plants twice as much as water as you normally would, directing water to the roots.

3. Cover the ground surrounding the lettuce with a thick layer of garden compost mulch.

Cover the square with a shade cage and give the plants plenty of water; as a general rule, water twice as often as you usually would. Remember, one of the best aids for growing a good crop is Mel's mix as it combines equal parts (by volume) of peat moss, coarse vermiculite and garden compost. It holds lots of moisture so the plant roots can take up all that's needed, yet drains well so the roots are less likely to become waterlogged.

Shade Screens

A shade cage (a structure with shade netting over, instead of garden fleece) will admit enough light for proper growth while keeping the temperature down considerably. A layer of mulch will also help moderate soil temperatures. You can also make use of natural shade or sun screens by locating a planting of spring crops to the north of your vertical growing frames.

Keep in mind that you're growing out of season, which means it is not the plant's natural inclination to grow then. You are urging these plants on, so be generous with your help and attention and don't expect too much. Just enjoy the challenge and experience!

Summer into Autumn

Gardeners sometimes wonder whether the extra effort involved in protecting summer crops from the first autumn frost is worth the effort. I think it certainly is, if you want an extra two or three weeks' worth of harvest from all those tender crops. Quite often the first frost is followed by a long period of clear, warm weather before the next frost. If you can protect your garden from that first frost, you can enjoy green plants, late fruits and fresh vegetables during one of the most pleasant periods of the year. Since most of these crops have a six- to eight-week harvest season, the extra two to three weeks gained amount to quite a bit. I would estimate more than a 25 per cent extension of the season.

All Together Now

To protect your crops from frost, you can start with a PVC arch or covered tunnel frame, and then cover it with a large sheet of clear plastic, crop cover or light blanket. Fasten down the corners so it

> **When all the summer crops grow in the same box frame, it's easier to protect them from late spring frosts.**
> 1. **Cover summer crops with a PVC arch or tunnel frame (Chapter 3 has DIY details).**
> 2. **Add a crop cover and fasten down the corners.**
> 3. **Or cover the crops with a mulch of loose straw.**

won't blow off during the night. Or the low-growing crops can be readily protected with a loose covering of straw that is easily removed the next morning.

To protect vine crops from frost, just throw a blanket or tarpaulin over the vertical frame so it's hanging down on all sides. This is one of the prime advantages of growing these crops on a vertical frame.

AUTUMN HARVEST

When autumn arrives, you and your garden have three options: to store food for the winter, extend the harvest or stop your garden. Whichever you choose depends on your time and inclination.

Keeping Secrets

I think the most economical and environmentally friendly way to extend the season is to store the harvest you have already grown correctly. There is almost no work and money involved, and the flavour and nutritional value of your home-grown vegetables can be maintained if the produce is healthy and undamaged.

Winter squash will store for long periods, especially if when harvesting you leave a section of stalk on to prevent rot entering through the top of the fruit.

HANDLE WITH CARE

The only secret of successful storage is actually very simple – learn each vegetable's best storage conditions and provide it. There are really only two: cool and dry, or cold and moist. The list of vegetables that need cool and dry conditions is easy to remember because there are only a few: pumpkins, winter squash and onions. The temperature should be around 10 to 15°C (50 to 60°F) and the humidity needs to be fairly low, at about 50 per cent. Try to find a cool corner of your garage, shed or cellar where the temperature stays above 2°C but below 16°C (above 35°F but below 60°F). Don't stack produce up in a big pile, but spread your vegetables out evenly on a shelf or container so air can circulate.

Handle produce as gently and infrequently as possible. When you're out harvesting, treat each vegetable as if it were an egg. Any bruise or cut will be the first spot to spoil. Lay each harvested vegetable separately in a box of sawdust or crumpled newspaper; don't pile them all together. Do not wash or scrub the produce. Leave the bottom of the root on root crops, and at least an inch of the top growth. For crops such as vine crops, leave as much of the stem on as possible. Only store produce that is in really good condition.

Store Root Crops

Vegetables in the group that need cold and moist conditions are all root crops: beetroot, carrots, turnips, potatoes and winter radishes, plus most of the cabbage family. This group also includes fruit – especially apples. The ideal storage temperature for them is as cold as you can get without actually freezing, say 2 to 7°C (35 to 45°F)

Actually, the simplest way to store root crops is not to dig them up at all. Roll a bale of straw over the planted area; this will break their tops and stop the plant's growing cycle while keeping the ground from freezing. When you're ready to harvest, simply roll the bale over, dig up a few vegetables and then replace the bale.

Write It Down

Don't forget to draw a diagram of what's left in the garden and where, so you won't be frantically digging around on a cold winter afternoon looking for the carrots but finding only radishes. The entire garden looks the same once the snow covers everything.

These carrots were lifted from their growing beds in autumn and stored in trays of moist peat moss or similar mix, kept in a garden shed. The roots can be used right into the following spring.

Regular summer radishes won't hold up too long in freezing weather while the winter radish will last almost indefinitely. Carrots and leeks also do quite well through the entire winter. If you're feeling adventurous, you can experiment with leaving different root crops in the ground to see which last through the autumn and winter so you'll know what to expect the following year. In many areas, slugs will attack root crops such as beetroot and carrots so it is worth lifting them and storing them. Use plastic trays lined with empty compost bags and filled up with barely moist sand or peat moss. Space unwashed crops out so they are not touching and store in a shed or garage.

Cosy Cover

Cabbage and other leaf and head crops can also be stored in the garden, using a loose, fluffy covering of straw or leaves. To keep the wind from blowing this loose covering around, try placing a 60-cm (2-ft) high fence of chicken wire around your garden areas and anchoring the wiring at each corner with stakes.

TEMPERATURE DIFFERENCES

On a cold night you can walk around your property and actually feel the differences in temperature. The cold air virtually rolls down the slope and settles in low-lying areas; in fact, this is called "cold air drainage". Surprisingly, this will happen even where there is not a great difference in elevation. Once you get the knack of watching out for frost and covering your plants when it threatens, you will see the advantages of locating a garden on the top or south side of a slope, rather than at the bottom of a low area. You will also see the advantage of grouping your crops according to their weather requirements. This makes it easier to protect them from either frost or freezing in both the spring and autumn. One of the greatest advantages of SMG is how easy it is to protect your garden since it is condensed into small, uniform areas.

It's much simpler and more cost effective to grow hardy crops for an extended season using a box frame with a crop cover that protects plants from just the severe weather fluctuations.

Autumn Frosts

When frost is predicted, be ready with insulating crop covers. Your best bet is to catch the local evening weather forecast. Another (perhaps better) source is the Internet, particularly where you can get up-to-date information relevant for your postcode.

First Hard Frost

A light frost blackens the outer leaves of most summer flowers and vegetables. It is indicated by a white covering on the lawn in very early morning. Summer vegetables can still be harvested if eaten right away. A hard frost will blacken and kill all summer flowers and tender vegetables. Plants, such as dahlias, that were bushy and colourful the day before are now just droopy skeletons with blackened leaves hanging like rags from the stems. This can be very disheartening for gardeners who come out in the morning to find that the garden has been devastated. A hard frost is indicated by a crunchy feel to the ground and a thin film of ice on the birdbath. This is the time when most gardeners declare an end to the season. But if you have hardy autumn vegetables, and you clean up the garden right away, your garden will still look attractive and inviting.

WINTER

Gardeners who are particularly ambitious and want to continue growing something all winter will need additional tools for providing special protection to a very select variety of plants. If you can keep the ground from freezing solid and provide sunlight in just a small area, in many parts of the country you can continue growing special varieties of lettuce and salad, hardy leaf crops, such as kale, and a number of oriental vegetables all winter long. It's also possible to plant some members of the onion family in the autumn in order to get a larger or early crop next spring and summer. Take local advice on which crops are usually worthwhile in your area but remember the weather will vary from year to year.

Mizuna is a hardy salad crop but given some cloche protection, either at the start or end of the growing season, this will improve the leaf quality.

Hardy Varieties

Salad from your garden during the coldest months of winter? You bet. A SMG box can provide fresh salad each week during the winter without a greenhouse. Here's how: select fast-growing vegetables for

Growing Winter Veggies

1. Select fast-growing varieties with superior cold resistance.

2. Select the sunniest sheltered spot.

3. Plant in a box frame with a cage to keep out pests such as pigeons.

your winter garden. Try any of the hardy salad greens and root crops, but look for special cold-tolerant varieties. Every seed company offers different varieties so look through catalogues and select those that are recommended for cold and winter growing. Look for names that have words in them such as 'Arctic', 'Frost King' or 'Snow Man' (I just made that last one up).

PICK A SPOT

Now pick the sunniest, most sheltered spot you can find for your winter garden. It doesn't have to be in the main garden; next to the house or garage is better, especially if you have white walls, since they will reflect quite a bit of heat into your miniature garden. Remember that the sun is very low in the sky during the winter, and the place that may have been in full sun during the summer could now very well be a very shady place in the winter. Don't place the box under the roof or gutter line, or you'll risk the chance that rain, sleet or snow will fall on it. You'll be in good shape if the area is sheltered from strong winter winds and if it gets a maximum amount of winter sunlight. It doesn't have to be a permanent spot either. First, lay down a sheet of plastic or sturdy weedproof membrane and in the spring you can pick everything up and return the area back to its former use.

Plant Closer

Install your winter box frame, fill it with Mel's mix and start your planting. Since the plants will grow very slowly compared to spring and summer and since you'll be harvesting every leaf almost as it is ready, you can plant your produce closer than the usual spacing, even as close as half the recommended distance.

Insulate

Provide some insulation around the winter box, by placing bales of straw all around. Provide a tight-fitting cover or make a double-layer cover with plastic to keep the soil and air from losing heat at night. Throw a blanket or tarp on the box for those extra cold nights.

PUTTING YOUR GARDEN TO BED

When it is time to put the SMG to bed, we do this the same way we put our children to bed. You wouldn't think of sending them to their room and paying no attention to them, would you? Instead, we encourage them to prepare for bedtime: to brush their teeth, get one last drink, fix the bed just the way they want it and then spend some time reading a bedtime story. Then it's finally lights out.

Well, treat your garden the same way. Don't leave it a mess with dead plants and debris lying about. Tidy it up and make it look good. Now is an excellent time to mix a little extra garden compost in each box and smooth and level it out so it will be all ready for the spring planting. That's never happened before with single-row gardening. Now it's not only possible, but also very practical.

The little extra work you do in the autumn will keep your garden attractive and neat-looking all winter and make your springtime garden easier to begin. You'll simply go out, rake off the mulch cover and start planting, either at the regular time or earlier if you use a crop cover.

> **It's worth recording some of the highlights of your gardening year. For example, varieties that did well and what you had too much of. It is also worth noting if crops had any soil-borne pests and diseases; if so, grow a different family of plant in that box frame next year.**

Grid Storage

You can remove, clean, fold and hang up the planting grids now or leave them on the boxes all winter, which will remind you of how much fun you have now with gardening. What I'm suggesting for the end of the season is really no different than what I recommend you do all season long. Keep your garden neat, tidy and attractive. If you keep it in tip-top condition (and that's not too difficult with a no-work garden), you will enjoy it so much more.

KEEP THE BOX NEAT

You'll enjoy SMG much more if you keep your garden neat and attractive at all times. Since you no longer have to hoe the weeds or dig and cultivate the soil, you'll have time for the pleasant things like trimming off yellow or dead lower leaves, dead blossoms, removing plants, dead and pest-damaged leaves or even entire plants.

But what about winter? Not much work to do after putting the garden to bed, but you might think about decorating the garden so it still looks nice all winter long or at least for the holidays.

9

Special gardens and gardeners

The Square Metre Gardening system makes it easy to create a garden anywhere, even if there is no soil. SMG is equally flexible for all types of users too. Box frames filled with Mel's mix make gardening fun for everyone, especially children and seniors.

Children will enjoy growing their own food in a SMG.

Beyond the garden gate

There's no heavy digging and no need for lots of tools, so the SMG method is perfect for schools and community gardens, also it can be built in courtyards and playgrounds where there is no natural soil.

Tricky locations are no barrier to creating a SMG and I've found my method is particularly suitable for getting both youngsters, including those with special educational needs, and seniors growing their own food. Here's a few thoughts on adapting the technique.

NO GARDEN

Sometimes a property may have limited outdoor space for a garden, so you'll need to think creatively and closer to your front or back door. A corner of a patio or balcony could contain several 60 x 60-cm (2 x 2-ft) boxes. These could be stacked up creatively at different heights to form a very attractive corner garden. The boxes could be placed on low tables of different heights or on supports to give each one a different height. If you install a vertical frame with netting along both walls or just tack the netting to the walls, it could fan out so it gets larger as it gets higher to expand the garden area even more. Another option, of course, is at the base of, or even on top of, a balcony or deck railing. You could install 15 to 30-cm (6- to 12-in) wide boxes on the floor or bolt them to the top or side of railings.

SHADY SOLUTIONS

If you have a heavily shaded garden, then you don't have too many choices. One solution is to locate several boxes around the house wherever they might receive enough sunlight. Your boxes could be on the ground or even on legs next to the house. If you had a southern exposure with enough sunlight, you could put a double-decker long box against the house. Other than that, the only choice would be, if the shade is cast by your own plants, to prune back or remove entirely some of the exisiting plants. If these suggestions don't work, then it's shade gardening for you.

HILLSIDES AND SLOPES

What if the only space you have for a garden is on a hillside or fairly steep slope? If it's facing south, it may be worthwhile to develop it for your Square Metre Garden. The limiting factors are how steep the slope is and how big your garden is going to be. You're in luck with a

LEVELLING A SLOPING GARDEN

1. "Cut and fill" is an efficient technique for making small adjustments in level to sloping ground. You can probably tackle minor changes in level yourself but for major changes in gradient, consult a professional landscaper.

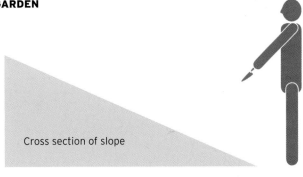

Cross section of slope

2. The beauty of this method is that the minimum amount of earth is moved around. A section is dug out (A) and then placed at the foot of the slope to create a base (B).

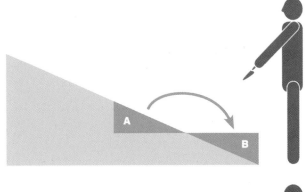

A
B

3. The ground is levelled off and you can now place a box frame there, line it and fill it with Mel's mix.

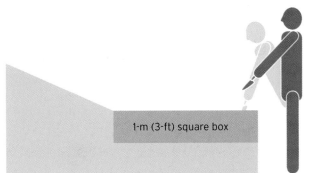

1-m (3-ft) square box

SMG because you can build boxes that will fit into the lay of the land, although keep to 30-cm (1-ft) square grids.

Basically, in order to have a level garden so your soil and water don't run off, you're going to cut a path into the slope wide enough to make a garden area. If you want a 1-m (3-ft) wide bed, you will have to reach in from both sides and that can be too much of a stretch from the uphill side. However, with a 1-m (3-ft) wide box, which will be higher than the downhill aisle, you will be able to reach in the full 1m (3ft) from the downhill side because you are standing up rather than kneeling down next to the box.

To get a 1-m (3-ft) wide level spot, you just cut into the hill and move the soil downhill to form the 1-m (3-ft) wide areas.

Think ahead about water availability, time, and the cost to dig and then level a pathway wide enough to hold both you and your garden. The steeper the slope, the harder it becomes.

DECKS AND BALCONIES

When creating deck gardens in a flat or roof garden, be sure to consider the people below you and how you're going to water. Your garden may not be a problem when it rains, but when it is sunny and bright and your garden water drips down on the neighbours while they are at their barbecue below, they may not look favourably upon you or your garden.

There are several things you can do about this situation. First of all, since Mel's mix holds water so well, it's highly unlikely you will overwater, which will prevent a lot of dripping or excess water leakage. Just in case, though, you can always choose not to drill drain holes at consistent intervals over the entire bottom of your SMG, but only a couple in one corner. Then, slightly slope the box towards this one corner and put a decorative vase or other container underneath to catch any drips that may leak out.

GRANDPARENTS

One of the greatest bonds that I have found between grandparents and grandchildren is formed during a gardening project, even if the visit is short. Give your grandchild a garden or just a square, let him write his name on the grid, encourage her to plant her garden, and you may find your grandchildren will keep in touch more often, just to find out how the garden is growing. This, of course, can work the opposite way when the grandparent visits the child's home and they plant a garden there. And, of course, there will be great anticipation for the next visit and what has happened in the garden. Selecting plants for children is quite simple; plants should be easy to grow, fast growing for quick results and something that will produce an exciting result.

KIDS' CORNER
Finger Spacing

For nine per square, take two fingers, spread them apart and draw two lines horizontally, which divides the square into thirds, and then two vertically, so that you've got nine sections. For those with smaller hands (kids love doing this), use your thumb and the trigger

finger, or take one finger and draw two lines separately going each way. Poke nine holes in the middle of your drawn squares and you're ready to plant your seeds.

It's even more fun marking the sixteen plantings per square foot. Remember, there is no measuring. Divide the square in half each way by drawing lines in the soil with your finger, the same finger movements (one vertical line and one horizontal line, each dividing the square in half) as described for four per square. Then, take two fingers, your trigger and middle fingers, and punch holes in the soil. They should be spaced about the same distance that your eyes are spaced apart. Without poking yourself in the eye, hold your fingers up to your face so the fingers are spaced just about right, and then, mark your soil. In each of the four squares, go bing, bing, with your fingers, marking two holes each time so there are four holes in each small square.

Children will enjoy growing a little bit of everything in their SMG. There is so much fun to be had using the finger-spacing method, planting out and watching the plants grow but they will learn a lot too.

Seed Lessons

Why are seeds different sizes and different shapes? That's a fascinating enquiry into nature you could make with your kids. Quite often their shape depends on how they were formed or nestled together in the seedpod. Does the size and shape have anything to do with their ability to sprout? Yes and no. In general, the smaller the seed the more delicate it is as a young plant and the greater the care it needs to successfully germinate and grow. The size quite often depends only on the plant species itself.

Which Part Sprouts First?

Is it the top stem with its leaves? For all seeds, the root sprouts first and goes down. How does it know to go down? Gravity! After the root gets started and secured with little feeder roots so it can start taking up moisture and nutrients, it calls up to the top and yells "all clear below", then the top sprouts and goes straight up against gravity. It is not because of darkness or light or any other reason, it is strictly gravity and the all-clear signal, of course.

As we get older, it may become harder to do certain things. With SMG, you'll see another big advantage when you harvest one square and add that trowel full of compost. There's no heavy digging! Gardening then becomes a very simple, easy and pleasant task. This means you'll probably never have to stop gardening if you're using the Square Metre Garden method.

GARDENING FOR SENIORS

Some people find it difficult to do hard, manual labour like digging up the existing soil, as well as getting down on the ground and then getting back up again. With SMG, the simple answer is to just raise the garden up to the gardener's height. It can be a sit-down garden, which is particularly adaptable for a person in a wheelchair or someone who wants to sit and garden. A little higher would be a stand-up garden if that makes it easier to tend; since there is very little maintenance, just nurturing and you are not standing for long periods of time. And the gardens, once they have a plywood bottom installed, can be moved to any location for the convenience and pleasure of the gardener.

You can now put various sizes of boxes on patios, near the back door, or any pleasant area around the house that is easy for a senior to tend to their garden. Of course, there is no longer the need to walk way out back carrying a bunch of heavy-duty tools. Now, it is just a matter of going to your garden and tending it with the minimal amount of effort, work and tools. There is no weeding, and because we are starting with a perfect soil mix, there is never any heavy digging. There is no need even to have spades or forks or any large tools, just one trowel.

Sometimes seniors enjoy out-of-season gardening because they have the time to tend their gardens during the tricky, out-of-season weather. This also gets them moving about out of doors more often, which is another asset.

SPECIAL NEEDS GARDENING

SMGs have gone a lot of places over the years from veteran hospitals to schools for the blind and deaf. Other worthwhile places we have installed SMGs are in prisons and troubled youth facilities. Building a small portable garden (in sizes from 60 x 60cm/2 x 2ft up to 1 x 1m /3 x 3ft with a plywood bottom added) allows people to participate who otherwise might not have been able to garden.

GARDENING IN SCHOOLS

One thing I've learned from teaching SMG over the last thirty years or so is that kids love to garden. They are so excited about growing plants. From the beginning, it was obvious that SMG is perfect for teaching arithmetic and all kinds of maths and that, in fact, anything in the scientific field is easily taught using gardening as the vehicle. But then I began to see that a teacher could readily relate all subjects to gardening. A side benefit is that, in addition to school subjects, the children learned the important values of sharing, nurturing and taking responsibility.

We have worked with all age groups from pre-school through senior school, using gardening as a teaching tool. Suddenly learning begins to have some type of meaning in their lives, and they can begin to see the value of the other subjects they have been learning in the past.

A plan needs to be made on what to do with the gardens during the summer holiday period. There are lots of solutions – all you need to do is discuss with the students, and that in itself becomes another learning experience!

COMMUNITY GARDENS

With SMG, it is possible to have pocket gardens anywhere in the community, even right in a city. It doesn't need to be a huge project or large area to convert space into a community garden. It is now possible to take just a corner of a community space or any other small space, perhaps even in an existing city park, and have a very small community Square Metre Garden. Each person can have from one box up to three. One of the best things about using SMG in a community garden is that since there are no weeds, the garden doesn't become an overrun eyesore by the middle of the summer. This means it is much easier to operate and get public and official approval. If you want to start a community garden, I would emphasise the need again to start small, gain experience, become successful and then expand during the second season or year.

Community gardens do require a set of guidelines for what participants can and cannot grow so they don't interfere with their neighbour's garden; the guidelines should also cover the hours of operation, use of water and maintenance of the gardens so they look neat and attractive. The use of pesticides and fertiliser was always a big concern with community gardens, but that issue can be totally eliminated with SMG.

In the layout of the garden, it would be nice to have several tables where people in wheelchairs could wheel right up to their assigned garden plot. Also, several benches and some shade are always a good feature so it becomes a sociable space.

GROUP PROJECTS

A SMG could be a demonstration project for many different groups, including children's gardens, scouts botanical gardens and garden clubs. A group could create a salad garden with all the ingredients: lettuce, tomatoes, root crops and edible flowers. Each square would have a nice sign stating what is there and how it is used in a salad. Another idea would be an herb display with signs and an invitation to touch the plants.

The nice part about the idea of using a SMG is it requires so little maintenance, yet produces such a spectacular showcase. It is an easy way of attracting new members or of putting on a demonstration at a function. Another nice thing about it is, at the end of a fair or show, four people can pick up the garden, put it into a van and take it home. In that situation, you can even include a shortened vertical frame so that it would still fit in the vehicle and yet would add a third dimension to your display.

HUMANITARIAN PROJECTS

For some, gardening is an enjoyable hobby, but for many it can mean the difference between life and death. One step up from starving, the worst condition in the world, is poverty and continual hunger—and that's where SMG comes in. We can help solve the hunger situation. We have a billion people who need help, and the solution is to teach them how to help themselves. They need to be shown how and then helped to start just one Square Metre Garden of their own; the rest will follow. We teach them to use straight garden compost in their gardens because of the lack of peat moss and vermiculite in many of these areas of the world; they can create compost for free, while improving their environment. We believe that, instead of governments and humanitarian organisations sending food, they should start educational programmes that teach people how to compost and how to create a SMG garden. It would cost less, produce more, allow people to become self-sufficient, take very little effort and yet deliver worthwhile results.

That is why the our Foundation is so intent on Square Metre Gardening. We feel it can truly make a difference in the everyday lives of so many millions of people.

> RICH WRITES...
>
> *Your method is awesome. My 3-year-old and I have a blast with two boxes*

ON MY SOAPBOX

Well, here I am, on my soapbox trying to solve worldwide problems when you just want to learn how to have a better garden. But what this book is also all about is how SMG can reach and help so many more people.

That's the significant and imperative message I want to bring to the world. Will you help me? You can, simply by encouraging others to start a SMG. Get involved in your community or stretch your involvement to the entire world. Anyone, anywhere in the world can now have a small square metre garden right at their back door. The nutritional value of the children's diet will improve dramatically, and step-by-step, as they expand their garden, that family will be closer to self-sufficiency and independence from government and private aid programmes. You know the saying, "Give a man a fish and you feed him for a day. Teach a man to fish and you feed him for a lifetime." The world hunger problem can never be solved until we help people help themselves, step-by-step, square-by-square. Then, maybe the saying will be, "Show a family how to Square Metre Garden, and they will feed themselves forever."

10

Vegetables, salads and herbs

So what do you want to grow? For some ideas, here is a plant directory that details how to grow individual crops. You could either look up your family favourites and see when to grow them or simply browse through looking for new tastes to try. For a quick overview of how your crop choices will fit into your box frames, there is a handy chart.

A bountiful harvest from each square is possible if you follow the SMG method.

At a glance

Check here whether the crops you want to grow need a vertical support, how many plants you need and how long they will occupy the square. You can also see which crops produce a harvest quickly.

Vegetables, salads and herbs

Crop	Height	Support	Plants per square
ALLIACEAE			
Allium ampeloprasum **Leek**	30 to 50cm (12 to 20in)	no	9
Allium cepa **Onion**	30cm (12in)	no	16
Allium sativum **Garlic**	30cm (12in)	no	4
Allium schoenoprasum **Chives**	15 to 30cm (6 to 12in)	no	16
APIACEAE			
Anethum graveolens **Dill**	30 to 60cm (12 to 24in)	no	4
Apium graveolens var. *dulce* **Celery**	40cm (16in)	no	4
Apium graveolens var. *rapaceum* **Celeriac**	40cm (16in)	no	1
Coriandrum sativum **Coriander**	30 to 45cm (12 to 18in)	no	16
Daucus carota var. *sativus* **Carrot**	30cm (12in)	no	16
Foeniculum vulgare dulce **Florence Fennel**	30 to 45cm (12 to 18in)	no	4
Petroselinum **Parsley**	15 to 30cm (6 to 12in)	no	4
ASPARAGACEAE			
Asparagus officinalis **Asparagus**	1.2 to 2m (4 to 6ft)	in windy areas, support each stem	1 or 4
ASTERACEAE			
Artemisia dracunculus var. *sativa* **French Tarragon**	45 to 60cm (18 to 24in)	no	1 or 4
Cynara cardunculus and *C. scolymus* **Cardoon** and **Globe Artichoke**	1 to 1.5m (3 to 5ft)	no	1 per box frame

Growing season	Weeks to harvest (from seed)	Notes
summer, autumn	16 to 32	
spring, summer	20	There are also varieties for autumn planting
spring, summer	20 to 30	There are also varieties for autumn planting
spring, summer	16	
spring, summer	6	Repeat sow each month until midsummer
summer, autumn	20	
summer, autumn	30	
spring, summer	5	Repeat sow each month until midsummer
spring, summer, autumn	10	For long roots to store, grow in a deep box
spring, summer	10 to 12	
spring, summer, autumn	14	Can last until winter in mild areas
spring, summer	3 years	Perennial, needs its own permanent bed
summer	n/a	Not raised from seed, perennial plant
spring, summer	25	Large perennial veg that need their own box frame

Vegetables, salads and herbs (continued)

Crop	Height	Support	Plants per square
ASTERACEAE (continued)			
Cichorium endivia **Endive**	20cm (8in)	no	1
Cichorium intybus **Chicory** or **Belgium Endive**	20cm (8in)	no	1
Lactuca sativa **Lettuce** and other **Salad Leaves**	15 to 30cm (6 to 12in)	no	4
BRASSICACEAE			
Brassica rapa var. *chinensis* **Pak Choi**	25 to 30cm (10 to 12in)	no	4
Brassica napus **Swede**	50cm (20in)	no	1
Brassica oleracea Acephala Group **Kale**	30 to 90cm (12 to 32in)	no	4
Brassica oleracea var. *botrytis* **Cauliflower**	45 to 60cm (18 to 24in)	no	1
Brassica oleracea Capitata Group **Cabbage** (summer)	30 to 45cm (12 to 18in)	no	1
Brassica oleracea Gemmifera Group **Brussels Sprouts**	75cm (30in)	Individual stems may need staking	1 per 2 squares
Brassica oleracea Gongylodes Group **Kohl Rabi**	15 to 20 cm (6 to 8in)	no	4
Brassica oleracea Italica Group **Calabrese** or **Green Broccoli**	45 to 60cm (18 to 24in)	no	1
Brassica rapa **Turnip**	15 to 20 cm (6 to 8in)	no	9
Raphanus sativus **Radish**	15 to 30cm (6 to 12in)	no	16
CHENOPODIACEAE			
Beta vulgaris Conditiva Group **Beetroot**	30cm (1ft)	no	9 or 16
Beta vulgaris **Chard** and **Swiss Chard**	30 to 45cm (12 to 18in)	no	4
Spinacia oleracea **Spinach**	15 to 30cm (6 to 12in)	no	9
CURCURBITACEAE			
Cucumis sativus **Cucumber**	2m (6ft)	Yes, vertical frame	1 or 2
Cucumis melo **Melon**	2m (6ft)	Yes, vertical frame	1 per 2 squares
Cucurbita pepo **Courgette** and **Summer Squash**	bush 45cm (18in) vine 1.2m (4ft)	vines need a vertical frame	bush 1 per box frame, vine 1 per 2 squares

Growing season	Weeks to harvest (from seed)	Notes
summer, autumn	12	Sometimes grown as winter salad
autumn, winter	12	
spring, summer, autumn	20 to 30	Some grown as winter salads
spring, summer, autumn	4 to 7	
summer, autumn, winter	16 to 25	
summer, autumn, winter	16 to 32	Can also be grown as baby salad or winter crop
spring, summer, autumn	14 to 20	
spring, summer, autumn	16 to 18	Autumn, winter and spring are also available
summer, autumn, winter	30 to 36	
spring, summer	10 to 12	
spring, summer, autumn	12 to 16	
spring, summer	8	There are also winter varieties
spring, summer, autumn	4	There are also winter varieties
spring, summer, autumn	8	Repeat sow every 3 weeks
spring, summer, autumn, winter	8	Baby salad to mature stems
spring, autumn, winter	10 to 12	Can be repeat sown in spring
summer	16	
summer	17 to 20	Needs a long growing season
summer	12	

Vegetables, salads and herbs (continued)

Crop	Height	Support	Plants per square
CURCURBITACEAE (*continued*)			
Cucurbita **Winter Squash**	vine 1.2m (4ft)	vines need vertical frame	vine 1 per 2 squares
FABACEAE			
Vicia faba **Broad Bean**	60 to 100cm (2 to 3ft)	stake stems of tall varieties	4
LAMIACEAE			
Mentha **Mint**	30 to 60cm (1 to 2ft)	no	1
Ocimum **Basil**	20 to 45cm (8 to 18in)	no	1 to 4
Origanum **Oregano** and **Marjoram**	20 to 45cm (8 to 18in)	no	1
MALVACEAE			
Abelmoschus esculentus **Okra**	45 to 60cm (18 to 24in)	Yes, needs vertical frame	1
PAPILIONACEAE			
Phaseolus coccineus, P. vulgaris **Climbing Bean**	1.5 to 2m (5 to 6ft)	Yes, use vertical frame	4 or 8
Phaseolus vulgaris **Bush Bean**	30 to 40cm (12 to 16in)	no	4 or 9
Pisum sativum **Pea**	60cm to 1.5m (2-5ft)	Yes, vertical frame or netting	8
POACEAE			
Zea mays **Sweetcorn**	1.5 to 2m (5 to 6ft)	Yes, horizontal netting	9 per box frame
ROSACEAE			
Fragaria **Strawberry**	15 to 30cm (6 to 12in)	no	4
SOLANACEAE			
Capsicum annuum **Sweet Pepper** and **Chilli**	30 to 60cm (1 to 2ft)	Taller varieties may need stems staking	1
Lycopersicon esculentum **Tomato**	2m (6ft)	yes needs vertical frame or stake stem	1
Solanum melongena **Aubergine**	75cm (30in)	Yes, stakes to support stem	1
Solanum tuberosum **Potato**	30 to 60cm (1 to 2ft)	no	1

Growing season	Weeks to harvest (from seed)	Notes
summer, autumn	24	Or grow a bush variety, 1 plant per box frame without vertical support
spring, summer	20 to 30	There are also varieties for autumn sowing
spring, summer, autumn	n/a	Perennial herb that needs roots contained
summer	16	Repeat sow before mid summer
spring, summer, autumn	n/a	Some perennial, buy young plants as alternative to seed sowing
summer	16 to 20	
summer	16 to 20	
summer	8 to 10	
spring, summer	10 to 14	
summer	10 to 13	Grow in their own box frame
spring, summer	n/a	Perennial, buy bare root plants
summer	20 to 25	
summer	20 to 25	Heights, spacing and support details here refer to cordon varieties, other options available
summer	25	
spring, summer	20	Plant sprouted tubers in extra deep boxes

Alliaceae *Allium ampeloprasum*

LEEK

Location: Full sun
Height: 30 to 50cm
(12 to 20in)
Spacing: 9 per square
for baby leeks, 4 per
square for winter leeks

GROWING SEASON
Spring: no
Summer: yes
Autumn: yes
Winter: yes

GROWING TIME
Seed to Harvest: 16 to 32
weeks
Indoor Seed Starting: 4 to 8
weeks before the last
spring frost
Earliest Outdoor Planting:
after the last spring frost

VARIETY GUIDE
For baby leeks, 'Volta' or
'Zermat' is worth looking
out for. For winter leeks,
try 'Apollo', 'Bandit' or
'Darwin'. If you want a
variety that does well for
both types, then 'Striker'
is versatile.

Grow leeks to use when they are young, pulling up baby leeks in summer to autumn, or leave them to bulk up into a winter veg.

Starting

Leeks are easy to grow from seed and transplant easily so they are best started off in pots or modular trays to plant out later on. Sow seeds in mid spring and young plants should be at the right stage by summer, then plant out into squares vacated by early crops.

Growing

Plant out into their final growing positions when the young plants are about 20cm (8in) high and the thickness of a pencil. Planting size isn't critical and they will wait until a square is free but you might need to trim the roots to 8 to 10cm (3 to 4in) and, if the leaves are very long, trim these to compensate. Water the square, then plant the leeks deeply about 10cm (4in) deep so some of the leaves are above soil level: either poke a hole in the mix with your finger or use a trowel. Nine plants per square will give you baby leeks, four per square will leave more room for thicker stems for winter harvest.

Keep the mix moist and weed-free. Leeks used to be free of pests but in recent years, leaf moth and allium leaf miner have caused problems so consider using a fine mesh crop cover in summer if these pests have been reported in your area.

Harvesting

Pull leeks from the ground when they are 1 to 1.5cm (½ to ¾in) in diameter or leave them until required. You can also pull up bunches of pencil-thick leeks to use a substitute for spring onions. Leeks are hardy but if the growing mix freezes, they are hard to harvest so lift them if freezing weather is forecast. Leeks will store well in a sheltered part of the garden.

Alliaceae *Allium cepa*

ONION AND SHALLOT

Location: Full sun
Height: 30cm (12in)
Spacing: 16 per square
for onions, 4 for
shallots

GROWING SEASON
Spring: yes
Summer: yes
Autumn: no*
Winter: no*

*there are varieties
for autumn planting
that overwinter

GROWING TIME
Seed to Harvest: 20 weeks
Indoor Seed Starting: 8 to
12 weeks before the last
spring frost
Earliest Outdoor Planting:
4 weeks before last spring
frost

There are many types of bulbous onions from large mild ones right though to small flavoursome shallots. All are easy to grow from seed or sets (small immature bulbs). Sets are quicker and will produce a harvest by summer from an autumn or spring planting but there is a greater choice of varieties as seed.

Starting

Push sets into the mix, pointed side up with their tops just showing. Water in, and that's all there is to it although, until they sprout, protect with a wire barrier to stop birds pulling out the sets. A shallot set will form a clump of bulbs, hence the wider spacing.

To raise from seed, start off indoors in early spring at 10 to 15°C (50 to 59°F), then transplant into modular trays and harden off. Or wait and sow seed outdoors in early to mid spring (but use a crop cover for early sowings).

Growing

Keep the area weed-free and water in dry conditions but withhold water when the top growth browns and starts to fall over. When bulbs start expanding, use your finger to remove some of the soil around each bulb and partially uncover it. This makes it easier for the bulb to expand. Onions can get soil-borne diseases so grow in a different place each year.

Harvesting

Pull the onions out of the ground and place on chicken wire laid out in the sun (if it rains, bring undercover to dry off). After several days, the tops, roots and outer skin will be dry. Clean off any loose skins or dirt by rubbing them between your palms, then store the best for later use. Use any onions with green or thick tops straightaway.

Hints and tips

A quick alternative to onions and shallots, is to grow salad or spring onions. They are pulled up as required once the stems are pencil thick. Sow seed directly outside every fortnight from spring right through to summer; extra hardy varieties are available for sowing in late summer to early autumn. Plants are ready to harvest 10 to 12 weeks from sowing. You can sow up to 30 in a square.

VARIETY GUIDE
'Centurion', 'Red Baron' and 'Troy' are reliable onions. For shallots, look for 'Red Sun' or 'Jermor'. For spring onions, try well-known 'Guardsman' or 'White Lisbon'.

Alliaceae *Allium sativum*

GARLIC

Location: Full sun
Height: 30cm (12in)
Spacing: 4 per square

GROWING SEASON
Spring: yes
Summer: yes
Autumn: no*
Winter: no*

*there are varieties
for autumn planting
that overwinter

GROWING TIME
Seed to Harvest: 20 to 30
weeks from planting
cloves
Indoor Seed Starting: n/a
Earliest Outdoor Planting:
16 to 28 weeks before last
spring frost

Hints and tips

Spare cloves can be planted up in pots of multi-purpose compost and the green shoots harvested and used as you would chives. Hardneck varieties produce a green flower stalk (called a "scape") that can be harvested and eaten fresh.

VARIETY GUIDE
There is a lot of regional variation in garlic varieties so buy one that does well in your area. 'Cristo' and 'Solent White' are softnecks suitable for both autumn and spring planting and store well. For a hardneck garlic, try 'Spanish Rocambole'.

Useable bulbs of garlic can be harvested from the smallest of spaces; all you need is a sunny spot free of weeds. Simply plant the individual cloves either in late autumn or early spring and then harvest bulbs in midsummer. Hardneck varieties have a central shoot that hardens off in summer; these do well in cold areas and have a strong flavour. If you want to store your garlic harvest for several months, grow a softneck variety.

Starting
Buy certified virus-free bulbs from a garden centre or mail order supplier rather than use supermarket garlic. Split up the bulb into individual cloves. Plant each clove upright with the flat base of the clove facing downwards. Push the cloves at least 2.5cm (1in) down with no tip visible or the birds might pull them up out of the ground.

Growing
Keep the square free of weeds. You only need to water in very dry conditions. As soon as the leaves turn yellow, harvest the garlic promptly; a delay can cause the bulbs to shrivel and there is more chance of disease.

Harvesting
Ease the bulbs out of the ground with a trowel. Dry the bulbs in the sun but bring them undercover if it is wet. Store in cool, dry conditions.

Alliaceae *Allium schoenoprasum*

CHIVES

Location: Full sun or
partial shade
Height: 15 to 30cm
(6 to 12in)
Spacing: 16 per square

GROWING SEASON
Spring: yes
Summer: yes
Autumn: no
Winter: no

GROWING TIME
Seed to Harvest: 16 weeks
Indoor Seed Starting: 10
weeks before last frost
Earliest Outdoor Planting:
after the last spring frost

This is a fun little plant with attractive flowers. The slim, round leaves are hollow and have a mild onion scent when cut. The pinkish-purple flowers are edible and appear in late spring and make a pretty garnish for salads. Chives are a member of the allium family, and oddly enough, it is one herb that hasn't really been used for medicinal purposes during its long history. It is simply a garden plant that has enhanced the flavour of savoury foods for centuries.

VARIETY GUIDE
It is usual to grow the species only. Garlic chives are a perennial with flatter leaves.

Starting

You can buy and plant out young potted plants in spring (four plants per square would be adequate) or raise your own plants from seed. Seed can be sown indoors in late winter and transplanted or sown direct outdoors in spring, once there is little danger of frost.

Growing

Keep the roots moist. Plants are perennial and the clumps will spread out. Every few years, lift and divide clumps, replanting the youngest and healthiest sections to rejuvenate the plants and to keep rust disease at bay.

Harvesting

Snip off the leaf tips down to 1cm (½in) from the ground; don't cut off more than one-third of the plant at any one time. Chives can be harvested anytime after the new leaves have reached 15 to 20cm (6 to 8in). The flowers make a lovely edible garnish; wait until you can see the flower buds, then clip around them or wait until they bloom.

Apiaceae *Anethum graveolens*

DILL

Location: Full sun
Height: 30 to 60cm
(1 to 2ft)
Spacing: 4 per square

GROWING SEASON
Spring: yes
Summer: yes
Autumn: no
Winter: no

GROWING TIME
Seed to Harvest: 6 weeks
Indoor Seed Starting: No
Earliest Outdoor Planting:
    8 weeks before the last
    spring frost
Additional Planting: 4-week
    intervals until midsummer
    for continuous harvest

VARIETY GUIDE
Look for varieties bred
for leaf production that
are compact such as
'Bouquet'.

It's worth growing dill from seed. It is rarely offered as plants and the leaves have a warm spicy flavour that go well with cucumber and potatoes. The feathery foliage and bright green-yellow flowers make dill an attractive annual herb early in the year, but most varieties will run to seed quickly if their leaves are not cropped.

Starting
Seedlings do not transplant well, so sow the seed in its final square in mid spring. Re-sow every month until midsummer.

Growing
Thin out seedlings so there are four per square. Keep plants in full sun and allow the mix to dry out slightly between watering when plants are young; later keep the mix moist. While leafy the plant is 30cm (1ft) high but once it sends up flower stalks it reaches 60cm (2ft). Pinch out the flower stalks to maintain leaf quality.

Harvesting
Cut off bits of leaf as required. Start as soon as the plant starts growing away as the leaves have more flavour before the plant flowers. The flower seeds can be collected and used as a flavouring.

Apiaceae *Apium graveolens* var. *dulce*

CELERY

Location: Sun, partial shade
Height: 40cm (16in)
Spacing: 4 per square

GROWING SEASON
Spring: no
Summer: yes
Autumn: yes
Winter: no

GROWING TIME
Seed to Harvest: 20 weeks
Indoor Seed Starting: 10 to 12 weeks before the last spring frost
Earliest Outdoor Planting: after the last spring frost

Celery is tricky to grow well but if you love the crunchy stalks and are prepared to pamper it, then why not give it a try? Modern self-blanching celery is grown in a block with the plants closely spaced so the crowded plants shade each other and lengthen and blanch the stems. This means there is no need for all that digging and trenching associated with traditional varieties, so you can see how well self-blanching varieties could fit into a SMG scheme.

Starting

As you only need a few plants, buy young celery plants and plant out after all danger of frost has passed (late spring to early summer). Celery plants should do well in a middle square as they can take some shade. If you want to raise your own from seed, start seeds off at 15°C (59°F). The seeds need light to germinate so sow on the surface of the compost and sprinkle with vermiculite. Mist the surface with a hand mister. Seeds can take two to three weeks to germinate. Prick out into modular tray or use small pots. Harden off plants when they have four to six leaves and plant out.

Growing

The plants need regular watering and are a magnet for slugs, so be sure to use a slug control such as slug pellets (organic versions are now available) and apply these regularly after rain. A fine mesh crop cover might be needed to protect against carrot fly.

Harvesting

Harvest the first plant; then you can tuck straw in between the remaining plants to keep the stems shaded. Aim to harvest all celery before the first frosts. If you want to clear a square, surplus plants can be lifted and stored in a cool, frost-free place for several weeks.

Hints and tips

An alternative to celery is leaf celery ('Parcel') – this gives you the celery flavour from the leaves for soups and stocks but not the edible stalks of proper celery. Grow it as you would parsley and pick little and often.

VARIETY GUIDE
A self-blanching variety such as 'Golden Self-Blanching' or 'Victoria' suits a SMG.

Apiaceae *Apium graveolens* var. *rapaceum*

CELERIAC

	GROWING SEASON	GROWING TIME
Location: Sun or partial shade **Height:** 40cm (16in) **Spacing:** 1 per square	**Spring:** no **Summer:** yes **Autumn:** yes **Winter:** no	**Seed to Harvest:** 30 weeks **Indoor Seed Starting:** 12 weeks before the last spring frost but consider buying young plants **Earliest Outdoor Planting:** after the last spring frost

VARIETY GUIDE
Consider 'Monach' or 'Prinz': both produce a good size of globe.

A close relative of celery, celeriac has a thickened stem base with a subtle, earthy flavour. Celeriac is being re-discovered by chefs and can be eaten raw with dips or cooked and used in soups or mashed with potato. The plant needs a cool, damp place to do well. For a good-sized "root" (known as a "globe"), plant one celeriac plant per square – a family might want two or three celeriac so perhaps this crop is one for a "preserving" box frame.

Starting

As you only need a few plants, buy young celeriac plants from a garden centre or online supplier and plant out after all danger of frost has passed (late spring to early summer). Plants should do well in squares that are shaded. You can raise you own from seed (*see* celery page 187) but it isn't really worth it. Harden off plants when they are 5 to 8cm (2 to 3in) high and plant out.

Growing

The plants need regular watering and are a magnet for slugs, so be sure to use a slug control such as slug pellets (organic versions are now available) and apply regularly after rain. Remove the lower leaves in late summer to help the globe swell to a useable size.

Harvesting

Harvest plants in mid autumn. Remove the leaf stalks to prevent the root shrinking. Roots can be stored unwashed as you would carrots. Scrub well before peeling and cooking; lemon juice will prevent the flesh discolouring.

Apiaceae *Coriandrum sativum*

CORIANDER

Location: Full sun to partial shade
Height: 30 to 45cm (12 to 18in)
Spacing: 16 per square

GROWING SEASON
Spring: late
Summer: yes
Autumn: no
Winter: no

GROWING TIME
Seed to Harvest: 5 weeks
Weeks to Maturity: 5 weeks
Indoor Seed Starting: no
Earliest Outdoor Planting: after the last spring frost
Additional Plantings: 4-week intervals until early summer for continuous harvest

O nce just a garnish for curries, coriander is now widely grown an ingredient in cut-and-come-again salad mixes to add a spicy kick. The cut-and-come-again method is the ideal way to grow coriander in a SMG as you can get three or four cuts from one sowing of 16 seeds in a square. You need to get a variety bred for the purpose such as 'Calypso', which is slow to run to seed (bolt) and has its growing point low to the ground so it can re-grow easily. Another slow-to-bolt coriander variety is 'Confetti', which has very fine feathery leaves that make an attractive garnish. If you wanted to let the plants grow on and mature you can start with just four seeds per square rather than 16.

VARIETY GUIDE
To harvest leaves, look for varieties that are slow to bolt such as 'Calypso' or 'Confetti'.

Starting
Sow seeds direct into a square as coriander does not transplant well. Sow after the last frost (mid to late spring).

Growing
It's important that the plant produces lots of leaves and does not run to seed too quickly. Growing it in a sheltered spot and keeping the ground moist but well-drained will help.

Harvesting
For cut-and-come-again, use scissors to cut back plants; when they are 10cm (4in) high, cut back to 2.5 to 5cm (1to 2in) from the base of the plants. For other varieties just snip off leaves as required. If your plant forms a good root, use to add flavour to soups. If the seeds fully ripen in your area and remain dry, then a variety such as Moroccan coriander is worth a try; sow once in late spring and harvest in late summer. Cut whole plants and hang to dry, and then shake the dried seeds into a paper bag.

Apiaceae *Daucus carota* var. *sativus*

CARROT

Location: Full sun, but tolerates partial shade
Height: 30cm (12in)
Spacing: 16 per square

GROWING SEASON
Spring: yes
Summer: yes
Autumn: yes
Winter: no

GROWING TIME
Seed to Harvest: 10 weeks
Weeks to Maturity: 10 weeks
Indoor Seed Starting: no
Earliest Outdoor Planting: 3 weeks before last spring frost

Hints and tips

The long root types are better if you want to store carrots; these can be grown in a high-rise box, at least 30cm (1ft) deep. Then lift and store in autumn.

VARIETY GUIDE
'Chantenay' and 'Nantes' types have short stubby roots. Round varieties are 'Parmex' or 'Rondo'. For long roots, 'Autumn King' is reliable. Some varieties offer some resistance to carrot fly: 'Flyaway' and 'Systan'.

The stubby and short root types are easier to grow where there is only 15cm (6in) depth of Mel's mix. There is nothing more exciting for kids (including kids my age) than pulling up a carrot they planted months ago! It's sort of like fishing – you don't know how big it is until you see it, but you hope it's a whopper.

Starting

Carrots do not transplant well so seed is best sown outdoors. The seed is so small that sowing them can be very tedious; practise dropping a pinch (two or three seeds) on some white paper until you get the hang of it. The alternative is to get some pelleted seed: this is coated with clay to make it bigger and easier to handle. You can also buy seed tape (strips of biodegradable paper with the carrot seed embedded). Sow two or three seeds in each of the 16 spaces in a square. Water soil and cover the square with a plastic-covered cage. Keep the ground moist at all times, even if it means daily spraying in sunny weather. Seed can take two to three weeks to germinate and seedlings are prone to slug attack so use slug pellets and weed well.

Growing

Carrots must have constant moisture, until they're almost mature, to grow steadily, but just prior to harvest reduce watering so the carrots don't crack from overly rapid growth. Carrot root fly grubs can tunnel into the roots so in most areas using a fine mesh crop cover is essential, and secure well at the edges.

Harvesting

Pull up carrots with the largest tops. If you're not sure which are biggest, dig around the plant with your fingers to test the size. Pick them early, when they're only half size and at their sweetest and most tender. To store carrots, wait until autumn before harvesting.

Apiaceae *Foeniculum vulgare* var. *dulce*

FLORENCE FENNEL

Location: Full sun
Height: 30cm (12in)
Spacing: 4 per square

GROWING SEASON
Spring: yes
Summer: yes
Autumn: no*
Winter: no

* For autumn crop sow direct in summer

GROWING TIME
Seed to Harvest: 10 to 12 weeks
Indoor Seed Starting: 4 to 6 weeks before the last spring frost
Earliest Outdoor Planting: 3 weeks before last spring frost.

Florence fennel forms a swollen stem base with a mild licorice flavour, but it needs a long growing season so is only for mild areas or a warm spot. Also, very hot, very cold spells or a shortage of water can cause Florence fennel to bolt before the base swells. If it is tricky to grow in your region, then grow the herb fennel so you can harvest the leaves as a herb, but do not let the herb fennel set seed as the seeds will come up the following year all over the place.

VARIETY GUIDE
There is little to choose between the different varieties in terms of taste or size.

Starting

Sow seed indoors into 7-cm (3-in) pots and then plant out when they have two pairs of leaves; do not wait for a rootball to form. If you have enough squares, one plant per square will produce a larger bulb. For an autumn harvest, you can sow direct in summer (late June to July).

Growing

Keep the roots moist and protect plants from slugs.

Harvesting

Cut the above ground bulb and trim off the leaf stalks. The feathery leaves can be eaten too. Harvest bulbs before autumn frosts. Use the bulb while it is fresh.

Apiaceae *Petroselinum*

PARSLEY

	GROWING SEASON	GROWING TIME
Location: Partial shade to shade **Height:** 15 to 30cm (6 to 12in) **Spacing:** 4 per square	**Spring:** yes **Summer:** yes **Autumn:** yes **Winter:** no* * Sow late for a winter crop	**Seed to Harvest:** 14 weeks **Indoor Seed Starting:** 12 weeks before last spring frost **Earliest Outdoor Planting:** 5 weeks before last spring frost

VARIETY GUIDE
For curly-leaf, 'Moss Curled' is a reliable classic. Flat-leaved types tend just to be sold as French or Italian parsley.

Parsley looks great in the garden, yields a continuous harvest, is extremely nutritious and doesn't need a great deal of care! All in all, parsley is a very worthwhile addition to your SMG. Chefs often say the flat-leaf varieties taste better, but the curly-leaf types are more attractive. Why not try both?

Starting
Seed can be tricky; allow two weeks for it to germinate, or buy small plants. Soak seed in lukewarm water for 24 hours before sprinkling ten seeds in a cup filled with vermiculite 12 weeks before last spring frost. Keep warm (15 to 20°C/59 to 68°F) until sprouted. Move to full sunlight as soon as first shoots appear; then pot up in small pots as soon as plants are large enough (usually one to three weeks). Plant outdoors five weeks before the last spring frost or anytime plants are large enough; plant them at the same depth they grew in the pot.

Growing
Keep the soil moist. Grow under a fine mesh crop cover, if carrot root fly is a problem in your area. A midsummer sowing will provide leaves to harvest into winter; use a crop cover, cloche or pot up a plant or two in the autumn and keep on a kitchen windowsill.

Harvesting
Cut outer leaves as needed, once they are 8 to 10cm (3 to 4in) high; for a large harvest, cut off the entire plant slightly above tiny middle shoots. Either way, the plant will continue to grow.

Asparagaceae *Asparagus officinalis*

ASPARAGUS

Location: Full sun **Height:** 1.2 to 2m (4 to 6ft) **Spacing:** 1 or 4 per square	**GROWING SEASON** **Spring:** yes **Summer:** yes **Autumn:** no **Winter:** no	**GROWING TIME** **Seed to Harvest:** 3 years so buy bare roots instead **Indoor Seed Starting:** n/a **Earliest Outdoor Planting:** plant bare roots 4 to 8 weeks before the last spring frost

Asparagus is a perennial and takes a couple of years before the first harvest, producing only one crop a year so I suggest you devote an entire box frame to asparagus and make it extra deep. When you invest in growing asparagus, consider the location carefully, as the plants can last for up to 20 years.

VARIETY GUIDE
For high yields pick a modern all-male variety such as 'Backlim', 'Franklim' or 'Gijnlim'.

Starting

The easiest and quickest way to start is to buy bare roots (crowns); these can be ordered from mail order veg specialists in autumn for planting in spring. Traditionally, you buy and plant two-year-old roots, one per square, but I've found that if you can afford to buy enough of the bare roots, four per square will produce a much bigger crop earlier. Put about 8cm (3in) of the mix down, mark your spacing (either the one or four per square), make little mounds at the plant location, and then drape the roots over each one of those little mounds. Then pour in the rest of the mix, about 8cm (3in) more to total 15cm (6in) deep, which covers the roots an inch or two. *See* page 100 for a step-by-step on planting the roots.

Growing

During dry summers, water weekly and weed. Cut the foliage to the ground in autumn as it turns yellow.

Harvesting

Cut asparagus spears in late spring, when the shoots are 10 to 15cm (4 to 6in) high; cut every other day for about six weeks but leave some spears to grow up or you will weaken the plants. Don't harvest from first-year plants, and only sparingly, say one or two shoots per plant, the second year. Thereafter, you can harvest as required.

Asteraceae *Artemisia dracunculus* var. *sativa*

FRENCH TARRAGON

| **Location:** Full sun
Height: 45 to 60cm
(18 to 24in)
Spacing: 1 per square | **GROWING SEASON**
Spring: no
Summer: yes
Autumn: no
Winter: no | **GROWING TIME**
Seed to Harvest: n/a instead
buy a young plant
Indoor Seed Starting: n/a
Earliest Outdoor Planting:
after the last spring frost |

Hints and tips

French tarragon with its long, thin leaves is the type to get as it has the best flavour. Taste a leaf before buying to make sure you are not getting the coarser Russian tarragon with more bitter leaves.

VARIETY GUIDE
There are no specific varieties of French tarragon available.

Fresh tarragon adds a delicate aniseed flavour to chicken and fish dishes, and the way to capture that elusive flavour is to grow your own. Tarragon is a perennial so worth growing in a SMG box frame dedicated to other perennial herbs such as sage and rosemary.

Starting

For culinary use, be sure to buy French tarragon (*Artemisia dracunculus* var. *sativa*) not Russian tarragon (*Artemisia dracunculus* spp. *dracunculoides*). True French tarragon is not available as seed, so buy a young plant in a small pot from a reputable herb nursery. Plant in the centre of a square.

Growing

Water carefully until the plant grows away; once rooted it is fairly tolerant to drought. If the plant growth slows, wait as it often starts growing again in early autumn. When the top growth starts to die down in autumn, cut away the debris and protect the crown of the plant with insulating material such as straw or bark chips. Plants can dieback, then re-grow, so you could try to spilt and pot up a root or simply buy a new plant in the spring.

Harvesting

Pinch out growing tips to use in the kitchen as soon as the plant is growing and producing new leaves. The subtle flavour is lost if the leaves are dried – aim to use fresh or freeze any surplus.

Asteraceae *Cynara scolymus*

GLOBE ARTICHOKE

Location: Full sun, sheltered
Height: 1 to 1.5m (3 to 5ft)
Spacing: 1 per box frame

GROWING SEASON
Spring: yes
Summer: yes
Autumn: no
Winter: no

GROWING TIME
Seed to Harvest: 25 weeks or buy young plants
Indoor Seed Starting: 12 to 16 weeks before the last spring frost
Earliest Outdoor Planting: after the last spring frost

Globe artichokes are impressive focal points in high summer and the edible buds are a delicacy. It has to be said this perennial crop is not the most efficient use of space for your SMG garden but if you have the space to dedicate a box frame to them they will certainly impress the neighbours.

Starting

As you only need a couple of plants and the seeds need warmth early in the year, buy young potted plants from a garden centre or online nursery. The alternative is to sow seed in late winter in a greenhouse or on a warm windowsill. Prick out the seedlings into 7-cm (3-in pots) and grow on; harden off the plants in mid spring.

Growing

When the plants are 10cm (4in) high, usually late spring, plant one out into the centre of a 1 x 1-m (3 x 3-ft) box frame. In a rectangular box, 60cm (2ft) deep but 3m (10ft) long, you could plant three in a row and they would make a screen. Keep the plants well watered. Flowering will be unpredictable the first year so it is best to remove the buds to help the plants build up their root systems. Thereafter globe artichokes will flower early to mid summer and you can expect ten or so flowers a year. In autumn, cut back the dead stems to the ground and mulch with straw.

Harvesting

Using secateurs or a sharp knife, cut the flower heads with a little of the stalk. Boil the heads whole for 20 to 30 minutes until the scales are tender. The delicacy is the fleshy heart under the bud or "choke". The choke, as its name suggests, is discarded. You can also eat the fleshy bases of each scale by scraping them with your teeth.

Other perennial vegetables

The cardoon (*C. cardunculus*) is a relative of the globe artichoke with large silvery leaves. Cardoons are grown for the fleshy edible stem bases. These are blanched in early autumn by wrapping cardboard around them and tying the tops of the leaves together with string. Jerusalem artichokes (not actually related to globe artichokes) are grown for their edible tubers; this vigorous perennial is not recommended for SMG as the plants are invasive.

VARIETY GUIDE
Look for a variety with no or few spines, such as 'Green Globe Improved' or the purple 'Concerto'.

Asteraceae *Cichorium endivia*

ENDIVE

Location: Full sun, partial shade
Height: 20cm (8in)
Spacing: 1 per square

GROWING SEASON
Spring: no
Summer: yes
Autumn: yes
Winter: sometimes

GROWING TIME
Seed to Harvest: 12 weeks
Indoor Seed Starting: 4 to 8 weeks before last spring frost or 12 weeks after the last spring frost
Earliest Outdoor Planting: after the last spring frost

Hints and tips

Endive and chicory can also be sown little and often as a "cut-and-come-again" technique. They add a bitter note to a mixture of salad leaves.

VARIETY GUIDE
Look out for self-blanching varieties of frilly endive, such as 'Moss Curled' or 'Wallone,' these should be less bitter. Look out for extra hardy varieties of broad-leaved endive such as 'Jeti' if you live in a cold area.

Endive leaf is a familiar ingredient in bags of salad mixes but it's worth remembering if you enjoy their bitter flavours that these plants can be grown at home too. The frilly endives are more suitable for summer sowing and are more decorative while the broad-leaved types are hardier and so a better choice if you want to carry on sowing for salads into the autumn.

Starting

Sow frilly endive in mid to late spring for a summer crop; either sow seed into a pot for planting out later or sow seed direct into a square. Sow broad-leaved endive in mid to late summer; sow a couple of seeds in a 7-cm (3in) pot and cut off the weakest one. A later sowing in early autumn is worth considering if you have a cloche.

Growing

By mid to late summer, when the frilly endives are the size of a fist, cover with an old dinner plate. This will exclude light and blanch the leaves to make them less bitter. It could take one week or two for blanching but check after one week as the plants are prone to rot. Plant out broad-leaved endive plants in late summer to early autumn: one per square if you want a large head or four per square if you want a supply of loose leaved.

Harvesting

Pick the leaves as required for winter salads.

Asteraceae *Cichorium intybus*

CHICORY, BELGIUM ENDIVE

Location: Full sun, partial shade Height: 20cm (8in) Spacing: 1 per square	GROWING SEASON Spring: no Summer: no Autumn: yes Winter: yes	GROWING TIME Seed to Harvest: 12 weeks Indoor Seed Starting: 4 to 8 weeks after the last spring forst Earliest Outdoor Planting: 8 weeks after the last spring frost

There are various types of non-forcing chicory: green chicory looks a bit like a lettuce with loose leaves. Red chicory or radicchio is the most colourful in autumn as the temperature begins to drop. There are also "forcing" chicories that are blanched, then forced to produce plump heads or "chicons" (pictured above).

Starting

Sow non-forcing types in early to mid summer for fresh salad from late summer to mid autumn. Sow seed into 7-cm (3-in) pots. For winter salads wait until mid to late summer. Sow a couple of seeds in a 7-cm (3-in) pot and cut off the weakest seedling with scissors if more than one germinates.

Growing

Plant out the chicory plants, from late summer to early autumn: one per square if you want a large head or four per square if you want a supply of loose leaves. Red and variegated varieties start to develop their distinct colours as the temperature begins to drop. Take precautions against slugs.

Harvesting

Pick the leaves of non-forcing types as required from late summer to October. Harvest forcing chicories about four weeks after forcing.

Hints and tips

To "force" chicory, sow in late spring. Lift the roots in late autumn and cut back the leaves to 2.5cm (1in) above the crown. Plant five roots in a 25-cm (10-in) pot. Exclude light and keep cool but frost-free for four weeks.

VARIETY GUIDE

Green chicory includes 'Bianco di Milano', which has loose heads for close spacing. Red chicory or radicchio includes 'Palla Rossa' and 'Rossa di Treviso'. 'Witloof Zoom' is a forcing variety.

Asteraceae *Lactuca sativa*

LETTUCE AND SALAD LEAVES

Location: Full sun to partial shade; shade in hot summers
Height: 15 to 30cm (6 to 12in)
Spacing: 4 per square

GROWING SEASON
Spring: yes
Summer: yes
Autumn: yes
Winter: sometimes

GROWING TIME
Seed to Harvest: 7 weeks
Weeks to Maturity: 4 to 7 weeks
Indoor Seed Starting: 7 weeks before last spring frost
Earliest Outdoor Planting: 4 weeks before last spring frost

VARIETY GUIDE
There are lots of varieties that change frequently, but start with 'Salad Bowl', 'Lettony' or 'Tom Thumb'.

Lettuce is easy to grow and extremely well suited for SMG—it grows quickly, prolifically and looks great. You can grow lettuce nearly all year-round but sowing and cropping in spring and autumn is easiest to start with. Summer can be tricky if it is hot and dry but not impossible. If you want to grow winter lettuce look for cold hardy varieties and use a crop cover.

There are several types of lettuce: Loose-leaf types such as 'Salad Bowl' and 'Lettony' produce a lot of leaves but little heart; these are good choices for cut-and-come-again mixes but can be grown on their own too.

Butterheads have round hearts and soft textured leaves with a buttery flavour. 'Tom Thumb' will produce four hearted lettuces per square. 'Cassandra' is a modern variety with good resistance to fungal disease while 'Buttercrunch' is an older reliable variety. Crispheads or "icebergs" are larger plants with crinkled outer leaves and a firm, crisp heart. Examples are 'Mini Green' and 'Blush'. Batavian lettuce looks similar but the heart is looser.

Romaine lettuce has long pointed leaves with a pale firm heart. They are sweet and crunchy and slow to run to seed; 'Little Gem' is the classic choice if you want a small-hearted one.

Varieties change frequently so choose the type you want to grow, then look at what is on offer either in seed catalogues or as young plants. As well as green you can grow red or bronze-leaved lettuce and many are speckled or streaked. The texture and leaf shape adds to their appeal, frills, crinkles and leaves shaped like oak leaves or pointed – all add interest.

Starting

You can buy young plants or raise your own plants from seed in pots or trays, then plant out. Seed can be sown direct outside too but you will get a more efficient use of space by transplanting young plants; an exception is growing lettuce as a "cut-and-come-again" crop. Lettuce will germinate well at low temperatures, but at 21°C (70°F) or higher, germination is erratic. If you cannot provide a lower temperature, buy plants or sow another salad leaf during hot spells. Harden off lettuce plants before planting outside. Plant a new square or two of lettuce every other week until early summer. Plant one lettuce per square for a large, vigorous variety or four per square for medium or smaller ones.

Growing

Keep the soil mix moist, but try not to wet the leaves as this can encourage the spread of fungal diseases. Watering in the morning is best as evening watering encourages slugs and diseases. Weed weekly and provide shade covers for plants in hot summers. Watch out for pests and diseases such as slugs, aphids (greenfly) and downy mildew. Tackle any problems promptly.

Harvesting

You can cut individual outer leaves with scissors and leave the rest to grow on; use the cut-and-come-again method or harvest the entire plant by cutting it off at the root. If you're going to cut outer leaves you can start when the plant is half grown. Harvest at any stage; if you wait until all the plants reach full size you will have to harvest almost all of them at once or they will go to seed.

LETTUCE IN SALAD MIXES

Growing a mix of lettuce and other salad leaves all together and cutting the leaves when very young, but leaving them to re-sprout and then cutting again, produces a long harvest of a variety of fresh leaves from just one sowing. This "cut-and-come-again" technique is perfect for SMG. This is method is ideal for getting a lot of salad out of a small raised bed; use seed and space 1 to 2cm (½ to 1in) apart and cover with 1cm (½in) sprinkling of your growing mix.

A good place to start is to try seed packets of mixtures of edible leaves, often called 'Saladini' or 'Mesclun', which usually include lettuce, endive and chicory plus other flavours. Soon you will want to move on to choosing and combining salad leaves yourself. Start with a lettuce such as 'Little Gem' or 'Green Salad Bowl' as the base then add your favourite flavours from the following list.

Rocket has a distinct, peppery flavour and attractively cut leaves. Plants go to seed very quickly, especially in hot weather. Sow little and often and pick frequently.

Spinach leaf for a mild, buttery taste. This is best in spring or autumn, as plants tend to bolt in midsummer.

Oriental greens such as pak choi and mizuna have a mild peppery flavour when young. The oriental mustards have a hotter flavour.

Chicory and frilly endive add bitter notes. Just grow a small amount and pick the leaves as required.

Kale is another colourful addition to salad mixes, with a subtle cabbage flavour.

Beetroot leaves or red chard leaves can be added to salads for colour when the plants are very young.

Many seed sown herbs can be grown as "cut-and-come-again" crop, e.g. coriander, basil or parsley.

The first batch of salad leaves can be started off under a crop cover. Sow small amounts at two-week intervals or wait until one sowing has germinated or reached a certain stage before sowing the next batch. This should help to spread them out over the season.

Water them regularly to keep the seedlings growing strongly without a check to their growth. Take precautions against slugs and snails eating the crop.

Cut small quantities of leaves, either as whole immature plants or as individual leaves over a period of a couple of weeks. Aim to have another square coming into production as soon as the previous one is exhausted.

At first, use scissors to cut immature plants or individual leaves as required. Choose the larger leaves from the outside of the plants, leaving small and young leaves in the centre to carry on growing. Later when the leaves are about 10cm (4in) long, cut the whole plant leaving a 2.5-cm (1-in) stump to re-grow. You should get at least two to four pickings from one sowing.

Brassicaceae *Brassica rapa* var. *chinensis*

PAK CHOI

	GROWING SEASON	GROWING TIME
Location: Sun or partial shade **Height:** 25 to 30cm (10 to 12in) **Spacing:** 4 per square	**Spring:** yes **Summer:** yes **Autumn:** yes **Winter:** no	**Seed to Harvest:** 4 weeks for baby leaf or allow 7 to 10 weeks for semi-mature to mature plants **Indoor Seed Starting:** n/a **Earliest Outdoor Planting:** 4 weeks before the last spring frost but 8 weeks after are less likely to bolt

Pak choi is a leafy veg with the bonus of edible, fleshy leaf stalks. The leaves and stalks are picked either when young or the whole plant can be cut at any time before flowering. Pak choi grows quickly and makes a good follow-on crop so it is a versatile addition to SMG. If you want plants at a semi-mature size, which is good for stir fries, then plant four plants per SMG square.

Starting

Pak choi is a handy follow-on crop after broad beans or peas have finished. So although seed can be sown direct into their final position, it is more efficient to start the seed off sown 13mm (½in) deep in 7-cm (3-in) pots; then they will be ready to follow an early crop. Seed germinates at 10 to 13°C (50 to 55°F) so pots can be kept outside in partial shade at the hottest time of the year.

Growing

Add a trowel full of garden compost to the square before planting. Give the mix a thorough soaking if it is dry. If the previous crop was peas or beans, cut off these plants at soil level and leave their roots to nourish the pak choi. Plant out four plants per square for semi-mature heads. Cover the crop with fine mesh to keep out flying insect pests. Keep the mix well watered and protect against slugs and snails; daily checking and picking off pests is needed. Pak choi has a tendency to run to seed (bolt) if sown too early, so choose a "bolt-resistant" variety or sow in the summer rather than spring.

Harvesting

Cut the head, leaving a stump to produce a flush of new leaves. Pak choi is not very frost-hardy, so cover later sowings with cloches.

Hints and tips

Pak choi also grows well as cut-and-come-again salad mix. Sow in spring for a crop of loose leaves; thin to nine per square for a crop of loose greens. Cut the leaves either as seedlings or as immature plants. Spring-sown plants are likely to bolt if left growing too long. Other Oriental greens treated in the same way include: mizuna, mibuna and mustards.

VARIETY GUIDE

'Joi Choi' is an excellent variety as the plants grow evenly, are slow to bolt and have some frost resistance. 'Tat Soi' is a small, green rosette type that rarely bolts and may survive outdoors in mild areas. For a decorative pak choi, opt for 'Rubi' with red leaves that are green on the undersides.

Brassicaceae *Brassica napus*

SWEDE

Location: Full sun or
  partial shade
Height: 50cm (20in)
Spacing: 1 per square

GROWING SEASON
Spring: no
Summer: yes
Autumn: yes
Winter: yes

GROWING TIME
Seed to Harvest: 16 to 25
  weeks
Indoor Seed Starting: no
Earliest Outdoor Planting:
  6 weeks after the last
  spring frost

VARIETY GUIDE
There is not much
difference in growth
habit and taste between
varieties. 'Marian' is a
well-established, yellow-
fleshed variety that
crops well with some
resistance to clubroot
and mildew. 'Magres' has
yellow flesh and has
some resistance to
powdery mildew.

Swede, originally an abbreviation for Swedish turnip, is a slow-growing member of the cabbage family that produces a large root for storing over the winter. It is only worth growing in a SMG box frame devoted to preserving vegetables; otherwise if you are short of space consider a quick crop of summer turnips instead. Swedes are very hardy so a reliable crop in cold areas and they cope well with high rainfall so often do well in poor summers.

Starting
Sow the seed direct from early to midsummer. As you don't need many plants, start in small pots or modular trays and sow the seed 2cm (¾in) deep; as you are sowing late you don't have to sow indoors. You can also buy young plants at garden centres.

Growing
The plants need very little attention; just make sure the roots do not dry out or they will be tough and woody. Weed regularly. Clubroot is a soil disease that can build up, but some varieties tolerate it.

Harvesting
Lift the roots as soon as they are the size of a fist, which is large enough for a meal. The first harvest is usually early to mid autumn but you can leave the roots to get bigger and harvest in winter – the flesh is often sweeter after a frost. Use the smaller or damaged roots first and store the larger, undamaged roots. Twist off the leaves and store the roots in boxes filled with sand. Keep swedes stored in a cool but frost-free place.

Brassicaceae *Brassica oleracea* Acephala Group

KALE

Location: Full sun to partial shade
Height: 30 to 90cm (12 to 36in)
Spacing: 4 per square

GROWING SEASON
Spring: no
Summer: yes
Autumn: yes
Winter: yes

GROWING TIME
Seed to Harvest: 16 to 32 weeks
Indoor Seed Starting: no
Earliest Outdoor Planting: 6 weeks after the last spring frost

Kale is the hardiest of the winter greens, highly nutritious and is ideal for extending the season. Simply plant out when a square becomes free in midsummer and start picking from late autumn onwards, through the winter and into spring.

Starting

Sow seed in mid to late spring in 7-cm (3-in) pots; then plant out in its final position during mid-summer. The alternative is to order young plants, as part of a winter veg collection. Keep the pots in a cool but frost-free place outdoors. Use a fine mesh crop cover to protect from flying pests. If the leaves start to change colour, e.g. redden when the variety is a green type, the plants may be running out of nutrients so pot them on into slightly larger pots.

Growing

To plant out into their final positions, first water the plants well. Make a slight depression and plant into the bottom. This allows easier watering in a dry summer, until the plants are established. They may flop after planting even if well watered, but will quickly recover. They are prone to pests but a fine mesh crop cover will help. Do not grow plants in the same soil year after year or plants can get a soil disease called clubroot.

Harvesting

Pick a few outer leaves from each plant, leaving the youngest leaves to grow on. Wash foliage carefully to remove any insects lurking in the wrinkles. Cover the crops with bird netting or use bird scarers to deter pigeons. By early spring, the plants will look scruffy but leave them until the immature flower shoots form; these are delicious and can be picked and eaten like sprouting broccoli.

Baby leaf

Kale can also be grown as a cut-and-come-again salad, either on its own or as part of a salad mix. Sowing can start earlier in spring but also a late sowing of kale in late summer will make good use of empty squares. Sow the seed direct.

VARIETY GUIDE
Compact varieties (30 to 60cm/1 to 2ft)) such as 'Dwarf Green Curled' and 'Starbor' suit small spaces. Tall varieties (!m/3ft) include 'Reflex' and 'Scarlet'. Heritage varieties include: 'Nero di Toscana', distinctive strap-shaped, blue-grey leaves with puckered appearance; 'Red Russian' has grey-green serrated leaves with purple stems, attractive in salad mix. Red kales such as 'Redbor' add colour to a box frame but sadly the red colour is lost on cooking.

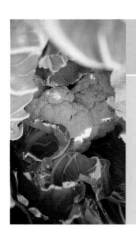

Brassicaceae *Brassica oleracea* var. *botrytis*

CAULIFLOWER

Location: Full sun but will tolerate some partial shade
Height: 45 to 60cm (18 to 24in)
Spacing: 1 per square

GROWING SEASON
Spring: yes
Summer: yes
Autumn: yes
Winter: no

GROWING TIME
Seed to Harvest: 14 to 20 weeks
Indoor Seed Starting: 8 weeks before last spring frost
Earliest Outdoor Planting: 4 weeks before last spring frost

Hints and tips

For white varieties in direct sun, bend or break large leaves over the top when heads start to form. Then tie or hold with a rubber band to cover and protect the head from exposure to the sun, which can turn the head yellow and speed up the buds opening.

VARIETY GUIDE
The standard summer cauliflower is 'All Year Round'; you can stagger the harvest by sowing early, mid and late in the season. But for SMG look out for the early variety 'Igloo', which can be harvested in mid-summer from an outdoor mid spring sowing. 'Tarifa' is another quick-maturing cauliflower that is ready in 11 weeks.

Growing cauliflowers needs extra care as they are sensitive to any check to their growth. In a SMG box frame, it is best to concentrate on summer types as these mature quicker and to seek out varieties that produce small heads ("baby" cauliflowers) at dense spacing. White cauliflower is the most popular type but there are also coloured heads for novelty. The white varieties usually need 14 to 15 weeks to mature but there is a lot of variation depending on sowing time, spacing and variety.

Starting

Sow seed 12mm (½in) deep in modular trays or pots in spring. The alternative is to buy young plants, taking care to avoid any that are potbound. Set out the young plants in the box frame four weeks before the last spring frost. Be extra careful when planting; cauliflower suffers more from transplanting stress than any other cabbage family member. Make a deep hole so the lowest leaves are on the ground and firm the plant in well.

Growing

Keep plant roots moist so they don't dry out. Weed weekly and mulch surface with garden compost in hot weather. Protect against all the usual brassica pests with a fine mesh crop cover. Clubroot is a soil disease that will build up if brassicas are grown in the same space year after year.

Harvesting

Cut off the entire head at its base with a sharp knife. The right time is as the head enlarges but before the buds separate or open. Do not delay harvest, as the head will grow fast and pass the ideal harvest point in just a few days.

Brassicaceae *Brassica oleracea* Capitata Group

CABBAGE (SUMMER)

Location: Full sun
Height: 30 to 45cm
(12 to 18in)
Spacing: 1 per square

GROWING SEASON
Spring: yes
Summer: yes
Autumn: yes
Winter: no

GROWING TIME
Seed to Harvest: 16 to 18 weeks
Indoor Seed Starting: 8 weeks before last spring frost
Earliest Outdoor Planting: 4 weeks before last spring frost

When growing in small spaces, start with baby summer cabbage or a spring cabbage (*see* Hints and tips). Traditional spacing for cabbages is 45cm (18in) apart but by growing a modern variety, one plant per square, you can get a useable baby cabbage head 8 to 10cm (3 to 4in) across. If you do not have a follow-on crop after the first head has been cut, you can leave the stalk, make a cross-shaped cut across the cut end, about 1.5cm (¾in) deep, add a mulch of garden compost to the soil surface and after six weeks you might get extra small cabbages.

Starting

The seed is easy to handle and is sown in mid spring or you can buy young cabbage plants instead. Sow one seed per 7-cm (3-in) pot or use a modular tray. Keep the pots or trays in a sheltered but frost-free spot, keep moist and protect against slugs and snails. Plant out in mid to late spring, when plants are 10 to 13cm (4 to 5in) tall with at least four leaves. Don't let young plants get any larger before planting them outside or they may not form a good head.

Growing

The plants need a regular supply of moisture but after the head has formed and while it is growing to full size, reduce watering or the head may grow too fast and split. Weed weekly; cut away any extra-large bottom leaves if they are yellow or if they are spreading to other squares. Cover cabbages with a crop cover of fine mesh to keep out flying insects in summer. Protect against slugs and snails.

Harvesting

Cut off the head with a sharp, serrated knife when the head starts to feel firm, usually in early to midsummer.

Hints and tips

Spring cabbage will keep your box frame productive until the spring sowings start. Sow seed in pots during midsummer in the same way as you would for a summer-cropping variety and plant out in early autumn. Space out four plants per square as you can cut them young. A cage of chicken wire will protect against rabbits and pigeons.

VARIETY GUIDE
For summer cabbages, look for quick-maturing varieties such as 'Hispi', which produces small pointed heads. Or the later variety 'Minicole' with solid round heads that stand well until needed. 'Red Jewel' is a red summer cabbage that yields well at close spacings. For spring cabbage, look out for varieties such as 'April', 'Pixie' or 'Spring Hero'.

Brassicaceae *Brassica oleracea* Gemmifera Group

BRUSSELS SPROUTS

Location: Full sun and sheltered
Height: 75cm (30in)
Spacing: 1 per 2 squares

GROWING SEASON
Spring: no
Summer: yes
Autumn: yes
Winter: yes

GROWING TIME
Seed to Harvest: 30 to 36 weeks
Indoor Seed Starting: 4 to 12 weeks before the last spring frost
Earliest Outdoor Planting: straight after the last spring frost

VARIETY GUIDE
The cropping times of varieties differ, so if you want sprouts for Christmas look for mid or late varieties such as 'Silverline' or 'Trafalgar'. For something a little different, 'Falstaff' is a red-purple variety, fairly short at 50cm (20in) high so it would make the box frame look decorative. Look out for new clubroot-resistant varieties such as 'Crispus' if you want to grow plants in the same spot year after year.

Even a couple of Brussels sprout plants will produce tasty fresh veg in the middle of winter and they are a good way to use your box frames in winter. You could, for example, use them as a follow-on crop from peas or beans. The plants do take up a lot of space; allow each plant two squares and make sure cage protection is at least 1m (3ft) high for most varieties.

Starting

For just a few plants, sow seed in 9-cm (3½-in) pots in spring and keep outside in a sheltered spot. Remember to water them. The alternative is to buy in some young plants. Either way, aim to get the plants in place when they are 15cm (6in) high, usually late spring to early summer. Add extra garden compost and dig a hole with a trowel and plant so the lower leaves are just on the surface of the growing mix. Firm the mix down well around the plants.

Growing

Keep the ground moist and weed-free. Keep piling the mix around the plant base and firming down, which will help prevent the plants falling over. You may need to support plants with stakes too. Pigeons can be a problem over winter. Clubroot is a soil disease that can build up if brassica crops are grown in the same ground each year.

Harvesting

The sprouts will remain in good condition on the plant for up to three months or so, so just pick them fresh as needed. Sprouts are best at the tightly closed stage, start at the bottom of the stalk and pull them off with your fingers or cut them off with a sharp knife. If cold weather makes harvesting tricky, uproot the stalk and pick off the sprouts indoors.

Brassicaceae *Brassica oleracea* Gongylodes Group

KOHL RABI

Location: Sun or partial shade **Height:** 15 to 20cm (6 to 8in) **Spacing:** 4 per square	**GROWING SEASON** **Spring:** yes **Summer:** yes **Autumn:** no **Winter:** no	**GROWING TIME** **Seed to Harvest:** 10 to 12 weeks **Indoor Seed Starting:** no **Earliest Outdoor Planting:** 6 weeks before the last spring frost

Kohl rabi is a continental relative of the turnip with a swollen stem base that looks particularly attractive in a SMG box frame and has a sweet flavour. Both kohl rabi and turnip are quick growing and best picked young, so you could use either of them to fill squares early in the year and then use the space later for broccoli or other later crops.

Starting

Sow seed direct into the square, starting in mid spring and, if you wish, sow a square every month through the summer. Sow 1.5cm (¾in) deep and keep the mix moist. Cut out weaker seedlings with scissors until there are four strong seedlings per square – you can thin to nine plants per square for smaller roots.

Growing

The plants need to grow without a check to their growth, so keep the roots moist. Flea beetle can be a nuisance, so use a fine mesh cover to keep them off the crop.

Harvesting

Harvest the crop when the swollen stem bases are golf-ball size, but cut before they are larger than tennis-ball size; larger stem bases often turn woody. Trim off the root end and the outer leaves. First pickings of small roots can be peeled and eaten raw; they are often grated in salads. Larger roots are peeled and then cooked just as you would turnip.

VARIETY GUIDE
The purple kohl rabi such as 'Kolibri' is particularly attractive in SMG box frames. If you want a green variety consider 'Lanro' or for baby veg opt for 'Logo' as it crops in six to ten weeks from sowing.

Brassicaceae *Brassica oleracea* Italica Group

CALABRESE, GREEN BROCCOLI

	GROWING SEASON	GROWING TIME
Location: Needs full sun, sheltered position **Height:** 45 to 60cm (18 to 24in) **Spacing:** 1 per square	**Spring:** yes **Summer:** yes **Autumn:** yes **Winter:** no	**Seed to Harvest:** 12 to 16 weeks **Indoor Seed Starting:** 12 weeks before last spring frost **Earliest Outdoor Planting:** 5 weeks before last spring frost

Hints and tips

For fresh winter pickings, it is worth growing sprouting broccoli. This crop also needs a fair amount of space for a long time, it can grow to 1m (3ft) so allow one plant per two squares plus you will need a couple of plants but it is only an option if you have plenty of box frames. Plant young plants out in the summer.

VARIETY GUIDE
There are lots of varieties of calabrese that change frequently; it is worth looking for early varieties such as 'Aquiles', 'Belstar', 'Green Magic' or 'Trixie' as these crop when fewer caterpillars are around. 'Romanesco' is actually a type of cauliflower with lime-green, pointed curds so although it is grown like calabrese there is not the extra second crop of side-shoots.

Calabrese is a type of broccoli with a large central flower head that is harvested in summer; the side-shoots then grow on to produce a secondary crop. Calabrese is sometimes known as green broccoli to distinguish it from the very hardy purple sprouting broccoli that produces small flower heads over a long season from winter to spring. You need a fair amount of space to grow calabrese but it is tasty and nutritious.

Starting

As you only need one plant per square, it is easiest to buy a couple of young plants from a garden centre or order from a mail order supplier. If you wish to grow from seed, sow in small pots with the seed sown 12mm (½in) deep in mid spring. Seed will germinate at 10°C (50°F) in seven to ten days. Plant outside approximately five weeks before the last spring frost, but check the seed packet for precise instructions as varieties do vary.

Growing

Like all members of the cabbage family, you're growing leaves and flowers, which need constant moisture. Never let the roots dry out. Weed weekly. Caterpillars can spoil the crop; use a fine mesh cover or a support with netting to keep out cabbage white butterflies.

Harvesting

Cut off the main central head at its base with a sharp, serrated knife, leaving as much foliage on the plant as possible. Harvest as soon as a head appears full and tight before the flower buds open. If you have several plants, don't wait too long to cut the first one after the heads start forming, even if it looks a little small. Within a few weeks, new side-shoots will form and grow from the original plant to provide you with a second helping.

Brassicaceae *Brassica rapa*

TURNIP

Location: Full sun
Height: 15 to 20cm
(6 to 8in)
Spacing: 9 per square

GROWING SEASON
Spring: yes
Summer: yes
Autumn: no*
Winter: no*

* Winter turnips can be grown into autumn/winter

GROWING TIME
Seed to Harvest: 8 weeks
Indoor Seed Starting: no
Earliest Outdoor Planting:
4 weeks before the last spring frost
Additional Planting: yes, can sow every 4 weeks

Summer turnips take as little as eight weeks from sowing to harvesting so they are perfect for growing in spare squares early in the year as they will be harvested and out of the way before many of the later crops need to be planted out. There are also winter turnips if you want larger roots for storing (*see* Hints and tips).

Starting

Sow seed direct into a square, starting in early spring or any time up to summer. Early sowings can benefit from cloches or crop covers. Sow seed 1.5cm (¾in) deep and keep the mix moist. Cut out weaker seedlings with scissors until there are nine plants per square or 2 to 3cm (1in) apart for baby turnips. You do not need to be too precise as the roots will push neighbouring plants apart as they grow.

Growing

The plants need to grow without a check to their growth; keep the roots moist. Flea beetle can be a nuisance, so use a fine mesh cover to keep them off the crop.

Harvesting

Harvest summer turnips when the roots are golf-ball size, but cut before they are tennis-ball size; larger roots often turn woody. Trim off the root end and the leaves.

Hints and tips

Winter turnips (also known as maincrop turnips) are slower growing than the summer varieties. For these just make one sowing, in mid to late summer and thin to four seedlings per square. Keep the soil moist and free from weeds until the roots are lifted in autumn or winter. Twist off the leaves and store the roots in boxes of sand in a cool, frost-free place such as a garage or shed.

VARIETY GUIDE
Quick-growing summer turnips include: 'Snowball' a mild-flavoured variety with round roots and 'Purple Top Milan', a flat-topped, purple and white turnip. If you want a green root variety consider 'Lanro' or for baby veg opt for 'Logo' as it crops in an amazing six to ten weeks from sowing.

Brassicaceae *Raphanus sativus*

RADISH

Location: Full sun to partial shade
Height: 15 to 30cm (6 to 12in)
Spacing: 16 per square

GROWING SEASON
Spring: yes
Summer: yes
Autumn: yes
Winter: no*

* Yes for winter varieties

GROWING TIME
Seed to Harvest: 4 to 6 weeks
Indoor Seed Starting: no
Earliest Outdoor Planting: 3 weeks before last spring frost
Additional Plantings: every 3 weeks

Hints and tips

Teaching a child to garden? Summer radish is the perfect first crop as the results are so quick; let each child pick a colour, and take it from there.

VARIETY GUIDE
For summer radish 'Cherry Belle' is a good variety with the classic round, red root; 'Amethyst' has round purple roots. For a longer, red root opt for 'French Breakfast'. Winter radish: 'April Cross' a long white root for eating fresh and raw; 'Black Spanish Round' stores well and is best cooked. 'Mantanghong' is round with a white skin and pink flesh – it stores well and has a mild, nutty flavour.

Summer radishes are a great crop for all gardeners—from experts to beginners. Who can pass up a vegetable that matures in only three to four weeks? There's a multitude of shapes from small and round to long carrot shapes. Winter radishes take six to eight weeks to mature and some of these types store very well. It's easy to plant too many radishes. They don't like being crowded, so the SMG method works well. Decide how many you can use each week and then plant no more than double that number every other week for a continuous, but controlled, harvest.

Starting

Sow seed outdoors. Plant a square every other week for a staggered but continuous harvest. Sow 1cm (½in) deep in spring, 2.5cm (1in) deep in summer. In hot weather, they benefit from some shade and lots of water. Winter varieties are sown in summer after the longest day or up to July.

Growing

Don't let radishes stop growing or dry out; lack of water causes hot-tasting and pithy radishes. Weed weekly; a crop cover of fine mesh is useful if flea beetle is a problem.

Harvesting

Pull summer radishes as soon as the roots are the size of a marble up to golf-ball size; the smaller you pull them, the sweeter they taste. Winter radishes can be left in the ground until the first frost; then either mulch to keep the ground from freezing, or pull up and store in damp sand after the tops are removed.

Chenopodiaceae *Beta vulgaris* Conditiva Group

BEETROOT

Location: Full sun or partial shade
Height: 30cm (12in)
Spacing: 9 or 16 per square

GROWING SEASON
Spring: yes
Summer: yes
Autumn: yes
Winter: no

GROWING TIME
Seed to Harvest: 8 to 12 weeks
Indoor Seed Starting: no
Earliest Outdoor Planting: 4 weeks before last spring frost
Additional Plantings: every 3 weeks

Beetroot is a wonderful vegetable to grow because it is so easy and both the roots and the greens (tops) are suitable for eating. It rarely suffers from pests or diseases and can cope with mild frosts.

Starting

Sow seed directly into the square. Each "seed" is actually a cluster of two to five individual seeds, so several seedlings will come up from each cluster. Sow 1 to 1.5cm (½ to ¾ in) deep, four weeks before the last spring frost (you can start earlier if you sow under a cloche). Beetroot will germinate at temperatures as low as 7°C (45°F). After the seedlings are about 2.5cm (1in) tall, cut off all except the strongest plant from each cluster. To have a continuous harvest, plant a new square every three weeks except in the hottest part of the summer. Instead of sowing seed direct, you can also transplant clumps of seedlings raised in modular trays.

Growing

Plants need constant and even moisture. Remove any damaged leaves, mulch with garden compost and weed weekly.

Harvesting

Pull up the entire plant with the largest top. If you're not sure of root size, dig around the root with your fingers to uncover the top to check the size. To harvest greens, individual leaves can be cut at any time, but don't take more than one or two from each plant. Start pulling up the roots when they are the size of a golf ball and continue until they are full size. Roots can be left in the ground into the autumn but they are vulnerable to slugs and hard winters; the alternative is to lift the roots and store in boxes of barely moist sand. Leaves are usable at any size but are most tender when young.

Hints and tips

The first spring sowings will produce baby roots by early summer; you can carry on making regular sowings for baby beetroots until midsummer. If you want baby roots and beetroot to store, make sowings in late spring to early summer at 16 per square and pull every other root as a baby root and leave the remainder to grow on.

VARIETY GUIDE

'Boltardy' is the classic early round beetroot, 'Burpees Golden' has golden yellow roots and 'Chioggia' is an old Italian variety – cut through the root to see red and white rings. For those who want a lot of even-sized slices, for pickling, look for varieties with long roots such as 'Alto'.

Chenopodiaceae *Beta vulgaris*

CHARD, SWISS CHARD

	GROWING SEASON	GROWING TIME
Location: Full sun, but can grow in partial shade or shade **Height:** 30 to 45cm (12 to 18in) **Spacing:** 4 per square	**Spring:** yes **Summer:** yes **Autumn:** yes **Winter:** yes	**Seed to Harvest:** 8 weeks **Indoor Seed Starting:** 7 weeks before last spring frost **Earliest Outdoor Planting:** 3 weeks before last spring frost

Hints and tips

Chard will survive several frosts even if it's unprotected, allowing an autumn harvest. If mulched with loose hay or straw it can be harvested into the winter. Often it will re-sprout in very early spring. Plants will only produce a crop in early spring the second year; later they will go to seed, so you do need to start new plants every year.

VARIETY GUIDE
The most popular is 'Bright Lights', a mixture with seven different colours of leaf stalk from red through pink, orange, yellow and white. The Swiss or silver chard has green leaves and broad white stalks; rhubarb chard has red stalks but it is worth going for a named variety such as 'Charlotte' for the brightest colour.

Chard is valued for its spinach-like leaves and succulent stems. It's one of the easiest vegetables to grow and can be grown in the sun or shade, all spring, summer, and well into autumn for a continuous harvest. In most areas it can even be carried over the winter. Chard is available in white- or red-stemmed varieties and is also available in many rainbow colours.

Starting

Each "seed" is actually a cluster of two to five individual seeds, so several seedlings will come up from each cluster. Sow in modular trays, 1cm (½in) deep, seven weeks before your last spring frost. Seeds will germinate in five to ten days at 20°C (68°F). Keep warm until seeds germinate; move to full sunlight as soon as first shoots appear. Harden off and transplant into the garden three weeks before the last spring frost. Water and cover with a cloche. Seeds can also be sown outdoors, 1cm (½in) deep in each square, three weeks before your last spring frost. Seeds germinate outdoors in two to three weeks. Water and cover with a cloche.

Growing

Water weekly, or twice weekly in hot, dry spells. Like all leaf crops, chard needs lots of water for luxurious leaf growth and tender stems. Weed weekly; cut off any yellow or overgrown outer leaves. Take precautions against slugs and snails.

Harvesting

Carefully cut off each outer stem at the plant base with a sharp knife when the leaves are 15 to 23cm (6 to 9in) tall. Leave the smaller inner leaves and stems to continue to grow. Continue harvesting outer leaves (stalk and all) every week or so. Don't let the outer leaves get too large before harvesting.

Chenopodiaceae *Spinacia oleracea*

SPINACH

Location: Full sun to partial shade or shade
Height: 15 to 30cm (6 to 12in)
Spacing: 9 per square

GROWING SEASON
Spring: yes
Summer: no
Autumn: yes
Winter: yes

GROWING TIME
Seed to Harvest: 10 to 12 weeks
Indoor Seed Starting: no
Earliest Outdoor Planting: 10 weeks before last spring frost
Additional Plantings: every 3 weeks from early to late spring

Spinach is a very popular and nutritious crop but can be tricky to grow. A rapid grower, spinach can be grown in a fairly small space but will quickly bolt (run to seed) in the summer heat, so it grows best in the early spring and then again in the autumn. Spinach is very cold hardy so early autumn sowings will often crop the following spring.

Starting

Sow seed outdoors little and often from early to late spring; it will germinate in one to two weeks. Plant seeds 1cm (½in) deep, water, and cover early sowings with a plastic crop cover or cloche. Spinach doesn't usually transplant well but if you have a problem with slugs, try sowing seed in modular trays and then planting out. Late sowings of a winter hardy variety can be made in late summer to early autumn.

Growing

Being a leaf crop, spinach needs constant moist soil. Weed weekly; mulch in warm weather. Don't work in the spinach square if the leaves are very wet—they are brittle and break easily. Take precautions against slugs. The leaves can be disfigured by wavy lines (leaf miner) and spots (downy mildew), so pick little and often.

Harvesting

Cut the outer leaves as needed; small inner leaves will continue to grow rapidly. Harvest as soon as the plants look like they won't miss an outer leaf or two. Keep picking and the plant will keep growing right up until hot weather. If it's a spring crop and you think the plants are going to bolt soon, cut off the entire plant. Spinach leaf can be grown as a baby leaf, cut-and-come-again crop.

Hints and tips

For a longer season of leaves for cooking, also grow a leaf beet crop (often called "perpetual spinach") to supplement any gaps in production of true spinach. Leaf beet is a biennial so less likely to bolt and its leaves are plentiful over a long season if picked regularly, older leaves will need the midrib stripped out.

VARIETY GUIDE
There are many named spinach varieties but most are similar as far as the home gardener is concerned. 'Medania' is a summer variety with some resistance to downy mildew and 'Giant Winter' as its name suggests is a hardy variety that will overwinter from an autumn sowing.

Curcurbitaceae *Cucumis sativus*

CUCUMBER

Location: Full sun or light shade, sheltered position, grow on a vertical frame.
Height: 2m (6ft)
Spacing: 1 or 2 per square

GROWING SEASON
Spring: no
Summer: yes
Autumn: no
Winter: no

GROWING TIME
Seed to Harvest: 16 weeks
Indoor Seed Starting: 6 weeks before last spring frost
Earliest Outdoor Planting: 1 week after last spring frost

Hints and tips

If you want gherkins to make pickles, get special small-fruited varieties such as 'Conda' and 'Venlo'. Grow them as you would ordinary outdoor cucumbers but pick the fruits when they are just 10cm (4in) long.

VARIETY GUIDE
The slicing types such as 'Burpless Tasty Green' used for salads or sandwiches are classics. However a recent development are the "mini cue" or "lunch box" varieties such as 'Cincino' or 'Green Fingers', which yield lots of small fruits that are popular with children.

There's nothing quite like picking and eating your own home-grown cucumbers. For SMG, choose vine varieties suitable for outdoor use that you can train up a support.

Starting

In mid spring, sow one seed per 7-cm (3-in) pot, 1cm (½in) deep and keep at 20°C (68°F) and seed should geminate in four to eight days. Grow on the young plant, harden off and plant out after the last frost date (early summer). Plant the young plant into a small mound so water drains away from the stem. Avoid disturbing the roots; water and use a shade crop cover if it is hot or a cloche if it is cold and windy. You can also sow the seed direct into the square in early summer if the weather is warm; use a cloche until the seedling is growing away. The alternative is to buy pot-ready plants in late spring but make sure to harden off before planting outside.

Growing

Never let the roots dry out; this can mean watering twice a week or more. Avoid wetting the leaves and stem as this can encourage rots. Automatic irrigation is worth considering. Keep training the vines on the netting. When plants reach the top of the supports, pinch out the growing tip to encourage side-shoots. Cucumbers are prone to leaf diseases and viruses, so remove badly affected plants.

Harvesting

Cut the stem connecting the fruit to the vine. Harvest fruits continually; if you allow any cucumbers to become yellow or overly large, the plant will stop producing fruit. Keep picking even if you can't use them. Don't eat the large fruits and leave the smaller ones on the vine, because in only one or two days the little ones will be big. Instead, compost the large cucumbers and eat the smaller ones.

Curcurbitaceae *Cucumis melo*

MELON

Location: Full sun, sheltered spot, grow on a vertical frame
Height: 2m (6ft) vine
Spacing: 1 per 2 squares

GROWING SEASON
Spring: no
Summer: yes
Autumn: no
Winter: no

GROWING TIME
Seed to Harvest: 17 to 20 weeks
Indoor Seed Starting: 4 to 8 weeks before last spring frost
Earliest Outdoor Planting: 3 weeks after last spring frost

Melons need four to five months of warm, sunny weather to produce ripe fruit so you will not succeed with them everywhere every year. But they are a challenge and an exciting crop if you have the right spot. Train them on vertical frames and make use of a suitable cloche or crop cover for extra warmth.

Starting
Sow seed indoors in mid spring: two seeds per small 7-cm (3in) pot, 1cm (½in) deep. Seed should germinate in five to ten days at 15 to 20°C (59 to 68°F). You can also buy young potted plants from a garden centre. Harden off and plant outdoors three weeks after the last frost date; it is worth pre-warming the planting square with polythene or a cloche several weeks before planting.

Growing
Water the plants in warm weather but reduce watering when melons are almost ripe to develop their sweetness. Keep the leaves and stems dry to try and avoid fungal diseases and mildew. Train the plants up the netting and pinch out the growing tip. Support the half-grown melon fruits in net slings; pinch out all new, small melons near the end of the growing season so that all the plant's strength goes into ripening the larger melons that are already set. Guard against slugs at every stage.

Harvesting
Melons release a scent when the fruit is ripe, and the netting pattern on the rind (if it's a cantaloupe) becomes very prominent. Twist the melon with one hand while holding the stem with the other. The stem will slip off easily when the melon is twisted

Hints and tips
Melons need more warmth than other fruiting crops such as tomatoes, peppers or aubergines and need higher humidity. If your local outdoor conditions are not suitable, consider growing them in a greenhouse or polytunnel.

VARIETY GUIDE
Be guided by what does well in your area, Cantaloupe varieties such as 'Ogen' and 'Sweetheart' stand a good chance of producing fruit in marginal regions. Also look out for varieties such as 'Emir', a cantaloupe that germinates at lower temperatures (15 to 20°C/59 to 68°F) as this can help you get an earlier start.

Curcurbitaceae *Cucurbita pepo*

COURGETTE AND SUMMER SQUASH

Location: Full sun, vertical frame for vine
Height: bush 45cm (18in), vine 1.2m (4ft)
Spacing: 1 per 3 or 9 squares for bush; for vines 1 per 2 squares

GROWING SEASON
Spring: no
Summer: yes
Autumn: no
Winter: no

GROWING TIME
Seed to Harvest: 12 weeks
Indoor Seed Starting: 4 to 6 weeks before last spring frost date
Earliest Outdoor Planting: 2 to 3 weeks after the last spring frost

Hints and tips

A single plant of a bush variety can fill a whole box frame but if you plant three bush plants per box frame instead, you will get more fruits overall because pollination is improved – but picking is tricky. However, if you are happy with 25 to 30 fruits from a box frame, stick with a single plant of a bush variety.

VARIETY GUIDE
Bush courgettes: 'Midnight' is spine-free, 'Parthenon' and 'Cavilli' fruit well even when pollination is poor. 'Parador' is a good yellow one. 'Black Forest' is one of the few climbing courgettes. Summer squash come in different shapes such as patty pans (which look like little flying saucers) or round fruits such as 'Summer Ball'.

Courgettes need a lot of room to grow, but even a single plant is prolific and easy to grow in warm summers. Most of the varieties are bush types and it is conventional to assign a whole box frame (1 x 1m/3 x 3ft) to one or three bush plants over the summer. Summer squash are grown the same way as courgettes but they offer more variation in fruit shapes and are easier to stuff.

Starting
Sow one seed in a 7-cm (3-in) pot, 2.5cm (1in) deep, indoors in warm conditions (20°C/68°F). Sow four to six weeks before your last frost date, harden off well and plant outdoors a few weeks after your last spring frost date. Seeds can also be sown direct in early summer; place a cloche or crop cover to warm the soil a few weeks before and them sow two seeds After sprouting, cut off the weakest plant if both seeds sprout.

Growing
When watering plants, keep the leaves dry to prevent powdery mildew. Weed weekly early on. Keep plants within bounds by re-directing growth; if you have a vine variety train it up the support. Plants can suffer from viruses (shown on leaves and by stunted growth); remove affected plants and destroy (burn or put in dustbin) but note some varieties also have natural leaf markings.

Harvesting
Cut carefully through the fruit stem but do not cut the main stem or leaf stems. Handle the fruits gently as their skins are soft and easily damaged. Start harvesting as soon as the blossoms wilt and carry on until the fruits are 15cm (6in) long. Sometimes you have to harvest at least three times a week; they grow that fast.

Curcurbitaceae *Cucurbita* species

WINTER SQUASH

Location: Full sun,
vertical frame for vine
Height: bush 45cm
(18in), vine 2m (6ft)
Spacing: bush varieties
1 per 3 or 9 squares, for
vines 1 per 2 squares

GROWING SEASON
Spring: no
Summer: yes
Autumn: yes
Winter: no

GROWING TIME
Seed to Harvest: 24 weeks
Indoor Seed Starting:
4 to 6 weeks before last
spring frost
Earliest Outdoor Planting:
2 weeks after last spring
frost

Winter squash can take over an entire box frame but you can control them by growing them vertically. The fruit can be picked in late autumn and stored to be used right through the winter. All winter squashes, including pumpkins, have thick skins that harden in the autumn, and are generally picked after the vines have been killed by frost. You don't get your crop until season's end, but since there is almost no fresh produce then, it is very welcome.

Starting

Sow one seed in a 7-cm (3-in) pot, 2.5cm (1in) deep, indoors in warm conditions (20°C/68°F). Sow four to six weeks before your last frost date, harden off well and plant outdoors a few weeks after your last spring frost date. Seeds can also be sown direct in early summer; first cover with a plastic-covered cage or cloche to warm the soil and sow two seeds. Cut off the weakest plant if both seeds sprout.

Growing

Keep the soil moist. Weed weekly early on; keep vines trained up the vertical frame. Plants suffer from same problems as courgettes and summer squash (*see* opposite).

Harvesting

Cut the squash from the main stem, leaving at least a 5-cm (2-in) piece of stem. Then set the fruit out in the sun to cure for a few days, protecting it at night when frost is in the forecast. Harvest after the first light frost, which will kill the leaves and stems but before a very hard frost. Store winter squash in a cool, dry place, check the skins often and use up promptly if you see any bruised or soft spots.

Hints and tips

Winter squash are very vigorous and will take over your box frame, so make sure you only grow winter squash vertically if you want to grow a mix of crops in one box.

VARIETY GUIDE
There are plenty of varieties; people often like the taste of the butternut types but these don't always fully develop and ripen within the growing season. So try small fruited types: the onion-type squash such as 'Uchiki Kuri' or an acorn squash such as 'Celebration'. For a good flavour and reliable storage, the large fruiting 'Crown Prince' is hard to beat.

Fabaceae *Vicia faba*

BROAD BEAN

Location: Full sun and
  shelter
Height: 60 to 100cm
  (2 to 3ft)
Spacing: 4 per square

GROWING SEASON
Spring: yes
Summer: yes
Autumn: yes*
Winter: yes*
* if sown in autumn

GROWING TIME
Seed to Harvest: 20 to 30
  weeks
Indoor Seed Starting: at
  least 8 weeks before last
  spring frost
Earliest Outdoor Planting:
  4 weeks after the first
  autumn frost

Hints and tips

Some years, plants from autumn sowings are more productive than those from spring sowings and other years, vice versa. Hedge your bets by sowing twice; autumn sowing can be done in October or later but aim to sow by November.

VARIETY GUIDE
'The Sutton' is a well-known short variety, useful in a SMG box frame. The heritage variety 'Crimson-flowered' has very beautiful flowers. For autumn sowing in a cold area, use the extra hardy classic variety 'Aquadulce Claudia'.

Unlike most beans, broad beans are hardy so you can sow them either in spring or in the autumn before you want them. As they grow early in the year, broad beans crop by early summer so can then be cleared to make room for a different later crop.

Starting

You can sow seed direct into the square by pushing the seed down 2 to 3cm (1in) or raise young plants in 7-cm (3-in) pots and then harden them off before planting out. An autumn sowing or early spring sowing will produce a crop by early summer but may need a crop cover if weather is particularly windy or cold.

Growing

Plants may need a bit of support to stop the plants flopping: a cane or stake should be sufficient. Weed the square and water when the flowers start to form. When the plants are in full flower, pinch out the top 10cm (4in) to encourage pods to form and to reduce problems with blackfly. Mice often eat the seeds. You might see brown spots on foliage, a sign of disease, but you often still get a crop even if the plants look scruffy.

Harvesting

Pick the pods as they mature, starting with the lower ones. For shelling, pick the pods when the seeds inside are just showing and are still soft. The beans are no longer at their peak when the scar (where the seed is joined to the pod) is discoloured. It is best to cut the pods from the plant, particularly early on, or you might damage the main stem or uproot the plant.

Lamiaceae *Mentha*
MINT

Location: Sun to partial
shade
Height: 30 to 60cm
(1 to 2ft)
Spacing: 1 per square

GROWING SEASON
Spring: yes
Summer: yes
Autumn: yes
Winter: no

GROWING TIME
Seed to Harvest: n/a; buy a
plant, it is a perennial
Indoor Seed Starting: no
Earliest Outdoor Planting:
6 weeks before the last
spring frost

Mint, and other members of the mint family, has the distinguishing characteristic of square stems. You can see this best by looking at the cut end of a stem. Mint plants come in many flavours, such as spearmint, peppermint, apple, lemon, some are variegated, and all mints give off a lovely aroma when the leaves are bruised or handled.

Mint is a worthwhile perennial herb but it is invasive so is best grown in a box frame separate from annual veg crops. It sends out tough runners that grow roots and leaves every few inches, and will crop up anywhere it can. To keep mint plants in bounds, cut a 15-cm (6-in) diameter circle around the plants in late spring and again in early autumn, and pull out any runners outside the circle. Try not to leave any small pieces in the ground—they too will sprout. In a SMG, sink a 30-cm (12-in) square or round plastic bucket; don't use a conventional plant pot with holes on the side or around the bottom. If using a bucket, drill some small drainage holes in the bottom. Pull the entire pot up in the autumn and take it inside as a houseplant. Mint is a good candidate for a standalone square 30 x 30-cm (1 x 1-ft) container so long as you remember to water it.

VARIETY GUIDE
There are lots of different flavoured mints; some are rather strong for culinary use so taste a leaf before buying. For a refreshing tea try peppermint or spearmint (Tashkent or Moroccan mint). For a delicate mint flavour for potatoes try apple mint.

Starting
Buy a small potted mint and plant anytime from early spring onwards; plants are hardy but harden off if plants were undercover.

Growing
Keep the roots moist, and lift and divide up the plant every year. Cut back, or pick regularly, to promote bushiness.

Harvesting
Harvest mint anytime after the plant has reached 15cm (6in) tall.

Lamiaceae *Ocimum*

BASIL

	GROWING SEASON	GROWING TIME
Location: Full sun **Height:** 20 to 45cm (8 to 18in) **Spacing:** small plant, 4 per square; large, 1 per square	**Spring:** no **Summer:** yes **Autumn:** no **Winter:** no	**Seed to Harvest:** 16 weeks **Indoor Seed Starting:** 6 weeks before last frost **Earliest Outdoor Planting:** after soil has warmed **Additional Plantings:** make one or two repeat sowings before midsummer

VARIETY GUIDE
'Sweet Genovese' is the classic basil variety for pesto or where you want leaves in quantity. 'Aristotle' is a good small-leaved Greek basil for garnish. For spicy flavours, try 'Siam Queen'. To make your SGM boxes more ornamental, look for purple-leaved types such as 'Purple Ruffles' or a basil with neat flowers.

Sweet basil with its cupped green leaves is the type used in salads and to make pesto. Other basils are used in Asian cuisines while in India, basil is planted around the temples and is a part of many religious ceremonies. Basil also comes in flavours such as cinnamon, liquorice and lemon, plus many leaf shapes and colours. Go ahead and experiment – grow a few different kinds and discover the wonders of this beautiful and delicious herb.

Starting

Start basil from seed indoors about four to six weeks before the last spring frost. Sow three to four seeds in modular trays or small pots, keep warm (at least 18 to 20°C/64 to 68°F) and then harden off thoroughly before planting out. Or choose potted plants at your local garden centre, but keep them sheltered until there is no more danger of frost. Once warm weather sets in, basil plants will grow quickly, but they won't amount to much if they get chilled early in the season. Basil plants will turn black and die at the slightest hint of frost so there is little point starting too early.

Growing

Choose a square in full sun. Pinch off flower buds to save the plant's energy for leaf growth. Also pinch out growing tips to keep the plants bushy. Slugs love soft leaves of basil but keeping the soil surface on the dry side will help deter them.

Harvesting

Pinch stems just above leaf nodes where new stems will sprout; start picking as soon as the plants are growing strongly. In fact, the more you pinch off leaves and stems, the more basil will grow.

Lamiaceae *Origanum*

OREGANO AND MARJORAM

Location: Full sun.
Height: 20 to 45cm
(8 to 18in)
Spacing: 1 per square

GROWING SEASON
Spring: yes
Summer: yes
Autumn: yes
Winter: no

GROWING TIME
Seed to Harvest: n/a
Indoor Seed Starting: no
Earliest Outdoor Planting:
after last frost

Oregano and marjoram are Mediterranean plants, so provide them with sun and warmth to bring out their flavours. They are pretty plants when young and there are variegated forms for extra interest but plants can grow straggly once they flower. Give plants frequent trimmings to keep them neat and so you can dry the leaves. Their flavour is stronger when dried than it is fresh.

Starting

As you only need one or two plants, buy a potted plant from a garden centre in spring. You can also lift an existing plant from your herb border and plant young healthy sections in a SMG.

Growing

Water plants during dry spells. Harvest or trim mature plants often to keep them in bounds. Lift and divide plants every two to three years. Oregano is usually pest- and disease-free but can be invasive.

Harvesting

Cut stems back to a pair of leaves, which is where new branches will form. Leaves can be harvested anytime during the summer months, but the flavour is best after the buds have formed just before the flowers open. When the leaves have dried, crumble them up between finger and thumb, then store in an airtight container.

VARIETY GUIDE
There is often confusion and mislabelling between oregano (*Origanum vulgare*), sweet marjoram (*O. majorana*) and pot marjoram (*O. onites*). So it is best to buy by choosing an aroma you like when you rub a leaf between your finger and thumb, or use a specialist herb nursery.

Malvaceae *Abelmoschus esculentus*

OKRA

Location: Full sun and shelter, with vertical supports
Height: 45 to 60cm (18 to 24in)
Spacing: 1 per square

GROWING SEASON
Spring: no
Summer: yes
Autumn: yes
Winter: no

GROWING TIME
Seed to Harvest: 16 to 20 weeks
Indoor Seed Starting: 6 to 8 weeks before last spring frost
Earliest Outdoor Planting: 1 to 2 weeks after the last spring frost

Hints and tips

Harvest the pods daily: pick the young pods that are no more than 10cm (4in) long. Older pods can be too tough to eat, but remove them so more pods will form.

VARIETY GUIDE
The variety you are most likely to come across is 'Clemson's Spineless', an Asian variety with green pods that needs support. 'Burgundy' has attractive red pods and 'Pure Luck' is an early one with green pods.

Okra is a pretty plant with edible pods that can be yellow, red or green. This crop needs hot weather and a long growing season, so in most cases it needs to be grown in a greenhouse or polytunnel and trained up supports. However, if you can provide a warm, sheltered site in a mild area – for example, you can grow melons and cucumbers outdoors – then it might be worth a try outside.

Starting

The easiest way to start is to order potted plants from a mail order seed supplier. To raise from seed, sow indoors at a temperature of at least 20°C (68°F) after soaking seeds in warm water overnight. Sow in modular trays 2.5cm (1in) deep; young plants can be transplanted into 9-cm (3½-in) pots and grown on at 15°C (59°F) before planting out in their final positions. If you are planting outside, remember to harden off young plants thoroughly, then plant out after the soil has warmed up usually late spring to early summer.

Growing

Keep the roots fairly moist, using warm water if possible; mulch in hot conditions. Warm conditions will encourage insect pests, so check plants daily and pick or brush off any pests promptly.

Harvesting

Once the flowers have bloomed, the pods grow very quickly, so check the plant daily for young pods as these have the best flavour and texture. Cut pods from plants with a pruner or knife; wear gloves and long sleeves when harvesting as the pods have fine hairs that can irritate the skin.

Papilionaceae *Phaseolus coccineus & P. vulgaris*

CLIMBING BEANS

Location: Full sun or partial shade, sheltered, vertical support
Height: 1.5 to 2m (5 to 6ft)
Spacing: 4 or 8 per square

GROWING SEASON
Spring: no
Summer: yes
Autumn: no
Winter: no

GROWING TIME
Seed to Harvest: 16 to 20 weeks
Indoor Seed Starting: 4 to 8 weeks before the last frost
Earliest Outdoor Planting: after the last spring frost

Prolific and easy to grow, climbing beans – whether runner beans or French climbing varieties – are a terrific crop for any garden. Some gardeners think that runner beans have better flavour. Both crop well but French climbing beans crop better early in the season, while runner beans crop better later on. Both need a vertical frame for support and once they start cropping provide a steady supply all season long, so a single sowing is adequate.

Starting

Sow beans indoors in pots, two to a 12-cm (5-in) pot, pushing them 2cm (¾in) deep. Keep the pots at 10 to 12°C (50 to 54 °F) until the seeds have germinated; then grow on at a minimum temperature of 7°C (45°F) until the plants are 15cm (6in) or so tall. Gradually harden off the young plants and plant out after there is no more danger of frost. Seed can be sown direct outside once the soil is warm enough but cover square with a chicken-wire cage to keep out birds until the seed germinate.

Growing

Protect plants from cold winds and slugs; encourage them to climb up the support. Water regularly during dry spells and pull out any weeds. Pinch out the growing tips when the plants reach the top of the support.

Harvesting

Break or cut each stem holding the bean pod, and do not pull on the plant when harvesting. Pick beans when they are still small and tender. Once the pods bulge with seeds, the plant will stop producing and the runner beans become stringy.

VARIETY GUIDE
Choose varieties with colourful flowers, such as the red and white 'St George', red-flowered 'Wisley Magic' or the pretty salmon-pink 'Celebration'. 'Moonlight' is a white-flowered variety that is a cross between a French bean and a runner bean; it is self-pollinating so you should get a crop whatever the weather is like at pollination time. French climbing beans tend to have green pods, such as 'Blue Lake', but it is worth looking out for yellow- or purple-podded types as these are ornamental and easy to see for picking.

Papilionaceae *Phaseolus vulgaris*

BUSH BEANS

Location: Full sun or partial shade
Height: 30 to 40cm (12 to 16in)
Spacing: 4 or 9 per square

GROWING SEASON
Spring: no
Summer: yes
Autumn: no
Winter: no

GROWING TIME
Seed to Harvest: 8 to 10 weeks
Indoor Seed Starting: 4 weeks before the last frost
Earliest Outdoor Planting: after the last spring frost

Hints and tips

If your bush beans get floppy and start spreading over adjacent squares, just run a string around them as a group to keep them confined to their square.

VARIETY GUIDE
For a quick cropping early bean try 'Speedy'; if you like slim pods go for 'Safari'. For eye-catching pods try 'Purple Teepee' and the yellow-podded 'Pencil Pod Wax'. Shelling beans such as 'Brown Dutch' or 'Canadian Wonder' are picked later on in the season for their seeds.

Bush beans, also known as "dwarf beans", grow low to the ground. Each plant yields one large crop all at once, with a smaller crop a few weeks later. They are invaluable in a SMG box frame as they are quick growing and there is no need for a vertical support. They are frost-tender but as they are short it is easy to protect them with a crop cover.

Starting

Sow beans indoors in batches anytime from mid to late spring; use one seed per 7-cm (3-in) pot or use modular trays. Seed will germinate at 10 to 12°C (50 to 54 °F) until the seeds have germinated, then grow on at a minimum temperature of 7°C (45°F). Gradually harden off the young plants and plant out after there is no more danger of frost, and use a crop cover if need be. Seed can be sown direct outside once the soil is warm enough but cover the square with a chicken-wire cage to keep out birds until the seeds germinate. Mice often eat bean seeds. A late crop sown directly into a square in early to midsummer will crop into early autumn.

Growing

Once the flowers start to form, keep the soil moist. Slugs are often a particular problem with low-growing beans.

Harvesting

Pick pods as soon as they reach 10 to 15cm (4 to 6in) long, but much depends on the variety. Do not pull too hard at the plants or they will come out of the ground. If growing a variety for dried beans, leave the plants as long as possible before harvesting.

Papilionaceae *Pisum sativum*

PEA

Location: Full sun in spring; shaded towards summer, supports **Height:** 60cm to 150cm (2 to 5ft) **Spacing:** 8 per square	**GROWING SEASON** **Spring:** yes **Summer:** yes **Autumn:** no **Winter:** no	**GROWING TIME** **Seed to Harvest:** 10 to 14 weeks **Indoor Seed Starting:** 8 to 10 weeks before the last spring frost **Earliest Outdoor Planting:** 6 to 8 weeks before last spring frost

Who doesn't like the taste of fresh peas? The high-sugar peas, or mangetout varieties are extremely high yielding as you can eat the entire pod. They can be eaten raw or cooked and are a must in my garden. Because they are such a treat to eat raw – you might need to make a family rule: pick and eat all you want but leave enough for dinner.

Tall climbing peas will need a proper vertical support but they crop well, while some of the shorter types can make do with a low wrap of pea and bean netting around bamboo canes.

Starting

Peas are fairly hardy, so you can sow direct outdoors once the soil temperature is around 5 to 10°C (41 to 50°F). Sow 2 to 2.5cm (¾ to 1in) deep and seeds should germinate in 10 to 15 days. In cold areas, or if mice are a problem, sow indoors in 7-cm (3-in) pots and plant out in mid spring.

Growing

Never let the pea roots dry out but keep water off the leaves; supply extra water when the plants are in full flower: this will help prevent powdery mildew. Weave the young growth in and out of the netting. Keep the area weed-free and mulch the soil surface if the weather gets warm to help conserve moisture.

Harvesting

Carefully pick or cut pods off their stems in early summer. The mangetout types should be ready when the pods are 5 to 7cm (2 to 3in) long, but leave shelling pea varieties until they have small round peas. Pick over plants every other day; pick everything that is ready, as if you leave the pods on the plants the yield will drop.

VARIETY GUIDE

Early peas such as 'Feltham First' grow fast, need little support and can be sown early and harvest by early summer. For a longer cropping time, try a maincrop such as 'Onward' trained around some pea and bean netting. Tall varieties such as heritage varieties 'Alderman', 'Purple Podded' and 'Carouby de Maussane' (a mangetout) need a proper vertical support but will crop over a longer period. Mangetout and sugarsnap varieties growing to around 60cm to 100cm (2 to 3ft) include: 'Oregon Sugar Pod' and 'Norli' plus a wide range of modern, high-sugar varieties.

Poaceae *Zea mays*

SWEETCORN

Location: Full sun, some support needed
Height: 1.5 to 2m (5 to 6ft)
Spacing: 9 per box frame

GROWING SEASON
Spring: no
Summer: yes
Autumn: no
Winter: no

GROWING TIME
Seed to Harvest: 10 to 13 weeks
Indoor Seed Starting: 4 to 6 weeks before the last spring frost
Earliest Outdoor Planting: after the last spring frost

Hints and tips

Sweetcorn can blow over in windy conditions, especially as Mel's mix is loose and fluffy. It's easy to put a support around the box frame ahead of time (see page 55). Ripe cobs can be attacked by birds; if this happens enclose the box frame with a chicken-wire cage.

VARIETY GUIDE
It's best to pick one variety that does well in your local area, so ask around. Varieties available change regularly but look out for 'Sweet Nugget', 'Lark' and 'Mirai 003'.

The taste of store-bought sweetcorn just can't compete with home-grown cobs. Plant a whole box frame of just sweetcorn so you can grow it in a block; this improves pollination and also makes it easier to support the plants. Most of the varieties for home use are planted one per square and only one crop can be grown per season because it needs a long time to mature and lots of hot weather.

Starting

Sow one seed per 7-cm (3-in) pot; use tall pots (recycled plastic vending-machine cups work well) to minimise root disturbance. Germinate at a minimum of 15°C (59°F). Harden off young plants and delay planting out until there is no danger of late frost (late spring to early summer).

Seed can be sown direct outdoors in late spring to early summer, but are vulnerable to mice, and in cold areas plants will not produce cobs by the end of the season. Protect outdoor sowings from birds with a chicken-wire cage until seed has germinated.

Growing

Water during dry spells and keep the box frame weeded.

Harvesting

When the silk at the end of the cobs first turns brown and the cobs feel full and slightly bumpy, harvest time is near. To check, peel away a small strip of the husk to expose the kernels. They should be plump and if you puncture one with your thumbnail and milky juice squirts out, then it's ready. Clear juice means the sweetcorn is not quite ready to pick. Use two hands to harvest – one to hold the stalk and the other to pull down and break off the ear – otherwise you may break the stalk. Each will produce one or two cobs. Eat cobs as soon as possible after harvesting for that just-picked sweet taste.

Rosaceae *Fragaria*
STRAWBERRY

Location: Full sun **Height:** 15 to 30cm (6 to 12in) **Spacing:** 4 per square	**GROWING SEASON** **Spring:** yes **Summer:** yes **Autumn:** no **Winter:** no	**GROWING TIME** **Seed to Harvest:** n/a **Indoor Seed Starting:** no **Earliest Outdoor Planting:** plant bare roots in autumn or potted plants in spring

Picking strawberries in early summer is a treat – only about half the harvest actually makes it into the basket! Since strawberries are so popular, most families like to plant an entire box frame with strawberries – that way it's easy to protect and harvest them. A pyramid box design works well for these low-growing fruits.

Strawberry plants are perennials and will fruit for at least three years; then yields will decrease and the plants need replacing. Each plant sends out "runners", i.e. baby plants which can be used as the next generation of strawberries in the garden but I recommend you cut them off as they take so much energy from the parent plant.

Starting
Buy certified virus-free strawberry plants from a mail order fruit specialist; these are usually bare roots despatched and planted in late summer to mid autumn. When the plants arrive, soak the plants in a bucket of water, then trim off the roots slightly. Plant four bare roots per square.

Growing
Once the growing season starts, keep the soil moist; increase the frequency of watering when strawberries are fruiting. To help prevent fruit going mouldy, keep flowers and fruits dry by careful watering directed at the roots. Birds and slugs will eat the berries, so netting and regular picking are essential. Keep the ground free of weeds. Cut off all the runners promptly. Plant viruses and soil diseases build up over the years, so replace the plants and the bed every three years.

Harvesting
Pick the fruit leaving a short piece of stem attached; use scissors for a clean cut. Handle the berries carefully as they bruise easily.

Hints and tips
Cover plants with bird netting just before the fruits ripen. Use hoops or a tunnel support so the netting is held well above the fruits; the netting should be fairly taut and well-secured around the edges.

VARIETY GUIDE
If you only have room for one variety make it a June-bearing type such as 'Darlisette', 'Sallybright', 'Sonata', 'Elsanta' or 'Malwina'.

Solanaceae *Capsicum annuum*

SWEET PEPPER AND CHILLI

Location: Full sun
Height: 30 to 60cm (1 to 2ft)
Spacing: 1 per square

GROWING SEASON
Spring: no
Summer: yes
Autumn: no
Winter: no

GROWING TIME
Seed to Harvest: 20 to 25 weeks
Indoor Seed Starting: 15 weeks before last spring frost
Earliest Outdoor Planting: 2 weeks after last spring frost

Hints and tips

If you pinch out the growing tip when young plants are about 20cm (8in) high, the plants will grow into stockier, bushier plants.

VARIETY GUIDE

For sweet peppers, look for 'Magno' or 'Orange Bell' for good yields of tasty orange fruit; 'Gypsy' has attractive and tasty red fruit, 'Corno Di Torno' has long red peppers for roasting. Some chilli varieties are much hotter than others, so it depends on what you like. 'Padron' is useful where the growing season is short as the fruits can be picked when immature and roasted or left to ripen. 'Basket of Fire' is both ornamental, edible and very prolific.

Both peppers and chillies are very ornamental additions to a SMG box frame with the bonus of edible fruits. They are both grown the same way but whereas a single chilli plant will provide all the fruits you can eat, it is a challenge to get more than a couple of ripe peppers per plant, growing peppers outdoors, so consider growing undercover such as in a greenhouse or polytunnel.

Both subjects offer a wide range of varieties so the size of plant and the shape, flavour and colour of the fruits vary greatly. However, particularly for peppers, it pays to look for early-ripening, high-yielding varieties that will produce ripe fruit by the end of the growing season in your area.

Starting

Buying young plants, either from a garden centre or by mail order, will give you a head start. More mature potted plants are also sold through the summer at garden centres or garden shows if you have late gaps to fill. If you do opt for seed, sow in late winter to early spring at 20°C (68°F) in small pots and grow them on at 15°C (59°F) until early summer. Plants are very frost sensitive so harden off thoroughly before planting out two weeks after the last spring frost; cloches and crop covers can help.

Growing

Keep the roots moist: a mulch of garden compost will help conserve moisture. Stems and branches needs a bit of support with canes.

Harvesting

Cut the fruit from the plants (don't pull or you'll accidentally break other branches). Leave about 2 to 3cm (1in) of stem on the fruit for a longer storage life. Wash your hands after handling chillies.

A red variety of sweet pepper with a mix of immature green fruits and red ripe fruits.

Solanaceae *Lycopersicon esculentum*

TOMATO

	GROWING SEASON	GROWING TIME
Location: Full sun **Height:** Cordon 2m (6ft), bush 30 to 45cm (12 to 18in), dwarf 15cm (6in) **Spacing:** Cordon 1 per square, bush 1 per box frame, dwarf 1 per 1 to 2 squares	**Spring:** no **Summer:** yes **Autumn:** no **Winter:** no	**Seed to Harvest:** 20 to 25 weeks **Indoor Seed Starting:** 8 to 9 weeks before the last spring frost **Earliest Outdoor Planting:** immediately after the last spring frost

Hints and tips

There are lots of alternative ways of planting and training cordon tomatoes. Turn to page 146 for the best Square Metre Gardening method.

Tomatoes are a popular crop and there are plenty of types to choose from, but just remember to get varieties suitable for outdoor growing. There are three different growth habits: tall, bush and dwarf and they take up different amounts of horizontal space. The tall ones are referred to variously as cordon, indeterminate or vines types. In other words, they have a tall stem that grows on and on; this type takes up the least amount of ground space but they need to be trained on a support, a stout stake, tomato cage or a vertical frame of netting.

Bush varieties have a determinate growth habit so their main stem stops naturally and then they spread outwards. They don't need the same vertical support as the cordons but they spread vigorously so they will take up the whole box frame and harvesting is not as easy as the trained ones. Bush varieties are useful where you have enough room to give them their own box frame and where inserting supports for cordons is difficult – if there is a solid paved surface under the box, for example.

In recent years, dwarf tomato plants bred for containers have become popular. 'Tumbler' and others with trailing stems would suit a 30 x 30 x 30-cm (1 x 1 x 1-ft) box. While other upright dwarf types can be used in a mixed box frame, as they are neat, but yields are low on such small plants.

Starting

The easiest way to start is to buy young potted plants in mid to late spring and harden off before planting outside. The alternative is to sow seed indoors in early spring at a temperature of 20°C (68°F). Sow a pinch of seed in a small pot and seed should emerge in ten days. When the seedlings are large enough to be handled, pot them up individually in 7-cm (3-in) pots and grow on at 15°C (59°F). Keep a careful watch over the plants because they grow quickly and any check to their growth at this stage will affect them later on. Harden off young plants for one to two weeks, and plant outside after your frost-free date. Plant one cordon plant per square. Bush types are planted in the centre of their own SMG box frame, while dwarf ones can be grown in their own square container.

Growing

Daily watering during dry spells is key to quality fruit: an automatic watering system is worth considering. Remove the lower leaves if they are dead or yellow. Keep adding a mulch of garden compost as the season progresses. Cordon varieties need their side shoots removed and to be supported, either by tying in to a 1.5 to 2-m (5 to 6-ft) stake or by training on to vertical netting (wide mesh tomato netting is ideal if you can get it but pea and bean netting will suffice). Pinch out the main growing tip in late summer once there are four to six trusses (shoots bearing flowers or fruit). Bush types may need trimming so you can access the fruits; also their stems benefit from some support with small canes so the fruit does not lie on the ground. If the disease tomato blight is forecast, use a clear polythene crop cover or a cloche to protect the plants. Tomato soil diseases can build up after a few years, so grow in a different square or box frame each year.

Harvesting

Gently twist and pull ripe tomatoes so the stem breaks (if the fruit is ripe it should easily break away) or, even better, cut the stem so as not to disturb the rest of the remaining fruit. If you leave fruits on the plant too long they will turn soft and mushy, so inspect daily; it's one of the pleasures you've been waiting for all year.

VARIETY GUIDE
First make sure you get an outdoor variety that will ripen in time in your area and of a growth habit (cordon, bush or dwarf) that will fit in with your SMG scheme. Then choose some different fruit sizes: a small fruit such as a cherry or baby plum, and a standard size for slicing and cooking. Dense-fleshed plum and beefsteak types are popular for cooking but these types do best under glass.
CORDON 'Gardener's Delight' (cherry), 'Sungold' (cherry, best undercover but possible outdoors), 'Moneymaker' (one for slicing).
BUSH 'Losetto' (cherry), 'Lizzano' (cherry), 'Tornado' (slicing), 'Red Alert' (cherry), 'Roma Improved' (large plum for cooking).
DWARF 'Tumbler', 'Sweet 'n' Neat' or 'Venus': these types have small, cherry fruits.

Solanaceae *Solanum melongena*

AUBERGINE

Location: Full sun, warm and sheltered.
Height: 75cm (30in)
Spacing: 1 per square

GROWING SEASON
Spring: no
Summer: yes
Autumn: no
Winter: no

GROWING TIME
Seed to Harvest: 25 weeks
Indoor Seed Starting: 14 weeks before the last spring frost
Earliest Outdoor Planting: after the last spring frost

Hints and tips

Aubergines can become top heavy but if you pinch out the growing tip when the plant is 20cm (8in) tall, then you will end up with a stockier, bushier plant later on.

VARIETY GUIDE
For outdoor growing try one of the following: 'Bonica' for the classic purple aubergines; 'Calliope' an early variety with egg-shaped fruits that are mauve with white flecks; or 'Ophelia', another early one with purple egg-shaped fruits on compact plants.

Aubergines are ornamental once in flower and their edible fruits come in a wide variety of colours and shapes. They take a long time to fruit – but if you buy fairly mature plants they are a good way to fill a spare square in early to mid summer. You do need a really sunny, warm spot for the fruit to ripen outdoors; they crop better when give more warmth, i.e. under cover.

Starting

It's easiest to start with young potted plants bought in late spring as the seed needs to be sown early in the year at a high temperature. But if you want a specific variety, then sow seed at a temperature of at least 20°C (68°F) in late winter to early spring. Prick out seedlings into individual small pots. Gradually harden off the plants before planting out after the last spring frosts; plants need to be at least 15cm (6in) at this stage to produce fruit by the end of the season. Warm the bed up before planting by putting out a crop cover or cloche a week or so before.

Growing

Plant roots need constant moisture, especially when fruits are forming and swelling. Weed weekly; add a thick mulch of garden compost when hot weather sets in. Provide a stake or a wide-mesh, open-wire cage support when the plant is half grown. Slugs and grey mould are the main problems, particularly towards the end of the season when it is damp.

Harvesting

Always cut the fruit from the bush rather than pull at them; watch out for sharp spines on the stems and fruits. Pick the fruits while they are still firm and the skin is shiny.

Solanaceae *Solanum tuberosum*

POTATO

	GROWING SEASON	GROWING TIME
Location: Sun or partial shade	**Spring:** yes	**Tuber to Harvest:** 20 weeks
Height: 30 to 60cm (1 to 2ft)	**Summer:** yes	**Indoor Tuber Starting:** 10 weeks before the last spring frost
Spacing: 1 tuber per 30 x 30 x 30-cm (1 x 1 x 1-ft) container	**Autumn:** no* **Winter:** no * Other varieties for autumn harvest available	**Earliest Outdoor Planting:** after the last spring frost

Potatoes need no introduction; we've all eaten them at some point but growing your own potatoes to get that melt-in-your-mouth new potato flavour is a real joy. As potato tubers are planted deeper than the conventional 15cm (6in) depth of a SMG box frame, the most efficient way to grow them is to make, or buy, one or more high-rise boxes. Boxes measuring 30 x 30 x 30cm (1 x 1 x 1ft), with drainage holes, work well for a crop of early potatoes.

Starting

Buy certified virus-free seed potatoes; for small quantities go to a garden centre in winter. Set the tubers out in a small tray (or empty egg box) with the end of the tuber with the most "eyes" (growing points) uppermost. Put the tray on an indoor windowsill in late winter so the tubers sprout healthy stubby shoots.

Growing

In early to mid spring, half fill with Mel's mix and plant the sprouted tuber with a trowel so it is covered with the mix. One tuber per 10 to 15-litre box is sufficient; three boxes produces a useful quantity. As the plants grow, keep adding more mix until it almost reaches the top of the box. If frost is forecast bring the boxes indoors or cover with a double layer of garden fleece. By late spring you should be able to leave the boxes out on the patio. Keep the mix moist.

Harvesting

When plants start to flower the tubers will be starting to form. Gently work your hand down into the mix to feel the potatoes; when they are about the size of a hen's egg you can pull these out and leave the plant to produce more. When the top growth dies down, tip the contents of the box out to harvest the tubers. Cook and eat new potatoes as soon as possible to capture their flavour.

Hints and tips

You can re-use the high-rise boxes for another crop of potatoes by planting in summer for harvesting in the autumn. Specially treated tubers are available by mail order for planting in midsummer. Simply refresh the existing mix with some extra garden compost.

VARIETY GUIDE
Concentrate on early or second early varieties such as 'Accent', 'Swift' or 'Charlotte' as these have less top growth.

11

Flowers

While the main purpose of a SMG is to grow food crops, adding a bit of extra colour to a square or two will give the whole box a lift. The following chapter highlights a few good ornamental plants to consider. Some have edible petals, others can be cut for indoor displays and a few are neat and packed with colour. Of course, there are lots of other flowers but opt for short-lived ones that only last a growing season rather than perennials. That way you can start each year with a a clear SMG box frame.

Sweet peas will bring summer colour and scent to a vertical frame in a SMG.

At a glance

From backdrops to edging, there is a flower for every spare square.

Flowers

Crop	Height	Support	Plants per square
BEGONIACEAE			
Begonia semperflorens **Begonia**	20cm (8 in)	no	4
BORAGINACEAE			
Borago officinalis **Borage**	60cm (2ft)	no	1 per 1 to 2 squares
CARYOPHYLLACEAE			
Dianthus barbatus **Pinks, Dianthus**	15 to 20cm (6 to 8in)	no	1 to 4
COMPOSITAE			
Calendula officinalis **Pot Marigold**	25 to 40cm (10 to 16in)	no	1
Cosmos bipinnatus **Cosmos**	30 to 100cm (1 to 3ft)	not usually	1
Dahlia **Dahlia**	30 to 100cm (1 to 3ft)	yes, all but shortest	1 to 4
Tagetes patula **French Marigold**	25cm (10in)	no	4
Zinnia **Zinnia**	30 to 45cm (12 to 18in)	no	1
LABIATAE			
Solenostemon scutellariodes **Coleus**	20cm (8 in)	no	1 to 4
Salvia horminum S. viridis **Clary**	40cm (16 in)	no	4
LEGUMINOSAE			
Lathyrus odoratus **Sweet Pea**	2m (6ft)	Yes, vertical frame	1
SOLANACEAE			
Petunia **Petunia**	15cm (6in)	no	4
TROPAEOLACEAE			
Tropaeolum majus **Nasturtium**	15 to 45cm (6 to 18in)	no	4
VIOLACEAE			
Viola **Pansy and Viola**	15 to 23cm (6 to 9in)	no	4

Growing season	Weeks to flower (from seed)	Notes
summer	25	Buy as plug plants or bedding, as seed is tricky
summer	6	Takes up space but helps pollination of fruiting crops
summer	16 to 20	General bedding pinks add easy summer colour
summer	10 to 12	Edible flowers easy to raise from seed
summer	24	Heights vary greatly depending on variety
summer, autumn	10 to 12	Lots of different types, some grown from tubers
summer	8 to 12	Neat and long-flowering, often grown with tomatoes
summer, autumn	16-20	Lots of different flower colours, needs warmth
summer	25	Grow for its variegated foliage rather than its flowers
summer	20	Easy to raise from seed
spring, summer	12 to 14	Can be sown in autumn, early spring or mid spring
summer	14	Buy as young plants, as they are tricky from seed
summer	14	Easy from seed but look for neat varieties
autumn, winter, spring	20	Most useful at start and end of the growing season

Begoniaceae *Begonia semperflorens*

BEGONIA

Location: Sun, partial shade to shade
Height: 20cm (8in)
Spacing: 4 per square

GROWING SEASON
Spring: no
Summer: yes
Autumn: yes
Winter: no

GROWING TIME
Seed to Harvest: 25 weeks
Indoor Seed Starting: 16 to 18 weeks before last spring frost date
Earliest Outdoor Planting: after the last spring frost

Hints and tips

If you order large packs of bedding begonias for planting schemes, then pot up a few spares and grow them on in pots so you can fill late gaps in your SMG.

VARIETY GUIDE
Most *B. semperflorens* are sold as mixtures such as 'Organdy Mixed', which comprises plants with pink, white and red flowers. If you only want four plants to fill a square, look for strong single colours such as a red or dark pink that will show up amongst green leafy vegetable crops.

These small-flowered bedding begonias will grow in shade as well as sun and take all summer weathers. Their neat habit makes these begonias just right for filling squares at the front or sides of a SMG box frame, bringing some reliable colourful flowers to set beside leafy crops.

Starting

Buy a pot of seedlings to prick out and grow on in modular trays or buy young plug plants or packs of bedding in spring. Growing from seed is not recommended; the seed is tiny and tricky to sow especially as it needs starting early in late winter at high temperatures 20°C (68°F). Begonias are very sensitive to frost, so make sure young plants are hardened off thoroughly before planting out after the last spring frosts.

Growing

Once planted out, the plants need little additional care apart from watering carefully at the base of the plants during dry spells. Slugs can be a problem, so take precautions against these when the plants are first planted out. In partial shade or shade the flowers will last right into the first autumn frosts.

Boraginaceae *Borago officinalis*
BORAGE

Location: Full sun, partial shade	GROWING SEASON	GROWING TIME
Height: 60cm (2ft)	**Spring:** no	**Seed to Harvest:** 6 weeks
Spacing: 1 plant per 1 to 2 squares	**Summer:** yes	**Indoor Seed Starting:** 4 weeks before last spring frost date
	Autumn: no	**Earliest Outdoor Planting:** after the last spring frost
	Winter: no	

Borage has pretty star-shaped flowers that attract bees, so having a plant in your SMG box frame will help with pollination of fruiting crops such as courgettes, runner beans and strawberries. In addition, the flowers are edible and have a cucumber flavour. They make an attractive garnish for a salad, can be floated in summer drinks or captured in ice cubes. The leaves can also be eaten raw but are hairy so they don't suit everyone, try first as a herbal tea.

Starting
Sow individual seeds in small pots in early to mid spring and then harden off plants. Plant out young plants as soon as possible after the last spring frost. Seeds germinate and plants grow quickly so you can leave sowing until late spring and still get flowering plants.

Growing
The plant tolerates some shade and dry conditions but if it gets stressed is prone to blackfly and also powdery mildew. Remove the affected parts promptly and there should be enough of the plant left. To keep up a supply of flowers, remove any faded blooms.

Harvesting
Pick open flowers early in the morning, once the dew has dried. There is no need to wash the blooms but check there are no insects inside. Place stems in a jar of cold water, or put the flowers in a plastic bag and store in the refrigerator until you are ready to use. The centre of the flower can taste bitter, so just use the petals.

Hints and tips

The mature plant can become rather straggly, so consider replacing it with another young borage plant from a later sowing. A word of warning: do not let the plants self-seed in your SMG, deadhead the flowers and collect up and burn any seed heads.

VARIETY GUIDE
The species *B. officinalis* with its blue flowers is the main one grown. There is also a white-flowered form, *B. officinalis* 'Alba', which is sometimes available from herb nurseries.

Caryophyllaceae *Dianthus barbatus*

PINKS

Location: Full sun **Height:** 15 to 20cm (6 to 8in) **Spacing:** 1 to 4 per square	**GROWING SEASON** **Spring:** no **Summer:** yes **Autumn:** no **Winter:** no	**GROWING TIME** **Seed to Flower:** 16 to 20 weeks **Indoor Seed Starting:** 16 to 20 weeks before last spring frost **Earliest Outdoor Planting:** after the last spring frost

Hints and tips

Dianthus thrive in the same conditions as Mediterranean herbs so they are great for adding colour where these herbs are grown. The pink flowers of dianthus look great with all types of basil including the purple-leaved types at the front or edges of a SMG.

VARIETY GUIDE
Look for eye-catching mixtures or single plants: most will be pink, white or red. Mixtures you might come across in mail order catalogues include 'Sweetness', 'Sugar Baby', 'Indian Carpet' or 'Baby Doll'.

Within the Dianthus group there are lots of different plants, including familiar cut flowers such as carnations and sweet williams as well as evergreen garden pinks grown as border edging. These are all lovely flowering plants but most are perennial or biennial so will occupy space in a box frame for too long. For a SMG box frame, it is best to go for a bedding dianthus that you can simply plant out in spring to enjoy the non-stop flowering display over the summer, then remove.

Starting

Buy dianthus as young plants in small packs in spring or buy a single potted mature plant in summer. Dianthus are tricky to raise from seed but as bedding plants they are fairly hardy so they don't need too much hardening off.

Growing

Dianthus are drought-tolerant and do well in a sunny spot in a well-drained mix; once planted and watered in they need little additional care. They have few problems.

Compositae *Calendula officinalis*

POT MARIGOLD

Location: Full sun or partial shade
Height: 25 to 40cm (10 to 16in)
Spacing: 1 per square

GROWING SEASON
Spring: no
Summer: yes
Autumn: no
Winter: no

GROWING TIME
Seed to Flower: 10 to 12 weeks
Indoor Seed Starting: 12 weeks before the last spring frost
Earliest Outdoor Planting: mid spring

Calendula is an easy flower to add quick cheer to your SQM box frame, perfect if you are teaching children to garden. The orange flowers look great with red or purple veg crops such as red-leaved lettuce, beetroot, red chard or purple basil. The flower stems can be cut for indoor arrangements and the petals are edible with a slight nutty taste to them. Use the petals as a garnish in salads or chop petals and mix with rice or butter to add a golden colour.

Starting

Pot marigolds are one of the easiest seeds to sow; either sow direct into the square in spring or raise them indoors in small pots. Germination is quickest at 15 to 20°C (59 to 68°F); seedlings should be ready to pot on in seven to ten days. Any pot-grown plants should be planted out promptly in spring but harden off for a few days first.

Growing

Plants are fully hardy and are self-supporting. Water plants during dry spells while they are establishing or they are prone to powdery mildew. Pot marigolds can self-seed; if you sow a named variety the seedlings may not be the same as the parents.

Harvesting

Pick flowers early in the morning, once the dew has dried. They can be used as a cut flower. If you want to use them as edibles, check they are healthy with no mildew on. Place stems in jar of cold water, or put the flowers in a plastic bag and store in the refrigerator. The centre of the flower can taste bitter, so just use the petals.

Hints and tips

It is well worth growing your own from seed as pot-grown plants on sale often suffer a check to their growth when planted out because they have grown so quickly in the pot.

VARIETY GUIDE

The original pot marigold was a bright orange simple daisy flower but now there are: apricot shades ('Apricot Pygmy'), mahogany-red ('Indian Prince'), yellow ('Lemon Zest'). For double flowers, try 'Orange King' and for attractive pointed petals, the aptlynamed 'Porcupine'.

Compositae *Cosmos bipinnatus*

COSMOS

Location: Full sun **Height:** 30 to 100cm (1 to 3ft) **Spacing:** 1 per square	**GROWING SEASON** **Spring:** no **Summer:** yes **Autumn:** yes **Winter:** no	**GROWING TIME** **Seed to Flower:** 24 weeks **Indoor Seed Starting:** 12 weeks before last spring frost date **Earliest Outdoor Planting:** after the last spring frost

VARIETY GUIDE
Look for the shorter *C. bipinnatus* varieties such as the mix 'Sonata' as these grow to 60cm (2ft) high. 'Double Click' has interesting double flowers in pink, red or white but is a bit taller at 90 to 100cm (3ft).

Cosmos have pretty summer flowers, usually pink or white but sometimes red, that flutter at the top of the feathery foliage like butterflies. They are good gap-filler plants and the flower stems can also be cut for indoor arrangements. As some cosmos plants are tall and floppy, place these at the back and give them a bit of support. Shorter types will shade crops less, so take this into account.

Starting

You can start with young plants; order these from seed companies for delivery in late spring or buy plants at garden centres. The alternative is to sow seed indoors: use modular trays or small pots, start in early spring at 20°C (68°F). Seed should germinate in five to ten days, then you can grow them on in cooler conditions. Harden off plants, then plant out after the last spring frost.

Growing

Plant out in the square and water in well. Once the plant is growing away, pinch out the growing tip to encourage a bushier, more study plant. Thereafter, there is little need to water the plants unless the weather is very dry; they are reasonably drought-tolerant. They also stand up well to wet summers. If regularly deadheaded, plants will carry on producing flowers until the first frosts.

Harvesting

Cut the stems as required for indoor arrangements. As long as you leave enough of the plant growing more flowers will be produced.

Compositae
DAHLIA

	GROWING SEASON	GROWING TIME
Location: Full sun or partial shade **Height:** 30 to 100cm (1 to 3ft) **Spacing:** 4 per square (small bedding dahlias), 1 per square (perennial dahlias)	**Spring:** no **Summer:** yes **Autumn:** yes **Winter:** no	**Seed to Flower:** 10 to 12 weeks **Indoor Seed Starting:** 6 to 8 weeks before last frost **Indoor Tuber Starting:** 4 weeks before last frost **Earliest Outdoor Planting:** after last spring frost date

Dahlias add plenty of colour from late summer to the first frosts of autumn. There are so many to choose from but the short or medium height types are best for a SMG box frame. The small bedding types have many advantages: they are good for colour, attract bees, there is no need for staking and you can start afresh each year. However, for dramatic large blooms *in situ* and for cutting, the more traditional perennial dahlias are hard to resist. Warning: dahlias are habit-forming!

Starting
Buy rooted cuttings or young plants in spring; harden off and plant after the last frosts. Mature plants bought in midsummer also make good gap fillers and will flower through the autumn. Seed-raised dahlias can be sown six to eight weeks before the last spring frost. Dahlia tubers can be planted in spring, although for a SMG it is best to pot these up and grow on first.

Growing
Water dahlias and protect plants against slugs when first setting them out. Once shoots begin to grow, give plants daily water, especially during the hot dry spells. To encourage bushy growth in taller varieties, pinch off the growing tip soon after planting. Support tall varieties. Deadhead to encourage more flowers. When the first frost has killed the top foliage, remove the remaining tuber from large dahlias – this can be kept frost-free overwinter and replanted next spring. There is little point in saving the bedding dahlias but you should clear out all the roots.

Harvesting
Cut dahlias when the flowers are fully open and check carefully for earwigs. Keep the vase topped up, as they take up a lot of water.

Hints and tips

Earwigs nibble at the flower petals and leaves. They are active at night but sleep during the day; trap them in upturned flower pots or plastic cups stuffed with straw attached to nearby supports. Empty the pots of earwigs in the morning.

VARIETY GUIDE
There are so many varieties to choose from but concentrate on varieties under 90 to 100cm (3ft). Varieties with purple foliage add extra colour; the classic one is 'Bishop of Llandaff' with its vivid red single/semi-double flowers but there are now lots of other flower colours. The Gallery Series, is only 30 to 45cm (12 to 18in) high with lots of double flowers; there are plenty of colours here too.

Compositae *Tagetes patula*

FRENCH MARIGOLD

Location: Full sun, partial shade
Height: 25cm (10in)
Spacing: 4 per square

GROWING SEASON
Spring: no
Summer: yes
Autumn: no
Winter: no

GROWING TIME
Seed to Flower: 8 to 12 weeks
Indoor Seed Starting: 6 to 8 weeks before last spring frost date
Earliest Outdoor Planting: just after last frost date

Hints and tips

Don't confuse these types of marigolds (*Tagetes patula*) with the edible pot marigolds (*Calendula officinalis*).

VARIETY GUIDE
There's a good choice of warm red, yellow and orange shades, ranging from the double-flowers of 'Honeycomb' (the colour of honeycomb but actually a mix of yellow and red) to the single-flowered: 'Dainty Marietta' (yellow with maroon blotch) or 'Roulette' (yellow with a subtle orange stripe).

Just about everyone will recognise the pompom flowers of the marigold; the slim and lacy foliage is distinctive and give off a pungent scent when cut or crushed. The smaller marigolds, known as French marigolds, are particularly suitable for the front or sides of a SMG box frame as they are so neat. Marigolds are often recommended as companion plants to tomatoes as they are said to discourage pests. Whether this works or not there is no doubt the two together do look great!

Starting

Seeds will germinate indoors at 20°C (68°F) very quickly, within seven to 14 days, ideal for a child's first foray into the wonders of growing plants from seed. Move the seedlings on to modular trays or small pots. Plants are frost-tender so harden off carefully and then plant out after the last frost date.

Growing

Water in the plants when young and keep the roots moist by watering in dry spells. Don't let marigold roots dry out – the plants will wilt and die quickly. If growing one of the taller varieties, pinch the growing tips back when the plant reaches about 8cm (3in) tall to encourage bushiness. Pinch or cut off spent blooms to encourage more flowers; this is also what to do if flowers get grey mould.

Compositae

ZINNIA

Location: Full sun, warm site.
Height: 30 to 45cm (12 to 18in)
Spacing: 1 to per square

GROWING SEASON
Spring: no
Summer: yes
Autumn: yes
Winter: no

GROWING TIME
Seed to Harvest: 16 to 20 weeks
Indoor Seed Starting: 12 weeks before the last spring frost
Earliest Outdoor Planting: after the last spring frost

Zinnias have been improved by recent plant breeding so now not only are there some lovely rich colours but zinnias now flower more reliably before the end of the season. To get the most out of their late flowering ability, they need a warm, sunny spot to do well.

Starting

Zinnias are worth trying from seed as the seed is large and easy to handle but the young plants do not like their roots disturbed so they need carefully potting on. Sow indoors at 13 to 18°C (55 to 64°F); seed needs light to germinate. Seed should germinate in seven days, then transplant seedlings into modular trays or long pots (you could try the middle of toilet rolls, and plant the whole thing). Harden off plants thoroughly.

Growing

Plant out after the last frost date and keep the roots moist. Zinnias don't suffer from any major problems, but they do need warm sunny weather to flower.

Hints and tips

Some of the taller types make good cut flowers but they do need some canes to support the stems.

VARIETY GUIDE

'Profusion' is a good compact mix of orange, white and pink flowers; sometimes the colours are sold separately. Taller varieties include 'Zahara Starlight Rose' (white flowers with eye-catching pink centres) and 'Purple Prince' with striking purple to deep pink blooms.

Labiatae *Solenostemon scutellariodes*

COLEUS

Location: Sun, partial shade or shade but needs some warmth or shelter
Height: 20cm (8in)
Spacing: 1 to 4 per square

GROWING SEASON
Spring: no
Summer: yes
Autumn: no
Winter: no

GROWING TIME
Seed to Foliage: 16 to 22 weeks
Indoor Seed Starting: 4 to 14 weeks before the last spring frost
Earliest Outdoor Planting: after the last spring frost

Hints and tips

Pinch the flowering stems out as soon as they form. The flowers are nothing special and by removing them you will keep the plants compact and the foliage looking fresher for longer.

VARIETY GUIDE
Packs of mixed young coleus plants are often sold unnamed in garden centres but you can also buy seed. 'Wizard' is a good mix of dwarf types.

A packet of mixed coleus seed or a pack of young plants must be one of the cheapest ways to get bright foliage colour into a bed. Seed can be sown all year-round if coleus are to be grown as pot plants, but these plants are tender so to plant outside in a SMG box frame it makes sense to sow in spring.

Starting

Buy young plants in spring or summer, or sow seed in late winter to mid spring. Sow indoors at a temperature of at least 20°C (68°F); the seed needs light to germinate. Seeds germinate in 10 to 14 days, then transplant into modular trays or small pots. Plants are tender so harden off well before planting out.

Growing

Separate out the different coloured plants and select the best colours and markings. Keep the roots moist. Pinching out young plants will make them bushier. They don't suffer from any particular problems but they do not thrive in windy locations.

Labiatae *Salvia horminum, S. viridis*

CLARY

	GROWING SEASON	GROWING TIME
Location: Full sun, partial shade	**Spring**: no	**Seed to Flower**: 20 weeks
Height: 40cm (16 in)	**Summer**: yes	**Indoor Seed Starting**: no
Spacing: 4 per square	**Autumn**: no	**Earliest Outdoor Planting**:
	Winter: no	10 weeks before the last spring frost

Clary is an easy hardy annual with a carefree cottage garden look. The "flowers" are in fact coloured bracts that last from mid-summer to early autumn. Seed can be sown anytime from spring to early summer, direct into the ground.

Starting

Sow seed outdoors, and thin out to four plants per square. Seed can be sown from spring to early summer; it should germinate within 14 to 21 days.

Growing

Keep the square free of weeds by hand weeding until the clary plants establish. Protect young plants from slug attack. Once the young plants establish they are trouble-free.

Hints and tips

Cut and dry the deepest flower colours and use them as everlasting flowers indoors.

VARIETY GUIDE
'Bouquet Mix' is a pastel mix of blue, pink and white. For a stronger colour, get a blue or purple variety such as 'Marble Arch Blue' or 'Blue Denim'.

Leguminosae *Lathyrus odoratus*

SWEET PEA

Location: Full sun, partial shade
Height: 2m (6ft)
Spacing: 1 per square

GROWING SEASON
Spring: yes
Summer: yes
Autumn: no
Winter: no

GROWING TIME
Seed to Flower: 12 to 14 weeks
Indoor Seed Starting: 4 to 12 weeks before the last spring frost
Earliest Outdoor Planting: 8 weeks before the last spring frost

Hints and tips

Can't decide from all the options when to sow your sweet peas? Why not make two sowings, three weeks apart (early to mid spring) for flowers through the summer.

VARIETY GUIDE
It is really just a case of choosing the colours you like or opting for scent. If you are buying for fragrance rather than colour 'Hi-Scent' ('High Scent') is a good one but its blooms are a wishy-washy pale cream to mauve. The varieties with the brightest, strongest colours such as deep-pink to purple 'Geoff Hamilton' (above) often have less fragrance. If you have room, grow one for scent and a variety with a strong colour or large flowers; once cut they can be mixed in a vase.

Sweet peas are an easy annual climber that will make use of space on a vertical frame. They will provide plenty of cut flowers from early to midsummer, especially if you cut them regularly. Note: sweet pea pods and seeds are posionous.

Starting

Grow your own from seed; the seed is large and easy to handle. You can sow in autumn and overwinter the plants for planting out in spring but for most gardeners it is easiest to sow in spring, either early in pots or in late spring direct into the ground. Three seeds in a 10-cm (4-in) pot, sown 12mm (½in) deep will germinate at 10 to 15°C (50 to 59°F) within 10 to 21 days. Harden off plants and pinch out the growing tip when the plant has three to four pairs of leaves, to stimulate side shoots.

Growing

Plant out up against a vertical support and protect against slugs early on. Encourage the plants to climb up the netting by weaving in the growing stems, later on they will cling on themselves using tendrils. Keep the roots moist during dry spells: this will help plants to grow strongly. If the roots get dry the plants are prone to powdery mildew and also the flower buds drop off.

Harvesting

The more you pick the sweet peas, the more new flowers will be produced. Get into the habit of picking every other day or at least twice a week to get the most out of your plants. Cut the stems with scissors rather than pull at them.

Solanaceae
PETUNIA

Location: Full sun
Height: 15cm (6in)
Spacing: 4 per square

GROWING SEASON
Spring: no
Summer: yes
Autumn: no
Winter: no

GROWING TIME
Seed to Flower: 14 weeks
Indoor Seed Starting: 8 to
10 weeks before first frost
Earliest Outdoor Planting:
after the last spring frost

The trumpet-shaped flowers come in just about every colour imaginable. Rather than opt for those with the largest flowers, look for neat, small-flowered forms as these will produce lots of flowers all through the summer. Colourful and drought-tolerant, these plants are useful to brighten up plantings of Mediterranean herbs or amongst fruiting crops such as peppers and chillies.

Starting

Seed is very tiny and slow to germinate so the easiest option is to buy small plug plants in early spring or small packs of larger bedding plants in late spring to early summer. Petunias are very tender so harden off plants thoroughly before planting out.

Growing

Water young plants until they start growing away; after that they are trouble-free if the summers are warm and dry. Deadhead to encourage more blooms, and prune back by half if the plant gets scraggly. Rain can spoil the flowers but deadhead them promptly and there is another chance new flowers will form.

Hints and tips

Look out for calibrachoa if you want a neater alternative to petunia; the flowers look similar but are less sticky to deadhead. You will find them on sale with other summer bedding plants during the spring. There's a wide range of flower colours including dark purple, terracotta, yellow and red.

VARIETY GUIDE
Any compact multiflora type will be suitable. Avoid vigorous cascading or groundcover types as these will encroach on nearby squares.

Tropaeolaceae *Tropaeolum majus*

NASTURTIUM

Location: Full sun
Height: 15 to 45cm
(6 to 18in)
Spacing: 1 per square

GROWING SEASON
Spring: no
Summer: yes
Autumn: no
Winter: no

GROWING TIME
Seed to Harvest: 12 weeks
Indoor Seed Starting: 8 to
10 weeks before the last
spring frost
Earliest Outdoor Planting:
after the last spring frost

Hints and tips

Nasturtium seed is big and easy to handle, making it a great choice for children to use. The seeds can be pushed into the mix in spring or sown in pots for planting out later.

VARIETY GUIDE
There are lots of different varieties ranging from orange, red and cream flowers; some trail while others are bushy. 'Empress of India' is worth looking out for because the rich orange flowers are set off by dark blue-green foliage. 'Alaska' is a mix of flower colours with green and cream foliage.

Nasturtiums are the most worthwhile edible flowers. They are easy hardy annuals to grow from seed and cope well with hot, dry sites. The flowers have a distinct peppery taste, a bit like watercress and they add colour to green salads.

Starting

Sow in 7-cm (3-in) pots anytime from early spring to early summer. Push them 1cm (½in) down into the sowing compost, or sow seed direct into a square.

Growing

Trailing types will grow up vertical supports or you can grow the compact bushy ones in any free square. Pick off pests such as blackfly, cabbage white caterpillars and slugs when seen. You get more flowers when the roots are kept on the dry side.

Harvesting

Pick newly opened flowers in the morning. Check for insects, then keep flowers cool until ready to use. If using in a salad, add any dressing first, then sprinkle the petals on top.

Violaceae *Viola* species

PANSY AND VIOLA

Location: Partial shade, shade **Height:** 15 to 23cm (6 to 9in) **Spacing:** 4 per square	**GROWING SEASON** **Spring:** yes **Summer:** no* **Autumn:** yes **Winter:** yes * Summer-flowering varieties are available	**GROWING TIME** **Seed to Flower:** 20 weeks: **Indoor Seed Starting:** 14 to 16 weeks before last frost **Earliest Outdoor Planting:** early spring or early autumn

All violas (which includes pansies) have pretty flowers that are edible, but the main reason to grow them is they are shade-tolerant and flower autumn into spring. Summer-flowering violas are available but they are not so widely grown as the "winter" ones.

VARIETY GUIDE
There are lots of varieties but those from the 'Sorbet' series are widely available and perform well over the autumn to spring.

Starting

Violas are usually bought as young plug plants or pot-grown plants. Growing from seed can be a challenge. Sow indoors 14 to 16 weeks before the last frost date. Barely cover the seed, then refrigerate for two weeks. Once exposed to room temperatures, seeds should sprout in ten days. Set plants out in early spring or in autumn to add early or late colour to box frames.

Growing

Keep plants cool and moist; this will attract slugs so protect young plants with slug pellets or a barrier. Deadhead plants for continuous bloom, and cut back leggy plants to stimulate new growth. Do not replant in the same place year after year or the plants will not thrive as soil diseases build up.

Harvesting

Pansies make an attractive cut flower; keep in mind that the stems are quite short. Violas, with their small flowers, make a great garnish for a salad or cake.

12

Appendix

Most edible crops are annuals so in most cases you will start afresh each year with a clean sheet (or box frame!). To help get your growing season off to a flying start, this final chapter contains a quick overview on my method and handy at-a-glance charts that you can refer to before sowing or planting.

That just about wraps up the SGM method, apart from this summary.

Mel's final summary

Well – there you have it! The Square Metre Gardening (SMG) system, based on a standard unit of a 1 x 1-m (3 x 3-ft) box frame around a grid of nine 30 x 30-cm (1 x 1-ft) squares. You can have several of these boxes for each member of the family or adapt the layout and dimensions to suit your situation, so long as you use the same size square (30 x 30cm/1 x 1ft) as a guide to plant spacing.

Here are the most important SMG features covered in chronological order. First, the initial siting, setting up and filling of your boxes, then going on to the all-important planting and spacing with a grid. Finally, the crop care and harvesting the SMG way comes into play.

Location

Your SMG can be located almost anywhere regardless of the local soil – the ideal place is close to the house so it is easy to care for the plants each day. Also, choose a sunny site for the highest yields and widest choice of crops. Some subjects will tolerate partial shade, or even prefer it in the height of summer, but a warm, sunny place offers the best start and allows you to start early and finish later in the growing season.

Size

The compact size of the box frame makes it quick and easy to protect plants from adverse weather and pests. Simple DIY frames can fit over the box and support a wide range of crop covers. Having a compact, defined area to tend means that even those with limited time or energy can still enjoy the benefits of gardening. My SMG system is ideally suited to schools, senior homes and community gardens – all over the world.

Soil and Fertiliser Requirements

We've eliminated all the things you used to have to learn about soil and the special requirements for each individual vegetable because now you're using nothing but Mel's mix. If you make yours according to the simple formula, you'll have a perfect soil for every single crop. You won't have to remove stones, or adjust the soil pH or apply special fertilisers. So we don't have to give you different or special

directions about soil for every single plant. You won't need to learn that this plant needs extra nitrogen or that plant needs extra potassium – because Mel's mix has everything each plant needs, and it is readily available for them. Those that need it, take it. Those that don't need it, don't take it. It's that simple.

Make up a batch of Mel's mix to fill your boxes at the start. You can then grow a wide range of crops without worrying about different soil types and fertilisers.

Conserving Resources

As we all become more aware of the need to "reduce, re-use and recycle" in all aspects of our lives, it's good to know that SMG can play a vital part as it is such as environmentally friendly way to garden. To start with the obvious: growing some of your own food rather than buying in produce helps conserve resources and the SMG system helps more people do this as you don't need much space. I've already outlined how you can use "free" wood for the boxes and how to make your own DIY frames for crop covers. For example, using a fine mesh cover to keep out flying insects saves you having to use chemical sprays. Lots of fancy tools and fertilisers are not required either: remember: bucket, scissors, pencil and cup!

You do need to buy in the ingredients for your Mel's mix and these include peat moss and vermiculite, but I still strongly recommend doing this because the results are so good and these purchases are a one-off. After that you simply top up with your own garden compost made from all the recycled and composted plant debris from your

A planting grid that divides each SMG box frame into nine squares will help you with plant spacing.

garden and kitchen. Water is a precious resource (even if it doesn't feel like it when it has rained for months!) but growing the SMG way means it is applied in a targeted way, where it is needed and as plants are grown close together there is less water wasted than turning on the sprinkler over a large plot.

The Planting Grid

It's very important to use the grid so you can see what space you have to fill and also so the individual plants are spaced within each square at the optimum spacing for growth and cropping. If your box frame doesn't have a grid, then it isn't a real SMG!

Watering

The general advice for watering in the Square Metre Garden is to make sure the soil stays moist and gives the plants as much water as they need. Although that sounds nebulous at first, you will soon become accustomed to which plants require more. Of course, it all depends on depth of the mix, the season, the weather, and the size and growth pattern of that particular plant. Anyone can see that a large bushy plant needs much more than a young seedling. Another important feature of Mel's mix is that it makes it hard to overwater plants because the mix absorbs surplus water.

Pests and Diseases

We don't go into detail of all possible pests and diseases of each individual plant. I've had gardeners tell me that when they read a long list of potential threats, they often decide they don't want to grow that crop – and that's a shame, because in all likelihood, they'll never see that pest or disease.

I think you have seen by now that SMG is not about all the problems and diseases of plant growth, but it is about healthy productive plants. Having said all that, nearly all plants are vulnerable to slug (and snail in some areas) damage so it is worth taking precautions against these, particularly when plants are young and when the weather is damp.

When to Plant

Charts and the directory entries will give information about when to plant both seeds or seedlings, indoors or out. They also indicate when to replant an additional crop in order to have a continuous harvest through the gardening year. These are only a guidelines to get you started. There is a lot of regional variation in frost dates and which varieties thrive well in certain areas, so supplement our guidelines with local knowledge and experience.

How Much to Plant

Start out by asking yourself, "How much do I really want to harvest (not plant) in the time period that this crop will be ready?"

For example, a planting of calabrese will all be ready to harvest over a period of just a couple of weeks in early summer (after that it will go to seed). So if you only want to have two heads a week, then plant no more than four or five plants for that two-week harvest period.

For crops that give you a continuous harvest, such as chard, parsley, tomatoes, courgettes or climbing beans, grow only enough plants to give you as much as you want to harvest each week. You don't have to feed the neighbourhood – although sometimes you have to offer a few tomatoes in order to get rid of your courgettes.

Harvesting Method

Be gentle when you harvest, if you're picking something with a stem, like a pepper, tomato, squash or even peas and beans. Cut the stem with your garden scissors while you hold the fruit with the other hand. Remember, with SMG our plants are growing in a very loose and friable mix, so it's important to be careful and not tug or yank on the plant.

Since you won't be overburdened with too much harvest in your SMG, you can take your time and enjoy the actual process. For leaf crops where you're picking individual leaves or stems – such as lettuce, spinach, chard or parsley – do the same thing. Cut the leaf or stem with your scissors, then place it in your salad bowl or harvest basket. A lot of people like to dip their harvest in the water bucket to wash it off – you could use a colander as your harvest basket. Then you can wash off the crops right in the garden and any water and soil will fall right back into the box frame.

Slugs and snails: the number one garden pests

The most common pests are slugs and snails. Often people don't realise what is eating their crops as these creatures tend to hide during the day; they are usually to be found at the corners and edges of the box frames. They come out at night to feed on a wide range of plants at every stage from seedlings to fruits ready to harvest. Precautions and controls include: slug pellets (organic or wildlife-friendly types are now available), barrier methods such as copper tape or you can simply go out at night with a torch and pick them off your crops.

A Word about Plant Families

I feel that all of your plants are just like your children and should be treated as such. So it's fun and worthwhile to visit some of the plant families and get to know them a little better. Some members of different families will surprise you, such as lettuce. Wouldn't you think that would be in the leafy vegetable family? But no, it's in the aster or sunflower family (Asteraceae) . . . And what about celery? It's in the same family as carrots, the Apiaceae, and although we eat the leaves and stems of celery and the roots of carrot both plants are attacked by carrot root fly. There's a lot you can learn from this. Often members of the same plant family need the same requirements and conditions of growing. If you become familiar with the plant families you won't have to learn and digest as much information about individual crops because, for example, all plants in the same family have the same pests, diseases and problems related to growing. Each family member usually has the same frost resistance and pretty much the same type of care. So if you learn the families and the care of each family, you'll have a more satisfying gardening experience.

Conclusion

Chapters 10 and 11 have a directory of just a few favourites of the multitude of flowers, vegetables and herbs you can grow in your Square Metre Garden.

Can you visualise how attractive a quilt-like garden can be when you plant something different in every square? Can you see how little you really have to know about plants and gardening to be successful? Start small and expand as you gain experience and success. Then spread the word and help others start their own SMG.

So good luck with your garden. Thank you for all your support.

This is Mel Bartholomew wishing you . . . Happy Gardening!

Mel

Keep in touch online

You can get up-to-date tips and reminders from our website <www.squaremetregardening.org>. Also you can send in your feedback and ideas: this always encourages others to get started!

Harvesting fresh salad from a cut-and-come-again mix is easy, if you cut the leaves with scissors and then simply leave the remaining stump to re-grow.

Planting charts

Use the following charts to work out a sowing order for your chosen crops based around the last spring frost date and first autumn frost date for your area.

Sowing and planting for spring & summer crops

A guide to which annual crops need planting out in spring from early spring to late spring. Take your local conditions and plant growth into account as well.

Crop	12	10	8	6	4	2	Last spring frost
8 to 10 weeks before the last spring frost							
Potato (early)		●					
Spinach		●					🧺
6 to 8 weeks before the last spring frost							
Onion & Shallot			●				
Broad Bean			●				
Dill			●				🧺
4 to 6 weeks before last spring frost							
Kohl Rabi				●			
Kale				●			
Parsley					●		
Calabrese					⌣		
Lettuce & salad leaves						⌣	🧺
Lettuce & salad leaves					●		
Cauliflower			●		⌣		
Cabbage (summer)			●		⌣		
Onions & Shallot	●				⌣		
2 to 4 weeks before last spring frost							
Pak Choi					●		
Turnip (summer)					●		
Beetroot					●		
Carrot (summer)						●	
Radish (summer)						●	🧺
Florence Fennel				●		⌣	
Chard, Swiss Chard			●			⌣	
Straight after last spring frost							
Coriander							●
Sweetcorn				●			⌣

KEY

Indoor growth period started with seed

Outdoor growth period stared with seed

Outdoor growth period stared with set

Outdoor growth period stared with tuber

Outdoor growth stared with plant

Harvest period

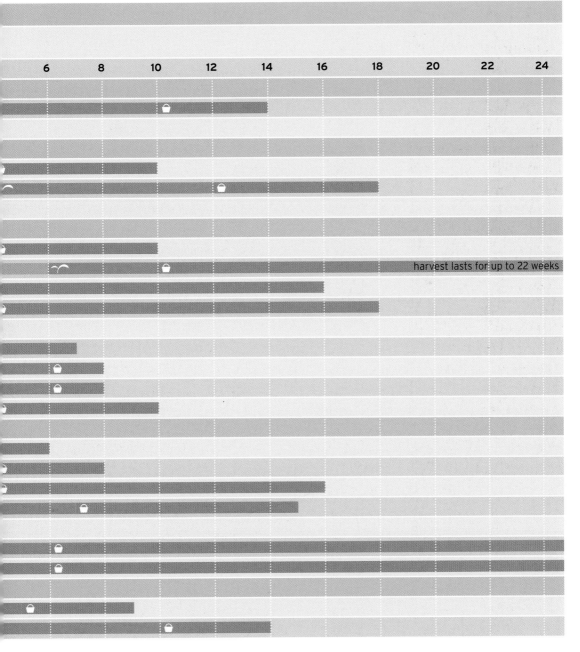

harvest lasts for up to 22 weeks

Sowing and planting for spring & summer crops (continued)

Crop	12	10	8	6	4	2	Last spring frost
Straight after last spring frost (continued)							
Climbing Bean			●				plant / harvest
Bush Bean					●		plant / harvest
Tomato		●					plant
Chives		●					plant / harvest
Celery	●						plant
Celeriac	●						plant
Brussels Sprouts	●						plant
Leek			●				plant
Endive			●				plant / harvest
After the last spring frost							
Cucumber				●			plant
Okra				●			plant
Sweet Pepper & Chilli	●						plant
Aubergine	●						
Courgette, Summer Squash (from seed)				●			
Courgette, Summer Squash (from plants)							
Winter squash				●			
Basil				●			
Melon			●				
Chicory							

KEY

● bar	Indoor growth period started with seed
● bar	Outdoor growth period stared with seed
● bar	Outdoor growth period stared with set
● bar	Outdoor growth period stared with tuber
⌒ bar	Outdoor growth stared with plant
◠ bar	Harvest period

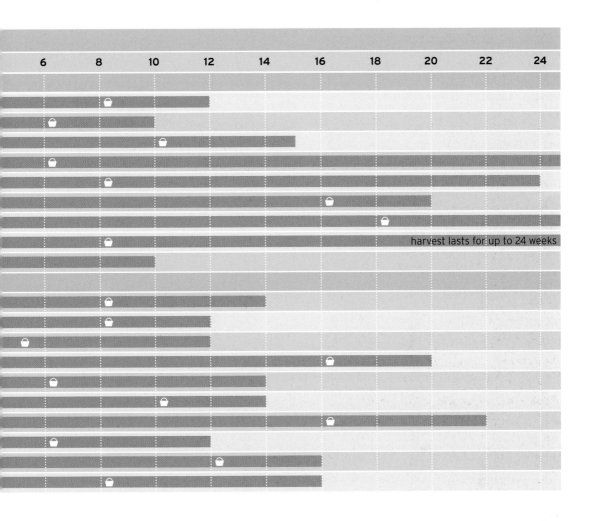

harvest lasts for up to 24 weeks

Indoor germination temperatures

Crop	Temperature				
	5°C (41°F)	10°C (50°F)	15°C (59°F)	20°C (68°F)	25°C (77°F)
ALLIACEAE					
Allium ampeloprasum **Leek**		■	■		
Allium cepa **Onion**		■			
Allium schoenoprasum **Chives**		■			
APIACEAE					
Apium graveolens var. *dulce* **Celery**			■		
Apium graveolens var. *rapaceum* **Celeriac**			■		
Foeniculum vulgare var. *dulce* **Florence Fennel**			■		
Petroselinum **Parsley**			■		
ASTERACEAE					
Cichorium endivia **Endive**			■		
Lactuca sativa **Lettuce** and other **Salad Leaves**	■	■			
BRASSICACEAE					
Brassica rapa var. *chinensis* **Pak Choi**		■			
Brassica oleracea var. *botrytis* **Cauliflower**				■	
Brassica oleracea Capitata Group **Cabbage** (summer)				■	■
Brassica oleracea Gemmifera Group **Brussels Sprouts**	■	■			
Brassica oleracea Italica Group **Calabrese**		■			
CHENOPODIACEAE					
Beta vulgaris **Chard** and **Swiss Chard**				■	
CURCURBITACEAE					
Cucumis sativus **Cucumber**					
Cucumis melo **Melon**			■		
Cucurbita pepo **Courgette** and **Summer Squash**					
Cucurbita **Winter Squash**				■	
LAMIACEAE					
Ocimum **Basil**				■	
MALVACEAE					
Abelmoschus esculentus **Okra**				■	■
PAPILIONACEAE					
Phaseolus coccineus, P. vulgaris **Climbing Bean**		■			
Phaseolus vulgaris **Bush Bean**		■			
Pisum sativum **Pea**	■	■			
POACEAE					
Zea mays **Sweetcorn**			■		

Indoor germination temperatures (continued)

Crop	Temperature				
	5°C (41°F)	10°C (50°F)	15°C (59°F)	20°C (68°F)	25°C (77°F)
SOLANACEAE					
Capsicum annuum **Sweet Pepper** and **Chilli**				▪	
Lycopersicon esculentum **Tomato**				▪	
Solanum melongena **Aubergine**				▪	

KEY ▭ Germination temperature range

Autumn planting schedule

If you want to extend your cropping season, plan ahead to sow for autumn harvests and also, if local conditions allow, plant hardy crops in autumn for earlier cropping the following year.

Crop	8	6	4	2	First autumn frost	2	4	6
Lettuce & salads (hardy)	◖⌒							
Endive	◖⌒							
Chicory (hardy)	⌒							
Onions	◖⌒							
Cabbage (spring)	⌒							
Strawberry	⌒							
Shallot			◖					
Broad Bean			◖					
Garlic					◖			
Chicory (forced)					◉			

KEY
◖ Planting period of seed
⌒ Planting period of plants
◖ Planting period of sets
◉ Lifting period for roots

Crops for an Autumn harvest

Summer crops still cropping until the first frost		Plants still growing outside ready for harvest or lifting after first frost
Celery	Radish (summer)	Leeks
Celeriac	Winter Squash	Parsley
Carrot	Mint	Swede
Endive	Oregano and Marjoram	Kale
Chicory	Pepper and Chilli	Brussels Sprouts
Pak Choi	Tomato	Turnip (winter)
Cauliflower	Potato	Radish (winter)
Calabrese		Beetroot
Turnip (summer)		Chard, Swiss Chard

Glossary

Annual A plant that completes its life cycle, from seed germination to producing new seed, in one year.

Biennial A plant that completes its life cycle in two years.

Blanch To exclude sunlight from leaves or stems so they whiten and become less bitter or softer. Light is usually excluded manually by thick paper, plates or soil depending on the plant, but some crops, e.g. celery, have self-blanching varieties where the growth habit shades the edible parts.

Bolt To produce seed prematurely, usually due to weather stress such as lack of moisture or too much heat. Most relevant for leafy crops, some varieties are described as being "bolt-resistant".

Certified stock Certain plant material such as strawberry plants and potato tubers that have been certified by a government body as being free of certain pests, diseases or plant viruses.

Cloche The word comes from the French for "bell" and refers to the glass bells used hundreds of years ago for protecting crops.

Crop cover Sheets, usually draped over a frame, to protect plants in various ways depending on the material.

Deadhead To remove faded flower heads from plants before they can set seed. This often stimulates the plant to produce more flowers or fruits.

Drip irrigation A system of small pipes that delivers water from a source such as a tap or storage tank direct to plants. Water either soaks through a perforated hose or leaks through special emitters placed near plants.

Follow-on crop A crop that is planted straightaway into a space after a previous crop has been harvested. Planning for follow-on crops will ensure you get more out of a smaller space.

Frost dates The dates of the last spring frost and the first autumn frost are key points in the garden calendar. The dates are not exactly the same each year, even in the same place, so an average of previous frost dates are used as a guide. Frost dates vary depending what region you live in, the lie of the land and the microclimate in your garden.

Garden compost Well-rotted, organic matter produced from your recycled garden plants when they are left in a compost bin. Use garden compost on outdoor plants, e.g. for a growing mix ingredient, as a mulch or to improve soil when re-planting.

Harden-off The process of gradually getting your seedlings or young plants raised indoors used to outdoor weather conditions. It takes about seven to ten days bringing them out during mild spells during the day and back in at night. Even hardy plants need hardening-off if they have been raised undercover.

Hardiness A hardy plant is able to withstand frost without protection, sometimes called frost-hardy, whereas a frost-tender plant cannot survive a frost unless protected.

Herbaceous Perennial plants with soft, not woody, top growth that dies back at the end of the growing season while the plant roots remain alive but dormant, ready to emerge again the following year.

Lift and divide A method for controlling the spread of herbaceous perennials usually carried out in spring or autumn. Roots are lifted out of the ground and the plant divided into sections, then the young healthy sections are re-planted or potted up.

Modular tray A handy item for indoor seed-raising. A plastic or polystyrene tray made up of individual modules or cells so each seed or young plant has its own space to grow and root.

Peat Formed by the partial decomposition of sphagnum or other mosses and sedges in acid, waterlogged conditions where there is a lack of oxygen. Peat moss (also known as moss peat or sphagnum peat) is derived from sphagnum moss and is spongy and fibrous. Sedge peat is formed from sedges (Carex) and other grasses and is more decomposed, so less useful.

Perennial A plant that lives on for over three years or more. Asparagus and globe artichokes are examples of perennial vegetables. Most vegetables are annuals.

Perlite Granular volcanic rock used as an ingredient in compost mixes to improve aeration, but it has no nutrients.

Pinch out To remove the growing tip of a plant to encourage side-shoots to grow to create a more compact bushy habit.

Prick out To move seedlings growing together to their own pots or trays with more space for them to develop. Prick out only the best and discard the weaker ones, but if growing a mix make sure you have the best examples of each.

Plug plants Small plants, at a stage between seedling and young plant, each growing in their own "plug" of compost.

Pollination The successful transfer of pollen from a plant's male flower to the female flower resulting in viable fruits or seeds.

Potbound Describes a container-grown plant with roots confined so long that they have filled the container and become matted.

Pot on To move a young plant into a larger pot before its roots get potbound.

Runner A trailing shoot that can root where it touches the ground; e.g. mint and strawberries can spread via runners and can become invasive.

Seed leaf The leaf or pair of leaves to appear after seed germination, they look different to the subsequent true leaves.

Sets Immature bulbs of onions or shallots used for planting.

Side-shoot A branch or stem growing from the main stem.

Sow direct (also direct-sow) To sow seeds directly into a soil or mix outside, rather than starting them in small pots first. Tender plants that are severely damaged or killed by frost, these plants need to be planted outside after the last frosts or given protection against late frosts.

Thin out To remove surplus seedlings so that the remaining seedlings have enough space to grow on and mature.

Transplant To move a plant from one growing place to another, usually from growing indoors to planting outdoors.

True leaves The second set of leaves that appear on a young seedling; these and subsequent leaves resemble the leaves of the species.

Tuber An underground stem or root used as a food-storage organ, e.g. potato and dahlia.

Variety (also known as a cultivar or cultivated variety) A variant of a plant species that retains its distinct characteristics when propagated.

Variegated Usually refers to plant foliage that is streaked, edged, blotched or mottled with a contrasting colour.

Vermiculite A natural mineral that when processed and heated becomes a lightweight, water-absorbent material that holds air well.

Index

Acknowledgements

Illustration
Schermuly Design Co.
Except p29 and 95 James Lindquist

Location Photography
We would like to thank photographer David Murray for the commissioned photography. Liz Dobbs for organising the location, props and plants.

Thank you also to Nick Hamilton for the use of the facilities at Barnsdale Gardens and with modelling. Also to Nick's staff: Jon Brocklebank, Susie Watson and Zak Adam who helped with construction, plant supply and modelling.

Picture credits
10 tl J. Paul Moore 11 tl LDI 14 bl LDI 20 tr Shutterstock / Beata Becla 24 c LDI 34 bl LDI 36 cl LDI 36 bl LDI 36 br LDI 37 tl J. Paul Moore 68 tr LDI 75 tl Shutterstock /audaxl 76 cl LDI 77 tl LDI 79 tl LDI 81 cl LDI 81 cr LDI 81 bl LDI 81 br LDI 82 br Shutterstock /Matt Hart 87 tl J. Paul Moore 87 cl J. Paul Moore 87 bl J. Paul Moore 88 tl J. Paul Moore 88 cl J. Paul Moore 88 bl J. Paul Moore 89 tl J. Paul Moore 96 tl J. Paul Moore 96 tr J. Paul Moore 96 bl J. Paul Moore 96 br J. Paul Moore 110 tr LDI 113 tl J. Paul Moore 113 tr J. Paul Moore 123 tl J. Paul Moore 125 tl J. Paul Moore 129 tr LDI 144 t J. Paul Moore 145 b J. Paul Moore 153 bl LDI 154 tr LDI 155 tl LDI 158 b LDI 159 br LDI 161 tr LDI 164 c J. Paul Moore 169 t J. Paul Moore 182 tl Shutterstock /Neil Roy Johnson 183 tr Shutterstock /BestPhotoPlus 184 tl Shutterstock / Denis and Yulia Pogostins 185 tr Shutterstock /lu-photo 186 tl Shutterstock /jokihaka 187 tr Shutterstock /Marek Pawluczuk 188 tl Shutterstock /Dancing Fish 189 tr Shutterstock /Shane White 190 tl LDI 191 tr Shutterstock / Dancing Fish 192 tl Shutterstock /Imageman 193 tr Shutterstock /elena moiseeva 194 tl Shutterstock /Lasse Kristensen 195 tr Shutterstock /Dancing Fish 196 tl Shutterstock /audaxl 197 tr Shutterstock /Lynn Watson 198 tl Shutterstock /asharkyu 201 tr Shutterstock /johannviloria 202 tl iStockphoto /AnglianArt 203 tr Shutterstock / MnemosyneM 204 tl LDI 205 tr Shutterstock /Vladimir Jotov 206 tl Shutterstock /carroteater 207 tr LDI 208 tl LDI 209 tr Shutterstock /Stefan Fierros 210 tl Shutterstock / chudoba 211 tr LDI 212 tl LDI 213 tr LDI 214 tl Shutterstock / KBF Media 215 tr LDI 216 tl LDI 217 tr LDI 218 tl Shutterstock /Claudia Holzmann 219 tr LDI 220 tl Shutterstock /Mazzzur 221 tr Shutterstock /Diana Taliun 222 tl Shutterstock /Kenishirotie 223 tr LDI 224 tl LDI 225 tr Shutterstock /Mars Evis 226 tl Shutterstock /Melica 227 tr Shutterstock /Samokhin 228 tl Shutterstock /Neung Stocker Photography 229 c Shutterstock /Denis and Yulia Pogostins 230 tl LDI 232 tl Shutterstock /Oleg Golovnev 233 tr LDI 238 tl LDI 239 tr LDI 240 tl Shutterstock /Hong Vo 244 tl Shutterstock /Tatiana Makotra 247 tr LDI 249 tr Shutterstock / jennyt

Vermiculite suppliers in the UK

LBS Garden Centre
Standroyd Mill
Cottontree
Colne
BB8 7BW.

Tel: 01282 873370
www.lbsgardenwarehouse.co.uk

Mail order supplier of vermiculite, as well as moss peat, multi-purpose composts and peat-free composts.

William Sinclair Horticulture
Firth Road
Lincoln
LN6 7AH

Tel: 01522 537561
www.william-sinclair.co.uk

They supply garden centres and other retailers, not home gardeners direct, but there is a postcode search on their website so you can find your nearest stockist.

Tomato Netting
Simpsons Seeds
The Walled Garden
Horningsham
Warminster BA12 7NQ

Tel: 01985 845004
www.simpsonsseeds.co.uk

Mail order tomato seed specialist that imports USA tomato netting.